The Male Image

Men's Fashion in Britain 1300–1970

PENELOPE BYRDE

B. T. BATSFORD LTD   London

To my mother and the memory of my father

First published 1979

© Penelope Byrde 1979

ISBN 0 7134 0860 X

Filmset by Keyspools Ltd, Golborne, Lancs
Printed in Great Britain by
The Anchor Press Ltd
Tiptree, Essex
for the publishers B. T. Batsford Ltd,
4 Fitzhardinge Street, London W1H 0AH

Contents

Acknowledgment

I would like to express my thanks to the many people who have helped me in the preparation of this book; firstly to Mrs Stella Mary Newton and Dr Aileen Ribeiro of the Department of the History of Dress, Courtauld Institute of Art, who very generously gave their time to advise me and read the manuscript. I am indebted to them and to Miss Margaret Scott for their comments and corrections.

Secondly I am grateful to all those who assisted me with information or advice on the text and illustrations: Miss Janet Arnold, Miss Jane Ashelford, Miss Elizabeth Birbari, Miss Mary Campbell of the Royal School, Bath, Miss Elizabeth Ann Coleman, Major G. M. B. Colenso-Jones, Mrs Valerie Cumming and Dr Brian Spencer of the Museum of London, Miss Mary Doering, Mr David Hinton of Southampton University, Mr Derek Hull and Mr David Wilson, Mrs Rachel Kirkham, Miss Diana de Marly, Mr Leonard Wallis of Savile Row, Mr Claude Wilkinson, and Mrs Joyce and the staff of Bath Reference Library.

My editors, Mr Michael Stephenson and Miss Paula Shea, have been unfailingly helpful and Mr Ian Chilvers gave me invaluable assistance in collecting many of the illustrations.

I have also received many suggestions and offers of help from my family and friends which I much appreciate; my special thanks go to Miss Lesley M. Young for her frequent advice, Miss Sarah Barnett who kindly typed the manuscript and Miss Margaret Cresswell who offered to read the proofs with me. Lastly I owe a debt of gratitude to my mother who probably alone knows the extent to which her patience, interest and help of every kind has made this book possible.

Author's Preface

The history of men's clothes is a vast subject which, in a work of this length, can only be covered in a general survey and with certain limitations. It has been written mainly from the point of view of English fashions and most of the illustrations and literary quotations are from English sources. There are, however, a number of references to European fashions and foreign works of art because in the period before 1500 there is comparatively little surviving evidence, either pictorial or documentary, for the study of English fashion and it has been necessary to look at material from other areas. In addition, some comments on men's clothing in other countries (such as France, Italy, the Netherlands, Scandinavia and the U.S.A.) have been included where it was thought interesting to draw comparisons with English dress or to place the fashions of this country in a wider context.

Secondly, the starting point for a detailed discussion of men's clothes has been made at the fourteenth century. The origins and evolution of garments before 1300 have been considered but treated only generally to provide the necessary background information. Since very little work has, as yet, been published on the dress of the early mediaeval period, the fourteenth century has been chosen as the most logical place to begin.

The subject has been approached in a series of chapters which deal with different categories of dress (such as the suit, the shirt or the necktie). Each chapter considers the function and importance of such items and traces their chronological development. In a separate section, the *Pictorial Survey* (a series of briefly-annotated illustrations) gives a general guide to the changes in men's clothing and the fashionable silhouette throughout the period covered. These chapters have been designed as units which may be used on their own or together.

List of Illustrations

Unacknowledged photographs are from the author's collection.

CHAPTER ONE

Introduction

Perhaps the two most striking facts about men's clothes in the present century are that they are essentially quite different from women's and that they are far more conservative in spirit. A notice in a typical English provincial department store in 1977, for example, advertised 'top quality Fashions, Furnishings, Menswear, Children's Wear, Television, Audio and Electrical'. In most people's minds 'Fashions' are clearly synonymous with women's clothes while men's can be placed significantly lower on the list and, by the general designation, 'Menswear', be more or less divorced from the concept of fashion altogether.

It is fair to say that men's dress during the last century and a half has been almost uniform in shape, colour and fabric. There have been few startling changes. As we shall see, the basic male wardrobe of a three-piece suit – coat, waistcoat and breeches or trousers – has, in fact, been established for over three hundred years. New fashions have consisted mostly of gradual and subtle alterations in cut or minor decorative detail. There has been no comparable or consistent version of the three-piece suit in a woman's wardrobe and her fashions have altered with considerable frequency during this period.

Until the beginning of the nineteenth century there was a closer parallel between male and female dress; many of the same fashionable tendencies were reflected in both because convention had not yet begun to restrict men to sober colours and conservative styles. Male fashions could be as fanciful, decorative and colourful as female dress since the same shades and textiles were used and admired. Male and female garments differed in construction but the use of delicate or patterned fabrics, a variety of colours and decoration with lace, ribbons and embroidery was not confined to one sex. In some periods men's clothes were actually more flamboyant and changed more often than their female counterparts. In the present century, after a long period of apparent dullness and lack of inspiration, a new and more lively approach to men's fashion began to emerge in the 1960's when more colour, informality and imagination became accepted, although very few new garments were invented. A closer link between male and female dress reappeared but they remained fundamentally different in character.

There has often been an affinity between the fashions of the sexes but at no time since the development of tailoring in the fourteenth century have their clothes been completely identical or interchangeable; sex has almost always been clearly differentiated by clothing. Male and female fashions are

related and comparable but are separate areas of study. It is sometimes thought that men are not really concerned with fashion at all because their clothes have so little visual impact: at best, their dress represents only a timid, diluted version of new trends in women's dress. This is a reasonable conclusion, but it pays insufficient attention to the nature of men's dress, to its functions and its means of expression. Men's clothes may not be so varied or exciting to the eye as women's but often they do not have the same aims and effects in mind.

The form, function and decoration of male and female garments are affected by two important factors: each sex is a different physical shape, and there have been significant differences in their way of life.

From an aesthetic point of view, women are by nature more suitable models for the draping of fabric; the female figure is both curved and malleable whereas a fit young man is more angular in shape, with hard, well-developed muscles. These physical differences are also apparent when the body is clothed, whether in loosely draped folds or tightly fitting garments (trousers, for example do not conceal but reveal the different shape of male and female figures).

Throughout its history, fashion has made a consistent attempt either to disguise or to emphasize the natural contours of the human body. Women's clothes have, in general, more scope because the female shape is more varied and interesting to look at. There is an almost infinite variety of ways of displaying the features of the bust, waist and hips. Since men have, by and large, no waist, no hips and a flat chest the garments that cover them will have a less sculptural quality and fewer opportunities for interesting effects. Men have the choice of either creating the illusion of curves (for instance by bulk and padding, as in the puffed trunk-hose of the later sixteenth century) or emphasizing the virtues of the male figure – height, powerful shoulders, flat stomach, slim hips and long legs – by wearing garments which stress these points. Normally men are just as anxious as women to display their figures to best advantage but male fashions can sometimes appear to be less dramatic because the qualities they underline are rather negative: they emphasize the lack rather than the presence of contours.

The different roles and lifestyles of men and women have had a direct effect on dress. For centuries the traditional woman's work of childbearing and homemaking has confined the majority of women to the home. Until quite recently many did not work for a living and the range of occupations was limited. As a result, although men travelled from home and had greater contact with the outside world, with its new ideas and changing fashions, it was the women who had the time to devote to dress and the opportunity to develop extreme forms of fashion. A restricting type of dress, such as a skirt in which it was almost impossible to walk, could be indulged in by those who were neither required to walk any distance nor given the chance to do so.

Men have usually led a more strenuous life than women, whether working, fighting or engaging in sport, and the shape of their clothes is

1 Rev. R. Walker by Sir Henry Raeburn c 1784 Men's clothes are rarely designed to hamper ease of movement.

very rarely taken to an extreme which would effectively hamper ease of movement [1]. Some male fashions certainly have appeared to be exaggerated and impractical and there has been no lack of tightly fitting garments, but it is hard to find a masculine equivalent of the boned, laced bodices and wide hoop-petticoats which so incapacitated women in the past.

Apart from the fact that women's clothes were not designed, as a rule, for active pursuits, they often were intended specifically to look more ornamental than men's clothes. At most periods dress has been worn as a symbol of social or financial status and the status symbol could extend to a wife whose function was both to be decorative and to display wealth in the form of jewellery and fine clothes. Men's dress was equally capable of playing this role but it has tended to be less of a full-time occupation for them; their appearance has generally been more subject to practical considerations.

In addition to the need for mobility (and it is hardly surprising that two significant influences in men's clothes have been military and sporting dress) male fashions have been influenced by what might be called moral or psychological trends: clothes usually indicate what people think about themselves and the conscious or unconscious image they are trying to project, and this has been as true for male dress as for female. A man's work or his profession is one of the most important aspects of his life and the man who earns his living by doing business, for example, will want to look both successful and reliable, with an unexceptionable and pleasing appearance. Too great an attention to the niceties of dress and the latest forms of fashion are associated, by tradition, with a certain lightness of mind or irregular priorities and tend to be avoided by the sober businessman. This might explain, in part, why men's fashions during the nineteenth century became so sombre and restrained. In the aftermath of the Industrial Revolution, the hero of Victorian society was the businessman whose dress embodied the virtues of middle-class respectability. The businessman has by no means been particularly emulated at every other period in the history of fashion but a certain moral fibre and self-discipline have almost always been attributed to men who excel at their work, or in sport or the armed services. These qualities are indeed often thought of as specifically masculine attributes, and men's clothes – particularly service uniforms – often express the idea that one can inspire confidence in the physical fitness, courage or discipline of the wearer simply by attention to cut, perfection of detail and a general air of restraint.

Women's clothes, on the other hand, have been more likely to emphasize the accepted feminine characteristics of softness, delicacy and fragility. Physically deforming clothes such as narrow-waisted garments or high-heeled shoes, which might make a woman appear attractively helpless, would cast doubts on a man's fitness or virility and are therefore seldom popular for men. Men do not necessarily aim to be self-effacing, let alone actually anti-fashion, in their dress but some of the traditional masculine ideals such as self-control, when expressed in dress, lead to understatement and subtlety which can be visually less arresting.

There is a further distinction between the clothes of men and women in the way they are made. Women's clothes have never been exclusively made or designed by their own sex. Apart from the undergarments sewn at home, women's clothes (including corsets) were made by men until the early eighteenth century, and even at a time of considerable female emancipation in the twentieth century at least half of the most distinguished designers of women's clothes have been men. The tailoring of men's clothes, by contrast, has always been the prerogative of men (although women have been employed in the actual making up or sewing of garments), which may have contributed to the conservative element in male dress of recent centuries. Men's tailoring is an old and established craft, based on long tradition and highly developed skills, which has become resistant to change and experiment. Cutting out a garment is the most important and skilled aspect of the tailor's craft, and good, well-fitting patterns became highly valued possessions.[1] Cut and fit required expertise, so the basic shape of men's clothes was altered rather slowly, and more attention seems to have been paid to perfecting existing techniques than to inventing new ones. Even with the decline in tailor-made garments this slow pace of development and spirit of conservatism remains in the mass production of men's clothing. At the same time, male fashions have continued to be designed by men without the same kind of collaboration between both parties and depth of interest which is usually given to women's clothes.

It has been pointed out that 'it is not in the nature of masculine fashion to change abruptly. Whilst there can be considerable variations of style and colour, dramatic alterations in the number of garments worn are not usual.'[2] The *Tailor and Cutter* also noted this phenomenon in 1897 and thought that 'men, as a rule, are most conservative in dress. They adopt new styles very gradually, and, as a rule, care more for ease and comfort, practical utility and neatness, than for any new fashion that can be submitted to them.'[3] Certainly it proved almost impossible to impose any large-scale reform of dress on men during the latter part of the nineteenth century. Many people – among them artists, writers, social reformers and political thinkers – had come to regard contemporary male fashion as ugly and impractical, even in some cases unhygienic. Trousers, in particular, were seen as shapeless, draughty 'tubes' and there were complaints about the general lack of colour or imagination; but the proposed alternatives such as knee-breeches for ordinary wear or Dr Jaeger's all-woollen sanitary suits were not received with widespread enthusiasm. The movement for the reform of men's dress was largely a failure, but then men at the time felt no deep desire or need to alter their image.[4] Amongst women, on the other hand, the dress reform movement was more successful because it was involved to some extent with the struggle for female emancipation. Many women resented the restricting nature of their dress and found the fashionable image of feminine elegance unacceptable; a rational alternative was readily received.

The innate conservativism of men's dress in the nineteenth and twentieth centuries stems in part from the fact that men were not in general

A £50 YEARLY BUDGET

1 Business Suit	£5 5 0	
1 Dress Suit	2 16 0	(8 gns. for 3 years)
1 Dinner Suit	2 9 0	(7 gns. for 3 years)
2 Waistcoats at 12/6	1 5 0	
1 Sports Coat	2 2 0	
2 pairs Daks	3 0 0	
1 Two-piece Suit	4 4 0	
1 Overcoat	1 15 0	(5 gns. for 3 years)
1 Raincoat	1 1 0	(2 gns. for 2 years)
2 Hats at 1 guinea	2 2 0	
2 pairs Shoes at 25/–	2 10 0	
6 Shirts at 12/6	3 15 0	
2 Sports Shirts at 8/6	17 0	
2 pairs Pyjamas at 16/6	1 13 0	
6 Ties : 4 at 4/6, 2 at 2/6	1 3 0	
12 pairs Socks at 3/6	2 2 0	
24 Handkerchiefs at 9d.	18 0	
2 pairs Gloves at 7/6	15 0	
1 Dressing Gown	1 1 0	(2 gns. over 2 years)
2 pairs Bathing Trunks at 12/6	1 5 0	
6 sets Underwear : 3 winter, 3 summer	4 13 0	
2 dozen Collars at 12/–	1 4 0	
1 Pullover	1 1 0	
Studs, etc.	3 0	
1 Umbrella	1 1 0	
	£50 0 0	

A £115 YEARLY BUDGET

2 Business Suits at £8 8 0	£16 16 0	
1 Dinner Suit	3 17 0	(11 gns. over 3 years)
1 Dress Suit	4 4 0	(12 gns. over 3 years)
2 Waistcoats at 21/–	2 2 0	
1 Sports Coat	4 4 0	
3 pairs Daks	4 10 0	
1 Two-piece Suit	4 4 0	
1 Overcoat	3 3 0	(9 gns. over 3 years)
1 Raincoat	2 2 0	(4 gns. over 2 years)
3 Hats at 30/–	4 10 0	
4 pairs Shoes : 2 at 42/–, 2 at 50/–	9 4 0	
6 Shirts at £1	6 0 0	
4 Sports Shirts : 2 at 15/6, 2 at 30/–	4 11 0	
4 pairs Pyjamas : 2 at 35/–, 2 at 65/–	10 0 0	
12 Ties : 6 at 6/6, 6 at 4/6	3 6 0	
12 pairs Socks at 6/6	3 18 0	
24 Handkerchiefs at 2/–	2 8 0	
3 pairs Gloves : 2 at 12/6, 1 at £1 1 0	2 6 0	
1 Dressing Gown	2 12 6	(5 gns. over 2 years)
1 Bath Gown	1 11 6	(3 gns. over 2 years)
2 pairs Bathing Trunks at 21/–	2 2 0	
6 sets Underwear : 3 winter, 3 summer	7 16 0	
2 dozen Collars at 12/– doz.	1 4 0	
2 Pullovers at 35/–	3 10 0	
1 Umbrella	1 15 0	
6 Silk Handkerchiefs at 7/6	2 5 0	
Studs, etc.	19 0	
	£115 0 0	

16

dissatisfied with their clothes or the appearance they presented to the world. The static, uniform quality of male fashion tends to be regarded as a negative force and almost a vice; yet it might be argued that it is a positive virtue. In an interview with *Observer Magazine* in 1977 Yves St Laurent said, 'men have a lot more confidence with their clothes than women. Because their clothes are always the same.'[5] He appeared to think that men have devised a good solution, in the suit, to the problem of ceaseless changes in fashion and he was aiming to create an equivalent for women's wardrobes.

Of course, men have not dispensed with fashion altogether. Their clothes have not altered in recent centuries as radically and as rapidly as women's but they have changed nevertheless. It may be that male and female fashions simply develop at a different rate. It has been suggested, for example, that the life span of a fashion for men is about twenty-five years,[6] whereas for women it is thought to be about seven or eight.[7]

It is generally accepted as a fallacy that men have never really been less interested in their appearance than women. However unjust it may be, people are and always have been judged by outward appearances and most of us cannot be indifferent to them, even if all we do is try not to look odd or incorrect. At every period men as well as women have aspired to an ideal of beauty or elegance. 'The idea of beauty which man creates for himself', wrote Charles Baudelaire in 1860, 'imprints itself on his whole attire, crumples or stiffens his dress, rounds off or squares his gesture, and in the long run even ends by subtly penetrating the very features of his face. Man ends by looking like his ideal self.'[8]

Baudelaire would argue that men look the way they wish to seem. The history of men's fashions is at least in part the history of their image of themselves.

2 Simpson (Piccadilly) Ltd 1937.
Two recommended budgets for a man's wardrobe, listing essential items.

CHAPTER TWO

Pictorial Survey

The *Pictorial Survey* is intended to give, in a series of illustrations, a visual impression of the development of men's fashions from the Roman period to 1970. The pictures are dated and arranged in a chronological sequence of centuries but a rigid division into periods or decades has been avoided. The brief captions explain points of interest so that the *Survey* may be used as a quick source of reference to the main changes in male fashion but the clothes are discussed in more detail in following chapters.

Pre-Fourteenth Century

3　Interior of a shop in Ancient Rome
The toga was worn by citizens of the Roman Empire. It was a draped overgarment of fine white wool, worn over a knee-length tunic. The mantle was a practical alternative to the toga for everyday wear and outdoor pursuits.

4　Bede's Life of Cuthbert (det) 953–959 A.D.
The basic male wardrobe consisted of a tunic, mantle and leg coverings. More than one tunic might be worn. The quality and decoration of the textiles were indicative of social or financial status (in this example the tunic is ornamented at the neck and wrists). The mantle fastened on one shoulder was a mark of royalty from an early date.

5

6

7

5 Bayeux Tapestry (det)
c 1080
King Edward the Confessor
and an attendant. Long tunics
and mantles were worn by the
nobility and upper classes for
ceremonial occasions. Short
tunics and hose were usual
for ordinary wear.

6 Lambeth Bible (det)
twelfth century
Male and female tunics
became longer and closer
fitting, with wider sleeves in
the twelfth century. The
tighter fit was achieved by
lacing and pinning the cloth
(rather than cutting the
garments to shape).
Embroidered decoration at
the hem, neck and wrists was
more fashionable.

7 Young Offa and Rex
Warmundus by Matthew
Paris, early thirteenth
century.
Upper and under tunics
remained long and unshaped.
The sleeves were loose in
the upper arm but could be
fastened close over the wrist.

8

8 Queen Mary's Psalter
c 1320
Two youths and two girls
holding hands with ribbons.
The shorter tunic gradually
began to be adopted and
tailored to fit the body.

9 Luttrell Psalter (det)
c 1340–45
During the 1340's the fashion
for short, tight tunics
developed. For the first time
garments were cut and shaped
to fit like an outer skin. The
new length revealed the legs
and the hose were made
longer and tighter. Hoods
were also tailored to a close fit
and the pointed tip was
gradually elongated.

10 Effigy of Sir Walter de
Helyon *c* 1360
The characteristic line of th
1350's and 1360's was long
and thin. The skirt narrowe
over the hips and the sleeve
developed long, ribbon-lik
streamers from the elbow.
The row of buttons on the
cote-hardi accentuated the li
The waist was tightly
emphasized and belts were
worn.

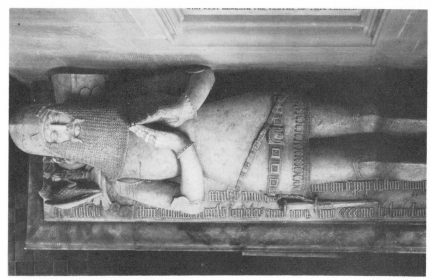

11 Effigy of Sir John Stanley *c* 1375
The tunic became even shorter and tighter during the 1370's and 1380's. The chest was padded into a bulbous shape and elaborate belts underlined the slimness of the hips.

12 The Wilton Diptych (det) *c* 1395
Richard II wears a long, loose, fur-lined gown or *houppelande*. It had a high collar and large wide sleeves. The silk in this example is patterned with Richard's personal emblems of the broomscod and the white hart. The bulky gown was adopted once the short, tight tunic reached its most extreme and became boring.

13   14

13 *Liber Cosmographiae* by John Foxton 1408
The houppelande or gown could be long or short and often was elaborately embroidered. The sleeves were large and bag-like. By this date the hose resembled a pair of 'tights' and were firmly fastened to the doublet (worn beneath the gown). Hair was cut in a short, bowl-shaped crop.

14 Poems and Romances in French (det) *c* 1443
The Court of Henry VI. Tunics shortened to mid-calf in the 1430's but remained bulky, with large sleeves. Outer garments of cloth were lined throughout with fur (which faced inwards). The hood or *chaperon* was worn on top of the head.

15 The Conquests of Charlemagne (det) by Tavernier *c* 1460
The fashionable male tunic was quite short by the mid fifteenth century although long gowns remained in use for official or ceremonial dress. Short capes could be worn. Shoes with long pointed toes were popular and contributed to a spiky, angular effect.

16 Two Men at the Court of Edward IV 1470–80
Hair grew longer in the 1470's and conical caps were pushed well over the forehead, giving men a thuggish air. The fashion for pointed toes and brief tunics reached its limit.

17 The English Ambassadors before King Maurus by Carpaccio *c* 1490
There was a reaction against the eccentric fashions of the 1460's and 1470's and a softer, more romantic image was introduced. It became possible to wear the skin-tight doublet and hose without a top covering and the doublet was slashed to reveal the shirt. A short, loose, coat-like tunic was a fashionable overgarment. A naturally rounded toe returned to men's footwear and caps were flatter.

23

Sixteenth Century

18 Bust of Henry VII by Pietro Torrigiano *c* 1500
The fashionable silhouette presented a squarer line. The four-cornered cap was worn with shoulder-length hair, a fur-lined gown or overcoat and broad-toed shoes.

19 The French Ambassadors to London by Hans Holbein 1533
The fur-lined overcoat continued to be worn over a knee-length tunic with pleated skirts, doublet and hose. The doublet was slashed to reveal the shirt beneath. Sleeves were padded to an enormous size in the upper arm. Scholars and ecclesiastics wore plainer, full-length gowns lined with fur and the four-cornered cap or *biretta*. Short hair was fashionable by 1530.

20 Portrait of a Man in Red.
German School *c* 1540–48
A longer line was
characteristic of the 1540's.
Although shoulders were still
enormous the torso appeared
to lengthen with a higher
neckband and lower
waistline. The skirt of the
tunic shortened to reveal the
trunk-hose. Shirts could be
embroidered at the neck,
centre front and wrists. Shoes
returned to a more natural
rounded toe.

21 Lord Darnley and his brother by Hans Eworth 1563 Large sleeves disappeared in the 1550's and the skirt of the doublet diminished in size. The height of the neckband increased and the frilled edge of the shirt collar gradually expanded. The trunk-hose were padded and stiffened to a round shape. There was a general liking for sombre colours.

22 Portrait of a Young Man by Nicholas Hilliard *c* 1588 The distinctive 'peascod belly' shape of the doublet became very pronounced in the 1570's and 1580's. The short puffed trunk-hose were worn with long knitted hose and shoulder-capes were at the height of fashion. The ruff was a separate starched collar set into formal pleats. Hair grew a little longer and fuller.

23 The Three Brothers
Browne and their Page by
Isaac Oliver 1599
The trunk-hose could be
made in two layers, a rounded
upper part and a lower, close-
fitting portion called
'canions'. After the mid
1540's the shoulder seams of
the doublet were covered by a
wing or welt. The circular
ruff could be replaced by a
small collar or falling-band
trimmed with lace. Tall-
crowned hats appeared in the
1590's.

24 3rd Earl of Dorset by William Larkin 1613 Longer baggy breeches succeeded the round trunk-hose. There was considerable emphasis on the legs and feet, stockings were embroidered, shoes were decorated with large rosettes and garters or ribbons were worn below the knee. Textiles were still richly woven or embroidered in coloured silks and metal threads. Lace-edged collars were stiffened to frame the face. Gloves with long gauntlet cuffs were elaborate and might be made to match the clothes.

25 1st Duke of Hamilton by
Daniel Mytens 1629
Breeches were almost
universal by 1620 and they
grew longer and slimmer
fitting. The waistline of the
doublet rose and the lower
edge lengthened. Slashes or
panes in the chest and sleeves
exposed the shirt below. The
lace collar softened and
collapsed on to the shoulders.
Hair gradually lengthened
and it was fashionable to
grow a longer lock or portion
on the left-hand side.

26 Lord John and Lord Bernard Stuart by Sir Anthony van Dyck *c* 1639 Long, narrow knee-breeches were usually worn with boots of supple leather. The high-waisted, deep-skirted doublet began to resemble a jacket. The lace collar reached its maximum width by the mid 1630's. Men's clothes appeared casual and romantic.

27 Family of Sir Richard Saltonstall (det) by David des Granges *c* 1645
The long, vertical look continued to predominate. Clothes tended towards plainer fabrics and sober colours during the Civil War and Commonwealth periods. Shoes returned to fashion for ordinary wear.

28 Colonel John Russell by
J. M. Wright 1659
At a time of war throughout
Europe the influence of
military dress was strongly
felt. Buff leather coats came
into widespread use for the
armed forces and soldiers
wore a sash or scarf draped
diagonally across the chest.
The shirt was revealed to a
startling extent. Hair grew
very long.

29 The Tichborne Dole
(det) by G. van Tilborgh 1670
By 1670 a new version of the
male suit of clothes was
established. The knee-length
coat and waistcoat replaced
the doublet and were worn
with knee-breeches. The
neckcloth or cravat was
preferred to the lace collar
and long wigs were adopted.

30 Homme de Qualité by
J. D. de Saint Jean 1694
The lines of the coat and
waistcoat were gradually
improved and refined. The
coat became tighter in the
waist and fuller in the skirt
(width was added by pleats in
the side and back vents).
Sleeves were cut with deep
wide cuffs. Pockets were set
low. Fur muffs were used by
seventeenth-century men and
the sword was an essential
accessory.

31 Joseph Collet by A. Chinqua 1716
The first decades of the eighteenth century saw a continuation of the trends set in the 1690's. The skirts of the coat remained wide. The waistcoat was slightly narrower and shorter; it was often made in a contrasting material and usually buttoned only at the waist. Shoes with square, blocked toes and tongues cut high over the instep were fastened by small rectangular buckles.

32 Club of Artists (det) by G. Hamilton c 1735
The coat began to curve back slightly at the front edges to reveal more of the waistcoat and breeches. In time, more attention was paid to the cut of the breeches which became closer fitting. Fashions in wigs altered frequently. Long and short bob wigs were usual for undress wear.

33 'Marriage à la Mode –
The Marriage Contract' (det)
by William Hogarth *c* 1743
Coats and waistcoats became
slimmer fitting and breeches
were tighter (they were worn
with rolled stockings). Red-
heeled shoes were usual for
court or formal wear until the
middle of the eighteenth
century. The tail of the wig
could be enclosed in a black
silk bag finished with a large
bow.

34 Francis Beckford by Sir
Joshua Reynolds 1755-56
The stock, a band of fine linen
fastened round the neck, was
the usual form of neckwear.
The front opening of the shirt
was edged with a ruffle and
laced ruffles were worn at the
wrist. Deep wide cuffs
remained a fashionable
feature of the coat sleeve (but
they were soon to become
shorter and narrower). The
three-cornered hat was often
carried under one arm.

35 Lord Willoughby de Broke and family (det) by J. Zoffany *c* 1762
An alternative form of coat was the 'frock' which had a turned-down collar and a slightly easier cut. It was worn on less formal occasions. As women's hair arrangements became fuller and higher the crown of the male wig rose a little in sympathy. The fashionable silhouette was long and slender.

36 Sir Brooke Boothby by Joseph Wright of Derby 1781
The increasing mood of romanticism encouraged less formal clothing. A simpler, countrified look was affected by the upper classes. Plain cloth was generally preferred to silks and lace ruffles were abandoned. The double-breasted frock and waistcoat were fashionable and drab (a light brown colour) was popular. Round hats were worn in the country.

37 David Anderson by Sir Henry Raeburn 1790 English riding clothes were adopted for fashionable day wear in the 1790's. The coat was cut in across the waist to improve the fall of the tails on horseback and the square line was balanced by a double-breasted fastening, high collar and wide lapels. Tight riding breeches were worn with boots.

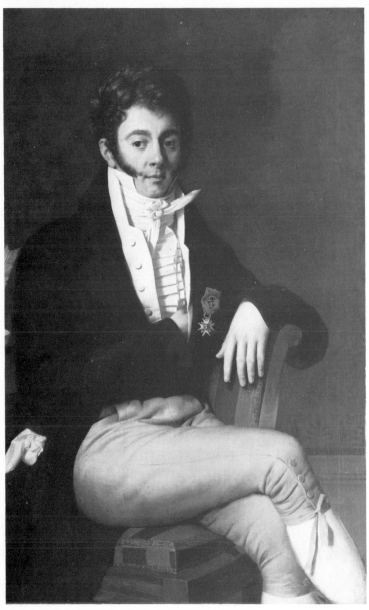

38 L. C. M. Dupaty, French School *c* 1810
The points of the shirt collar, or deep neckband, almost encased the lower jaw and the neck was entirely swathed by the cravat. The wig was discarded in the 1790's in favour of natural hair, worn short and unpowdered (intended to look carelessly windswept).

39 Baron Schwiter by Eugène Delacroix 1826
Black was worn with dramatic effect against a stark white neckcloth and heightened the romantic appearance of men's dress. Sombre colours and more practical clothes also heralded the coming industrial age. Trousers were in general use by 1825 and breeches were discarded for all but Court or very formal wear.

40 Portrait of a Gentleman
by W. Huggins 1842
By the 1840's men's clothes
had shed their romantic
appearance and took on a
more worldly air. Brighter
colours and lustrous textiles
appeared in waistcoats and
cravats. The frock coat was
usual for daytime wear and
did not match the trousers.

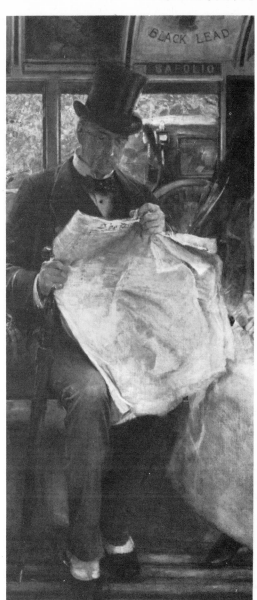

41 The Last Day in the Old Home (det) by R. B. Martineau 1862
During the 1860's the coat was made to button high to the neck and the waistcoat was almost concealed. The morning coat was usually single-breasted with three or four buttons and an outside breast pocket. Clothes appeared less formal—shirt collars were lowered and could be turned down over the cravat.

42 Chichester, Lord Carlingford by J. Tissot 1871
Trousers were cut straight in the leg, without interesting curves and had no centre creases until the 1890's. The necktie could be knotted or folded over the shirt front and secured by a pin. Whiskers were prominent and were worn in a variety of shapes.

43 The Bayswater Omnibus (det) by G. W. Joy 1895
The frock coat, worn with a top hat, stiff wing collar, bow tie and spats, was the correct dress in town and for business wear. By the 1890's a furled umbrella might be carried instead of a stick.

44 Bank Holiday by
William Strang 1912
Lounge suits gained in
popularity and by 1900 could
be worn for most informal
daytime occasions. The
jacket, waistcoat and trousers
were made to match and the
informal bowler hat could be
a similar colour. Separate
starched collars (single or
double) were always worn.

45 H. R. H. The Prince of
Wales by John St Helier
Lander *c* 1922
The Prince first wore 'the
multicoloured Fair Isle
sweater with its jigsaw of
patterns' in 1922. Pull-overs
(with knickerbockers or 'Plus
Fours') were worn chiefly for
golf and were extremely
popular between the Wars.
Tweed caps were usual for
country and sporting wear.

46 J. B. Priestley by James P.
Barraclough 1932
The lounge suit was
established for ordinary day
wear but on informal
occasions the waistcoat could
be replaced by a V-necked
pull-over. Collar-attached
shirts began to be worn. The
bow and long knotted ties
were the most common styles
of neckwear.

47 T. S. Eliot by Wyndham Lewis 1949
The wider trouser legs of the 1920's and 1930's were balanced by a squarer-cut jacket, padded in the shoulders, which was fashionable until the early 1950's. After the Second World War a new elegance was achieved by wearing very dark suits with plain white shirts.

48 Mr and Mrs Clark and
Percy (det) by David
Hockney 1970-71
Men's clothes were affected
by new attitudes and ideas in
the 1960's. Although the
conventional suit hardly
altered there was more
freedom of choice in colours
and textures and informal
clothes were increasingly
popular. Open-necked shirts,
pull-overs and flared trousers
or jeans were preferred at a
time when established rules of
etiquette were questioned and
rejected. Hair was grown
much longer.

CHAPTER THREE

The Suit I: to 1670

The general term 'suit' is used to describe a set or series of garments designed to be worn together at the same time, made in one colour or material, with similar decoration. The pattern for the modern suit for men – coat or jacket, waistcoat and trousers – was established in the later seventeenth century with the fashion for wearing a coat, vest and knee-breeches to match; but the general idea of wearing a set or combination of specific garments dates from a very much earlier period. The concept of a suit of clothes (at an earlier period called a 'robe') was accepted well before the mediaeval period and was probably a feature of primitive clothing. Remains of Bronze Age garments excavated from graves in Denmark, for example, fall into a consistent pattern of undergarment, cloak, cap and footwear which must have been worn by most men at that period.[1] In the fourteenth century the Great Wardrobe accounts of Edward III listed 'suits of clothes' of three, four, five or six garments each, and the term continued in use during the next three centuries. Samuel Pepys in the seventeenth century refers to his 'suits' both before and after the period when the coat, waistcoat and knee-breeches came into fashion.

The suit is composed of the main body garments which cover the upper and lower torso; at their simplest these took the form of a tunic, a mantle (or draped overgarment) and leg coverings [4]. As clothing developed it became usual to add an under layer of linen (shirt, drawers and hose) next to the skin and an outer layer (mantle, super-tunic or overcoat) for warmth and protection out of doors. The suit of clothes normally consisted of more than one layer, and two tunics were a common feature. The garments were often made to match, and although different shades, textures and types of ornament might be combined they were rarely without a common theme.

It was from these three basic items – the tunic, mantle and leg coverings – that most male clothing later developed. They constituted the essential male wardrobe in the Middle Ages but they have not always been worn together. In the Roman period, citizens of the Empire were privileged to wear the tunic and toga while Teutonic races of the colder north of Europe wore tunics, mantles and long, loose trousers called *bracae*. Roman citizens regarded the bracae (a typical feature of 'barbarian' costume) with contempt and were ashamed to cover their legs (although short, knee-length breeches for riding were permitted) [49]. During the early mediaeval period, the dress of working men was distinguished by practical short tunics and leg coverings, but those of higher rank wore long tunics and hose (stockings) rather than breeches [51].

Until the present century all clothes were made from the four natural fibres of wool (or hair), silk, linen and cotton. Linen and cotton were, in the main, confined to underclothing. Silk was a delicate, expensive fabric worn mostly by the higher ranks of society and then often restricted to ceremonial or formal wear. The most common and useful material for upper garments was wool which was available to every social class (in Latin literature, wool is often a synonym for clothing [2]). The special qualities of the fibre make it particularly suitable once it is woven into cloth and 'fulled'. It is warm and light but hard-wearing and elastic (which enables it to be shaped and moulded to the human figure) and it is to some extent weather-proof. Cloth can be woven in different weights and textures for use in cold or warm climates (the Roman toga, for instance, was made of a fine woollen fabric). Like leather, wool is a material that is readily available wherever animals are reared for meat; and since sheep feed on natural pasture they have for centuries been an economical source of material for clothes.

In the early history of clothing, the techniques of weaving were superior to those of cutting or sewing cloth. The process of weaving was established at a very early date and the fragments of cloth among Bronze Age finds indicate considerable skill and experience.[3] The construction of garments was relatively simple, based on the rectangular lines of the cloth as it was taken from the loom. The fabric was not cut into fanciful shapes and very little of it was wasted. Instead of cutting it to fit the natural contours of the body, the cloth was draped or hung about the figure with only the most essential stitching and fastening [51]. Male and female tunics were closer fitting during the twelfth and thirteenth centuries but this was achieved by means of pinning, lacing or buttoning. A major development came about in the fourteenth century with the evolution of tailoring techniques; for the first time cloth was cut to make garments fit like an outer skin [52]. Tailors adapted their skills to the problems imposed by this new concept of fashion, and techniques developed rapidly: by the early years of the fifteenth century, dress design had reached one of the high points in its history. Although men soon became bored with extremely tight-fitting clothes and looser garments returned to fashion for a time [12], fashionable dress in Western Europe had never reverted to untailored garments or the draped arrangements which have continued to be worn in the East.

It was with the introduction of shaped and fitted garments that the distinction between male and female clothing began to make itself felt. Until the early fourteenth century the clothes of both sexes were comparatively similar: each wore long, unshaped tunics and mantles. By the middle of the fourteenth century, however, most men had adopted the short tunic (previously worn by the labouring classes) and the legs were exposed to view. The hose became a more important garment for men and needed to be longer and better fitting. Knitted stockings were not common until the later sixteenth century and the hose were made from cloth or linen cut to the shape of the leg. They were held up by ties or 'points' fastened to the short tunic or 'doublet' above and, when tightly pulled, ensured a

49 Trajan's Column (det) Rome, eleventh century A.D. Soldiers wearing short breeches.

50 Saxon carving, ninth century A.D.

smooth fit [53]. The doublet was therefore indispensable to the hose; both were covered by an upper garment until the late fifteenth century and were considered indecent without it. Thus a pattern was set for the male suit of clothes, of doublet, hose and upper tunic. Men continued to wear long over-garments but essentially their clothes were bifurcated and there was no compulsion to conceal the legs. Women, however, retained the full-length skirt until the second decade of the twentieth century.

Before the radical changes of the fourteenth century there was less variety in the form and construction of clothing than in the quality or texture of materials, colours and decoration. These were the features which differentiated one man's appearance from another and served to indicate his position in the social hierarchy. Rank or occupation were distinguished clearly by the textiles worn. The finest grades of cloth or silk (which were often imported) were the most expensive and frequently were prohibited to the poorer classes, who dressed in cheaper, coarser home-spun cloths. Sumptuary legislation made every attempt to codify and regulate the social structure by restricting luxury clothing (even specifying the textiles and cut of garments permitted to different classes); but many of these laws were never enforced and their effectiveness is questionable.

Certain dyes were costly and highly prized – in particular, purple or crimson – and they remained the prerogative of a privileged few. In Roman

times it was rare to see an entire garment of purple (worn only by the Emperor or highest officials) and the colour was reduced to one or two bands or stripes which carried their own significance as a badge of social or political rank.

Textiles and clothing were varied still further by decoration – patterns woven into the cloth, embroidery, applied braid or metal ornaments sewn on to the clothes. The dress of the early Middle Ages especially seems to have been distinguished in these ways. There was little difference in the form of the tunic worn by upper and lower class men but the clothes of the higher ranks could be elaborately embroidered (for example, at the neck, hem and on the sleeves).

Mediaeval moralists frequently attacked the extravagance and luxury of contemporary fashionable dress, which appears fairly restrained to modern eyes; but it was probably the expensive materials, fine embroidery and costly fur linings which aroused their anger. Mediaeval clothes were lined throughout with fur [14], which was a precise indication of social status and one of the most important articles of luxury. Furs were worn by men of every class but the type varied according to rank and was regulated by sumptuary laws. In the Middle Ages furs fell into several different categories, the highest of which carried as much if not more prestige than mink and sable do today. The poor could only afford cheap furs, such as

51 Holkham Bible (det), early fourteenth century
Men wore long, unshaped tunics and closely-fitting linen caps or 'coifs' which tied under the chin.

49

lambskin (or 'budge'), while the middle and upper classes bought the more expensive squirrel ('gros vair' or 'miniver') and royalty or the very rich wore ermine and sable. (Some garments had cuffs and revers of fine fur, but for the sake of economy were lined elsewhere with a fur of inferior quality.)

During the past three hundred years the main items of a man's suit have retained their essential character and original names (apart from the change from knee-breeches to trousers in the early nineteenth century). Until the last decades of the seventeenth century, however, the garments in a suit of clothes altered considerably in form and combination and were known by a bewildering variety of names. Many of the early terms for articles of clothing are difficult, sometimes impossible, to identify with accuracy, especially in the periods from which relatively little information survives. There were, for instance, many forms of the mantle and tunic although at times the differences between named styles seems to have been very slight; in addition, some garments may have been known by more than one name (in the way that 'sweater, 'jumper', 'pullover' and 'jersey' can all be applied to the same article today). In tracing the development of the male suit of clothes, this chapter will denote the garments by general terms such as 'tunic', 'mantle' or 'leg-coverings' except when specific names can be positively identified in order to convey their essential form and to avoid confusion.

The Development of the Suit of Clothes

The earliest form of clothing was made from animal skins which were hung and wrapped about the body. When man discovered that the hair or fleece of animals could be twisted into thread and then woven into a piece of cloth it became possible to construct garments of a different nature. The most basic article of clothing, common to all primitive people, was a blanket or rectangular piece of cloth. This could be worn straight off the loom, either as a mantle over the shoulders or wrapped round the waist as a kind of skirt.[4] The Bronze Age finds in Denmark included several recognizable items of clothing:[5] in most of the graves were found the remains of cloaks, either semi-circular or oval, and a form of undergarment. This undergarment was a piece of woollen cloth, more or less rectangular, which appears to have been wrapped round the body and fixed with a belt at the waist and leather straps with bronze *tutuli* over the shoulders. A similar version was worn round the waist as a loin-cloth. These were accompanied by a cap and strips of cloth wound round the feet.

A curious feature of the Bronze Age garments is that the cloth was cut into a number of small, uneven pieces which were then sewn together. It has been suggested that this pattern was a deliberate attempt to imitate the animal skins used previously for clothing; but perhaps at such a relatively unsophisticated time the rough bits were simply easier to deal with than the straight pieces of woven cloth. These garments probably represent a fusion of two different cuts, one based on the irregular shape of animal pelts and the other on the rectilinear form of cloth from the loom.[6] In later periods the cut of the mantle was nearly always based on the rectangle. It could be worn as an unshaped piece of fabric or shaped into an oval or semi-circle by rounding off the corners.

A further development of the primitive blanket was the evolution of a tunic. Men began to come to terms with the potential of loom-woven cloth and found that if a slit or hole was made in the centre of the mantle it could be passed over the head and worn in the manner of a poncho; if they also joined the sides (leaving the seams open at the top for the arms to pass through), the garment could be closed. A sleeveless tunic could also be made from two smaller rectangular pieces of cloth (rather than folding one over in half); these were joined at the top and side edges with openings left for the head and arms, so that there were two side seams and a seam passing over the tops of the shoulders. Later, unshaped sleeves (rectangular or square) were inserted at the armhole, but many sleeved tunics, in particular those dating from the Coptic period (sixth and seventh centuries A.D.) were woven in one piece on the loom. The garment was woven sideways-on, so to speak, so that the width of the loom represented the length of the tunic; the weaving began with the end of one sleeve and finished at the end of the other. A gap or vertical slit was left for the neck-opening, and when complete the cloth was folded over and joined at the sides to form a perfect T shape. Tunics of the Roman period never had separate inserted sleeves; they were either woven in one with the garment or remained sleeveless.

The tunic was the basic article of clothing for Roman men [3]. It reached to just below the knee but was belted at the waist and could be pulled up and shortened for active pursuits. More than one tunic could be worn at a time and probably several were put on in cold weather. The most common material was wool, although linen was also used. In its natural state wool is a creamy colour, but it can be bleached white; whiteness and brightness were admired by the Romans, so the best quality cloths were those most finely bleached. Less expensive clothing was distinguished by its off-white colour, and class differences were immediately discernible by these shades. In addition, Roman citizens wore two purple stripes (*clavi*) on the tunic, from neck to hem passing over each shoulder. The stripes varied in width and appear to have been a mark of distinction, indicating rank or occupation; but their exact meaning is not altogether clear and it may have differed from one period to another. By the third century A.D. the stripes, although still worn, had lost their significance;[7] but they continued in use for some time and a vestige remained on tunics of the Coptic period.

The toga, which was the most ancient article of Roman clothing, was worn over the tunic by free-born citizens of the Empire (working men and those of low rank wore it only for festive occasions). It was a draped overgarment of fine wool, usually white, although some togas had a purple border. An all-purple toga was worn by the Emperor for ceremonies, and a dark-coloured, brown or black toga was the custom for mourning. The *toga praetexta*, which was white with a scarlet or purple stripe at the lower edge, was the dress of both officials or magistrates and boys until the age of sixteen. Young men then adopted the plain white *toga virilis*.

The toga was a stately garment arranged according to a set pattern; the correct draping was complicated and must have required assistance from another person. It consisted of a large piece of material which appears to have been about 5.55m. (18½ feet) long and 2.1m. (7 feet) wide, shaped approximately in a semi-circle or oval (the rounded corners allowed it to be draped more effectively). Its exact shape and proportions have not yet been fully established and there were several styles or arrangements fashionable at different periods. One form was draped diagonally around the body, passing over the left shoulder and under the right arm, while a later version passed around the back of the neck, over the right shoulder and arm and then on to the left shoulder. The folds could be arranged variously and it appears that the drapery of the toga grew increasingly elaborate and formalized. It is difficult to assess the extent to which the toga was worn in Britain during the Roman occupation. It is probable that new citizens adopted the privilege with enthusiasm, but it was, for the most part, only worn by the higher ranks on important occasions.[8] Many Roman citizens found the toga cumbersome and inconvenient and laws had to be introduced by several Emperors to ensure that it was used for formal wear. A practical alternative for ordinary daily wear was the mantle, which could be used as a protective outdoor garment.

By the early third century A.D. the toga had diminished in size and importance. The tunic was worn longer (to the calf) and had longer, close-fitting sleeves. In works of art from this period two tunics can be seen in use, the upper tunic being slightly shorter than the lower one.

The most important difference between the dress of the Romans and that of the races they conquered in the north of Europe, were the leg coverings or bracae worn by the latter. These long, unshaped trousers were fastened about the waist on a running string. They are known to have been worn by the Gauls (although they were not invented by them) and were later brought to Britain. The bracae were practical for country work and riding in the cold northern climate but they were despised by the Romans. During the occupation of Britain the Romans resisted adopting the garment, although it seems to have been incorporated gradually into the soldier's wardrobe and was eventually accepted. The Romans themselves wore a form of breeches called *feminalia* for riding and fighting, but these were short (to the knee) and were considered to be quite distinct from the barbarian trousers [49].

The first five centuries A.D. saw the evolution of basic Western European dress from a gradual fusion of northern and southern elements. The Roman tradition of long, dignified robes was maintained for ceremonial wear by the upper classes, while the simple, short tunic remained in use for poorer, labouring men. The tradition of rigid symbolism in Roman dress continued to be observed and clothes were intended to signify a man's status or occupation. An important new influence was felt in Europe with the conversion to Christianity, when a different attitude to clothing was introduced. Whereas the ancient Greek ideal had been to reveal the body and celebrate its natural beauty, the Jewish and subsequently the Christian faith strove to hide or disguise its natural contours. The effect was to muffle the figure in layers of unshaped garments. Although the basic forms of clothing remained similar their general character was changed. There was a new feeling of density in dress and the outlines of the body were diffused.

Few conclusions can be drawn about fashionable dress during the early mediaeval period since very little evidence survives in the way either of actual garments or of contemporary illustrations or literary references. Nevertheless, examples of jewellery and woven textiles still preserved suggest that the decoration of clothing was skilled and splendid. Rich colours, fine textiles, precious stones and metals were all incorporated in the dress of the higher social ranks.

A standard male wardrobe was gradually established and consisted of an over tunic and an under tunic (which reached the knee and had long, close sleeves), a short or long mantle, breeches, hose and shoes. Tunics were made of wool or linen (depending, to some extent, on the climate or season). Emperor Charlemagne, at the beginning of the ninth century, wore a linen under tunic or shirt, but the shirt as a piece of underclothing was not yet common and only came into general use two centuries later. The tunic was almost invariably belted at the waist [50], although the upper tunic could be worn loose. By the eleventh century a flourishing silk industry was established in Sicily and the fabric was worn by the upper classes all over Europe.

The breeches continued to be made in the form of loosely fitting trousers and were worn with stockings (hose or *chausses*) of linen or woollen cloth. The hose reached to the knee or just above it and were often made without feet, having instead a strap which passed under the instep. The breeches and hose could be bound with strips or bands of cloth wound spirally or criss-crossed round the leg from the ankle to the knee. Several different styles of mantle were in use and some were lined with fur. In general, long tunics and long mantles were reserved for the dress of the nobility and for ceremonial wear.

A useful and detailed source of information from the later eleventh century is the Bayeux Tapestry, thought to have been embroidered in about 1080 (but depicting the story of the Norman invasion of England in 1066). The monarchs, Edward, Harold and Duke William, when enthroned, wear long tunics and mantles, as do the important noblemen [5]. Other characters are dressed in knee-length garments, and Harold and William also appear in these at active moments in the story. Considerable attention is paid to leg coverings; the hose appear in different colours and some are cross-gartered. The dress of the Norman French and the English is fairly similar but the cut of the hair distinguishes their appearance. The French wear a distinctive short cut with the hair shaved at the back of the head.

The general character of male and female dress of the tenth and eleventh centuries reflected something of the intense and rigid spirit of the Romanesque style. The early twelfth century saw the beginning of a gradual relaxation towards a more decorative elegance typical of the Gothic period. By the mid twelfth century there appears to have been a clear departure from the basic T-shape cut of clothes – the carved figures on the cathedral at Autun, for example, illustrate a more varied line.

The new features in male dress were a lengthening and tightening of the tunic and the introduction of longer, wider sleeves. The wardrobe of two tunics remained the custom: the short version was worn by labouring men and by the upper classes when engaged in active pursuits such as hunting, [9] but the fashionable tunic was longer and fitted closer to the body. It is evident that tightly fitting clothes became very popular, but the effect was not yet achieved by tailoring; garments were gathered in and fastened at the side under the arm, by lacing or pinning the cloth (and buttons were used in the later thirteenth century). Works of art from the period (such as the figures on the West portal of Angers cathedral) illustrate these details and always show the folds which were caused by gathering the fabric (whereas in the fourteenth century a completely smooth fit was created by shaping the garments). The lacing or fastening may well have been considered ornamental. The belt or girdle played an important part in emphasizing the fitted waist of the tunic and was worn as a decorative accessory to dress (although some upper tunics continued to be worn unbelted).

There were variations in the style of the tunic, and the long skirt could be slit at the centre front to the level of the thighs. The upper tunic tended to be slightly shorter than the under one. Embroidered decoration at the hem, neck and sleeves became more usual. The sleeves of the under tunic were fitted close to the arm and it appears that they were often sewn up each time they were put on. Sleeves of the upper tunic were cut longer (to extend over the hand and sometimes well beyond the ends of the fingers) and could be turned back to form a cuff. The fashionable sleeve widened to a bell-shape towards the wrist and some examples were of such an exaggerated size that the lower part of the cuff hung almost to the level of the hem.

The long breeches or 'braies' were shortened and by the later twelfth century were worn as knee-length drawers of linen, as an undergarment. The hose reached to mid-calf; stockings constructed on a mediaeval pattern similar to these are still worn by Carmelite nuns. [10]

The increased length and width of fashionable dress may have been encouraged by the growing production and availability of fine textiles. [11] In turn, the textile industry was probably affected by new contacts with the East made during the Crusades, when large sections of the male population travelled long distances from Western Europe.

During the thirteenth century there appears to have been an increase in the splendour of dress rather than alteration in its form (Matthew Paris, for instance, expressed disgust with the foppery of fashionable clothes [12]). The most luxurious textiles, such as brocaded silks and cloth of gold, were still confined to formal or ceremonial use, but fine quality woollen cloth was worn with great effect. The heavy draperies and sculptural folds of long and ample garments created a stately and opulent effect, but the cloth could be lightened by additional colour and sparkle. Tunics were embroidered in polychrome silks or gold and silver thread, with pearls and precious stones. Another form of decoration was to sew small metal ornaments, devices or badges (stamped out of silver or silver gilt) on to the clothes. These 'bezants' may have been used in the twelfth century – and the origin of the custom probably dates from a much earlier, prehistoric period – but it was during the thirteenth and fourteenth centuries that they were particularly fashionable. Edward III's Great Wardrobe accounts make reference to ornamental devices such as letters, orange trees and swans, and a number of examples (dating from before 1361) have been excavated at Wisby in Sweden. Contemporary illustrations show hoods covered with decorative spots, and these are probably another variation.

Buttons became fashionable in the late thirteenth century as a means of fastening and as ornaments. The idea of wearing a row of buttons was new and very popular, but since they were at first rather precious and expensive the fashion was restricted to the privileged classes. University doctors, for example, were entitled to wear as many buttons as they wished and the tradition has persisted to this day in the long row of small buttons still worn on the Roman Catholic priest's 'soutane'. In the thirteenth and fourteenth centuries, buttons were worn at the neck, on the shoulders, at the centre front of the tunic and on the sleeves [10]. At one time it was thought that buttons from this period were purely ornamental, but it is evident from contemporary manuscript illuminations, effigies and fragments of fourteenth-century clothing recently excavated in London that buttons which fastened through buttonholes were in use for practical purposes too. Those found on the site of Baynard's Castle in London were made from small scraps of cloth tightly knotted in a ball but it is likely that more elaborate buttons of precious metal, stones or glass were worn by men of high standing.[13]

The male 'surcoat' began to be strikingly patterned in the early thirteenth century. The surcoat was a long, loose, sleeveless tunic worn over the mail armour (which was made of interlinked metal rings) for warfare or tournaments. The covering protected the armour from damp (and possible rust) in the north of Europe and from the heat of the sun in hotter climates; it also served as a means of identification, displaying the wearer's colours or coat of arms. Since mediaeval armour disguised a man's appearance, especially when the closed helm came into use after about 1217, the patterned surcoat made it possible to distinguish friends and enemies.[14] The colours and designs were painted on coarse linen cloth, but woven and embroidered patterns may also have been used. The surcoat was split at the front for riding and was shortened to knee-length by the middle of the century.

Mail armour was worn over a thick padded or quilted tunic (the 'gambeson' or 'aketon') which prevented chafing and eased the weight of the metal on the shoulders. The tunic was made from several layers of linen or woollen cloth sewn firmly together. Although the surcoat and gambeson were items of military rather than civilian dress their shape and structure exercised some influence over fashionable male clothing.

The tunic remained long and unshaped, with or without a belt, but there was a variety of sleeve styles. A popular sleeve in the thirteenth century was cut in one with the garment in the dolman fashion; it was loose in the upper arm but could be wrapped over the wrist and fastened to give a close fit. Wrapped sleeves were still to be seen in the early decades of the fourteenth century [51] which generally saw a continuation of late thirteenth-century shapes and styles. Garments were loose-fitting and ample, using a large amount of cloth. The sleeve of the under tunic was worn long, straight and close to the wrist and showed beneath the shorter, looser sleeve of the upper tunic. The oversleeve could have a wide cuff and the decoration of both sleeve ends consisted in bands of embroidery or braid.

By the beginning of the fourteenth century changes were beginning to take place; Italian frescoes of the period, for example, depict fashionable young men in tunics with a small standing collar instead of the plain slit at the neck-opening. The collar was to increase in height and became a distinctive feature of fashionable male dress in Italy in the 1330's. Another important change, beginning to take place at the end of the 1320's was the adoption of the short tunic previously worn by working men [66], while the full-length tunic was discarded for all but the most formal occasions. As the tunic shortened it became closer-fitting and began to be tailored or shaped to the body; it was slightly waisted with a full skirt (probably made with insets of material or cut on the cross grain of the fabric), had tight sleeves and could have a low, curved neck-opening [52]. The bodice of the tunic fitted the torso well and appears to have been slightly padded in the chest. The new length, of course, revealed the legs, so the hose were made longer and tighter. Women's clothes at this time displayed similar features of shaping, with a close fit over the bust and waist and a fullness in the skirt, but their tunics remained full-length.

By the middle of the 1340's, then, a new male wardrobe had evolved. It was now customary for all men to wear an undergarment or shirt of linen with short linen drawers. Over these came the short under tunic or 'doublet' (the term was in common use in England by the 1370's, and in France was called a *pourpoint*). The doublet was a short, padded waist-length jacket with a low neck, tight sleeves, and no belt. It was a lined or double garment which by the 1360's was often quilted, and the technique seems to have passed directly from military dress into civilian use. The doublet was always firmly constructed to bear the strain of the points which were tied through eyelet holes at the tops of the hose [53].

The upper tunic took several different forms (both open and closed) but one of the most common was the 'cote-hardi' [10]. This was a short coat or tunic with a low, rounded neck and a row of buttons at the centre front which fastened it tightly to the body; a narrow girdle or belt emphasised the fitted waist. Mantles were worn for outdoor wear but could be made to match both the upper and the lower tunics. The process of shortening and tightening continued throughout the 1340's. In the early years of the decade, 'mi-parti' became fashionable. Parti-coloured clothing was made from two different materials, usually one patterned and one plain or in two contrasting colours. The hose were also given this treatment.

Further changes in the appearance of men's clothes took place during the

52 Luttrell Psalter (det)
c 1340–45
By the mid-fourteenth century male tunics were short and tailored to fit the body. A belt carrying a purse and dagger was worn on the hips.

53 Hastings Hours (det)
c 1480
Long fitted hose were attached to the doublet by ties or 'points'. Until the late fifteenth century the doublet and hose were always covered by a tunic or gown.

54 Tomb of Sir Richard Vernon 1517
An open-fronted gown, skirted tunic, four-cornered cap and broad-toed shoes were fashionable by this date.

second half of the fourteenth century. There was a new development in the shape of the tunic in the 1350's. It was still worn short (the length gradually decreasing to the level of the thighs) but the skirt was narrowed to a close fit over the hips and extra padding was added to the chest. The new length and fit were taken much furthur than any previous fashion and caused a sensation. The idea of deliberately exhibiting a silhouette was eagerly seized upon, although Churchmen and moralists thoroughly disapproved of the way in which the contours of the body were so blatantly revealed. Contemporary writers went so far as to attribute the French defeat at the battle of Crecy in 1346 to a Divine punishment for their pride in wearing such short, indecent clothes.[15] On the other hand, the epic poem, *Sir*

Gawain and the Green Knight, (which appears to belong to this period) conveys all the pleasure taken in a fashion which so successfully displayed the best features of the masculine figure.

The Green Knight was an impressive sight:

> For though at back and at breast his body was broad,
> His hips and haunches were elegant and small.

The poet goes on the describe how he was dressed:

> And garments of green girt the fellow about –
> A two-third length tunic, tight at the waist,
> A comely cloak on top, accomplished with lining
> Of the finest fur to be found, made of one piece,
> Marvellous fur-trimmed material, with matching hood
> Lying back from his locks and laid on his shoulders;
> Fitly held-up hose, in hue the same green,
> That was caught at the calf, with clinking spurs beneath
> Of bright gold on bases of embroidered silk.[16]

The characteristic line of the 1350's and 1360's was long and thin, accentuated by the row of buttons on the upper tunic, the elongated end of the hood and the hanging oversleeves. The pointed tip of the hood was gradually drawn out to a long pipe and the sleeves developed ribbon-like streamers from the elbow [**10**]; with the decorative use of serrated edges ('dagging') these features contributed to the Gothic character of later fourteenth-century dress. Men's tunics were extremely tight and elegant in the 1360's and there appears to have been considerable use of the bias cut in the tailoring of clothes. Contemporary artists were obviously aware of the stresses and pulls caused by such a close fit and almost always painted in the inevitable creases and wrinkles across the waist and chest [**10**]. Sleeves also were tightly fitting in the upper arm and set in to a narrow, shaped armhole.

During the 1360's a new sleeve construction came into fashion. The head of the sleeve, which was cut wide and round, was attached to the bodice in a large circular seam spreading towards the centre front and back; it looked rather like a plate and the sleeves in fact were called '*à grandes assiettes*'. A doublet, thought to have belonged to Charles of Blois in about 1364, still exists in the Musée Historique des Tissus in Lyons and has sleeves of this type. They were made in two parts joined by a seam at the elbow. The forearm fastened with twenty spherical buttons, from wrist to elbow, and there were thirty-two buttons at the centre-front opening of the garment. The doublet, or pourpoint, was slit at the side seams over the thighs and had seven ties (points) for the hose on the inner lining at hip level.[17]

During the 1370's the torso remained tightly moulded, with the aid of padding and quilting (in both the skirt and the bodice), and the neckband or collar began to rise. The tunic of the 1370's and 1380's was, if anything, even tighter and shorter and the slim fit over the hips was marked by a broad and elaborately wrought belt [**11**]. The minimal length of the tunic made it necessary for the hose to reach the fork, and by the late 1390's the separate stockings could be joined to form one garment, similar to a modern pair of 'tights' [13].

A new version of the upper tunic which came into fashion for both men and women was the *houppelande* [12]. It was mentioned in French wardrobe accounts as early as 1359[18] but was not common in England until the 1380's. This overgarment (called a 'gown') was worn above the close-fitting doublet and hose and could vary in length. Its distinctive features were a loose fit, long, large sleeves and, later, a high collar. The gown was pleated or gathered across the chest and belted high over the waist; the rising neckband encircled the neck and part of the face and the hem swept down to a train at the back (the short version ended at the thighs) [13].

The houppelande could be made of fine woollen cloth or plain and brocaded silks, lined throughout with fur and decorated with embroidery and dagged edging. The squire in Chaucer's *Canterbury Tales*, for example, had a short gown with long, wide sleeves:

> He was embroidered like a meadow bright
> And full of freshest flowers, red and white.[19]

The idea of being embroidered like a field of flowers was a favourite theme in fourteenth-century literature and Sir Gawain, a few decades earlier, had worn such beautiful robes that:

> It certainly seemed to those assembled as if spring
> In all its hues were evident before them.[20]

Some of the brocaded silks also were very splendid, and the finest were woven in Italy which (rather than France) was the fashion centre of Europe at this period. Francesco Datini, a cloth merchant of Prato in the late fourteenth century, spent large sums of money on his clothes; apparently his prestige required a sumptuous appearance.[21] One of his inventories of 1397 included:

4 doublets
10 long gowns:
     5 old ones for every day
     2 with fur linings
     1 'old, unlined one for writing'
     2 very grand ones for great occasions, both red
     (one lined with squirrel, the other with taffeta)
5 cloth cloaks
2 shorter riding capes
9 hoods

His undergarments consisted of:

6 pairs of breeches
5 pairs of long hose of cloth or linen:
     3 were blue with leather soles
     2 were black, to wear with slippers
8 or 10 pairs of linen undersocks.

It was the custom for rich men to employ a tailor, with one or two workmen, to spend several days or weeks in the house to make new clothes for the whole family; [21] middle-class families usually ordered one new set of clothes each year. [22]

The years from the 1390's to about 1420 cover the International Gothic period, a title which refers to a common style in painting, architecture and dress throughout Europe (national or regional differences in clothing did not become noticeably apparent until the second decade of the fifteenth century). The International Gothic style in dress had a well-defined character. The period marks the point at which people grew bored with the extreme tightness of clothes, and their reaction was expressed in the widespread adoption of the bulky houppelande. The sleeves of this garment were enormous and varied considerably in style; the two most common fashions were huge and open-ended sleeves with a hanging cuff, or large and bag-like sleeves with a cuff closed tight at the wrist [12, 13]. Almost all sleeves were lined with fur.

There was an air of grandeur and dignity about early fifteenth-century dress, for not only was it enriched with embroidery and woven patterns, ornaments and fur but it was also extremely weighty with its yardage of heavy woollen cloth or brocaded silks and furred linings. Yet true to the Gothic spirit it also had a light, fluttering, sparkling quality. Clothes were decorated with elaborately cut edges and ribbon-like streamers; a wide range of bright clear colours was worn and embroidery included the sewing on of small metal ornaments which gave the cloth an additional lift. It was a period of extravagance and exaggeration but also of imagination and exuberance.

By the 1420's much of this high-spirited romanticism began to fade and there was a gradual toning down of expression. At this date regional differences became more marked and in particular there was a growing divergence in taste between the north and south of Europe. Dress in the south and in Italy was distinguished by a tendency towards discipline, restraint and a general classicism, whereas the north of Europe appeared to have a natural affinity with the Gothic spirit and preferred a harder, more elaborate and rather eccentric line.

The 1420's and 1430's marked the disappearance of high necks, serrated edges and voluminous garments. Tunics were worn shorter (by the 1430's reaching to about mid-calf) and sleeves, though magnificent, were not enormous [14]. In Italy, for instance, a shorter tunic with a wide bulky hem was fashionable in the 1420's, making men's legs appear long and thin; also the neck-opening was dropped low at the back which with a short, full haircut, made necks look longer than usual. The general effect was a somewhat bird-like aspect. In the north of Europe, especially in the Low Countries, fashionable clothing was characterized by a more solid simplicity; there is a monumental quality about the typical weighty bourgeois dress so often seen in early Netherlandish painting. The over tunic was cut fairly full with a low-set waistline and bag-shaped sleeves which made the wearer seem round-shouldered. The doublet and hose beneath remained tight-fitting, although the centre front of the doublet was beginning to be left open to reveal the shirt. The hose continued to be made with or without feet; they were worn sometimes as two separate stockings but it was more usual for them to be joined at the crotch and attached by points to the doublet. By the first decade of the fifteenth century the shortness of the doublet had made it necessary to cover the front opening, at the fork, with a flap or pouch, called the codpiece, which was tied to the hose [53]. The codpiece was to remain in fashion until the last quarter of the sixteenth century and was displayed in varying degrees of prominence. C. W. and P. Cunnington suggest that the name derives from 'cod', an old term for bag;[23] in the sixteenth century the words 'cod and yard' were used by contemporary writers (such as Richard Hakluyt) to refer to the male genitals.[24]

Until the last decades of the fifteenth century the doublet and hose were covered by an over tunic, but it was possible for working men, when actively engaged, to dispense with it temporarily (as an equivalent of working in shirt sleeves today). At times it was also necessary to loosen or untie at the back the points attaching the hose to the doublet; it was often difficult to bend over otherwise, and any strenuous movement put undue strain on the fastenings. This was regarded as a practical but not very dignified measure and it distinguished the labourer from the man of breeding.[25]

During the fifteenth century there was some diversity in the length and shape of the overgarment. In general it took two forms, the short over tunic (which decreased in length as the century progressed) and the long, bulky gown. The gown reached the calf or ankle and was a formal, dignified garment, worn by officials and men of standing or on special occasions; it could be put on over an upper tunic [15, 53]. The shorter over tunic was the more usual form. Both were made of cloth or silk lined with fur. Styles changed with the fashion but there were three general variations: it could be cut with a separate, close-fitting bodice and a flared skirt, joined by a seam at the waist; it could be semi-circular, widening towards the hem and falling into folds or pleats which were confined at the waist by a belt (or secured from inside by an arrangement of stitches or tapes); or it might be a sleeveless, tabard-like garment (also pleated at the back and front). Sleeve shapes varied a great deal.[26]

The fashionable silhouette of the 1440's was more slender and elegant than before. Much of the previous bulk was pared down and in the Netherlands, for instance, there was a tendency towards angularity with a squarer, padded shaping in the upper arm. The tunic was worn above the knee and the waist was tightly confined with a belt. These trends were taken further during the 1450's when the tunic became very short, the position of the waist was a little higher and shoulders were made to look broader (enlarged by a ball-shaped padding in the sleeves of both short and long tunics). The result was a slightly swaggering air but, on the whole, there was an increasing elegance and refinement in men's clothes. Well-fitting, bias-cut hose and narrow, pointed shoes were worn with the shorter hemline. Fashions in northern Europe were influenced by the Burgundian Court, especially during the reign of Philip the Good (who died in 1467). Philip was noted for his elegance and had a personal preference for black, but both black and purple were popular colours.

During the 1460's northern European dress became even more eccentric, increasing in spikiness and angularity [15]. The short, square-shouldered tunic (emphasizing the length of the legs), tall caps and very long-toed shoes all contributed to this image [16]. The short tunic reached its briefest length by 1470 but in the middle years of that decade a different line began to emerge. The fashionable silhouette lost much of its aggressively linear quality and was replaced by a new simplicity and softness. The grotesque padding of the tunic was also discarded, in favour of a more slender shape. By the 1480's men's tunics and doublets were beginning to look casual and romantic. The doublet was worn very short and left open at the centre front to expose more of the shirt, and the sleeves were slit at the elbow and along the forearm to allow the shirt to spread more comfortably and soften the line [17].

It became possible, during the 1470's, to wear the doublet and hose without the covering of an over tunic [53] and by the following decade the practice was widespread. This was, in effect, a fashionable 'playing at democracy' with its imitation of working-men's dress. It was also an expression of the new interest, in Italy, in classical works of art, for the skin-tight doublet and hose resembled the nude figure; the allusion to antique statues was reinforced by the loose draping of large mantles over the body, in the manner of a Roman toga or ancient Greek draperies. The seemingly nude image was at first considered rather shocking but soon became very popular and it was undoubtedly a glamorous fashion for younger men with good figures; it was a neat, athletic, youthful look.

During the 1490's however, the starkness of this line was broken up by a certain amount of surface patterning and fabrics were decorated with small scores and slashes. There was also a squaring of the silhouette together with an increasing softness and roundness in the shape of the garments. The doublet, for example, lost its collar and was cut with a low, squared neck-opening; in Germany, the centre-front opening formed a deep, low-cut V which was laced across the chest over a soft, full shirt. The hair was worn long, to the shoulders, and shoes were cut in a rounder, more natural shape. In the final years of the century the squatter line was completed by a new version of the over tunic [18, 54]. The tunic, worn over the doublet and hose, had sometimes been open at the front; from this fashion there developed a short, loose overcoat or gown which reached the knees and fastened in front, with turned-back lapels or revers. By 1500 this had become the most fashionable type of upper garment (from which the gown of the university graduate was, in turn, to develop) and it was worn throughout Europe.

The first two decades of the sixteenth century saw a continuation of the square silhouette. The shoulders and upper sleeves were cut wide and full to give an impression of squashy bulk over the mock nudity of the tight doublet and hose. There continued to be marked regional differences in European fashions; Germans visiting the English Court, for example, were thought to look unnecessarily indecent in their extremely tight hose (which revealed the shape of the buttocks) and their low-cut doublets open to the waist over low-necked shirts. Long and short tunics remained in use, the long gown, as before, being reserved for more dignified or ceremonial occasions.

By 1510 the nude effect was passing out of fashion and in England the tunic with long, pleated skirts made its appearance [54]. The front had a deep U- or V-shaped opening which could be filled in with a piece of matching material rather like a woman's stomacher. The skirt was parted at the centre front, below the waist, to reveal the codpiece which was fashionably prominent (with the addition of padding, stiffening and decoration) until the mid 1570's.

A very popular form of decoration was slashing which had appeared in a modest form at the end of the fifteenth century but was at its height during the 1520's and 1530's. Small, ornamental cuts or slashes were made in the material of the overgarments to reveal the white linen shirt or a coloured lining beneath [19]. Very often the shirt was pulled through the slits in small puffs and the slashes were decorated further by pinked or snipped edges (which were left raw).[27] The practice of slashing probably originated from cutting slits in leather garments to allow greater ease of movement. In the 1530's slashed leather jerkins or over doublets (with or without sleeves) became a popular and practical fashion, and they were worn universally until the following century.

The tunic or doublet changed its general shape during the 1530's, to become closer-fitting and shorter in the skirt; the low, square neckline began to disappear and was cut higher to the throat. The overcoat, with large, puffed upper sleeves was still popular; often it was lined with fur, and snow leopard or spotted lynx were particularly fashionable [19].

A long-bodied look was characteristic of the 1540's when further noticeable changes took place in the male wardrobe [20]. As the position of the waist was lowered a little and the neckband rose, the torso appeared to lengthen; at the same time, the hem of the tunic rose and by the mid 1540's it revealed a new version of the hose. A form of short breeches appeared and the hose were now divided into two parts. The stockings fitted the legs from ankle to mid-thigh and were attached to a looser, upper portion called the trunk-hose, which reached from the thigh to the waist. The trunk-hose, as a rule, were made to match the doublet and over-tunic; the stockings did not necessarily match but could be worn in a harmonizing or even a contrasting colour. Knitted hose were not made in England until the mid sixteenth century (although they were known elsewhere at an earlier date), but they came into common use during the second half of the century.

During the 1550's, the large sleeves of the early decades disappeared. Detachable sleeves which were tied in at the armhole with points came into general fashion and from the mid 1540's onwards the shoulder seams of the tunic or doublet were covered by a narrow wing or welt (and sometimes a padded roll of material) which concealed the join [23]; this feature was often also included on garments with set-in sleeves, as an added ornament. At this period short cloaks worn over the doublet or upper tunic were very fashionable, and they continued to be worn as part of the suit (especially for formal wear) until the second half of the seventeenth century. The cloak was frequently made *en suite* with the doublet and trunk-hose, in cloth, velvet, satin or brocaded silks.

Black and red were two popular colours of the sixteenth century and were often worn together in the 1540's. The heraldic effect of this combination is very noticeable in the portraits of Holbein. After the mid sixteenth century Spanish fashions were the predominant influence on European dress; black was the keynote of Spanish elegance and there was a general liking for sombre colours. Fashionable English dress in the 1560's favoured a combination of black, cream and coral which is often found in Elizabethan portraits.

The shape of the male suit of clothes in the second half of the century was increasingly rigid and formalized [55]. Both the doublet and the trunk-hose were padded and stuffed into a rounded shape which set the masculine silhouette into rather artificial lines. The skirt of the tunic grew even shorter during the 1550's and a decade later the waistline itself began to rise. The waistline finally came to rest at a new angle, higher at the back than at the front where it dipped to a point with a slight swelling over the stomach. The distinctive 'peascod belly' shape became very pronounced in the mid 1570's and was worn until the end of the century [22]. The shape was achieved by stiffening and padding the doublet with bombast, a stuffing of cotton, flock, rags or other material. The trunk-hose were padded in the same way. In the 1550's they were still fairly restrained, but they were more puffed by the 1560's and in the second half of the decade became extremely full.

Another important development was the increased height of the neckband (at its highest in the 1560's, when it almost encased the lower jaw) [21]. The neckline of the doublet was surmounted by the frilled edge of the shirt and as the neckband rose this frill expanded, in both width and height, to become a separate starched collar or ruff, set into formal pleats [22]. The use of padding and starching gave an inflexible aspect to men's clothes in the 1560's. This was a common image all over Europe since male fashions of the mid sixteenth century were virtually international; men in England, for example, differed little in appearance from their Italian counterparts.

During the 1570's several variations in the shape and form of the trunk-hose were fashionable. The trunk-hose could be made in two layers (with the stockings, there were three items of hose in all); the upper layer, from waist to thigh, remained full and rounded, but could be combined with a closely fitting lower portion (canions) which covered the thighs. Canions varied in length and sometimes were little more than a tight, narrow band to which the trunk-hose were attached above the knee. By the 1580's the shape of the trunk-hose was very exaggerated; they were either very short and puffed or long and narrow and the two versions could be worn together [**23, 55**]. Breeches in the form of longer, baggy trunk-hose came into fashionable use during the last quarter of the century. These 'Venetians' were constructed with two side seams – on the inner and outer sides of each leg – and had much less padding, to give a softer, slightly longer line.[28] Breeches may have been introduced originally for more informal wear, such as riding or hunting. By the last decade of the sixteenth century greater attention was paid to knitted stockings and they were worn in many different colours with ornamental clocks at the ankle and decorative garters round the knee.

There was a similarity in the rigid, exaggerated shape of both male and female dress of the 1580's and 1590's [**55**]. Both wore the long, pointed bodice with a narrow wasp-waist and leg-of-mutton sleeves. By the end of the century however, the men looked more romantic. There was a casual

55 A Procession of Queen Elizabeth I (det), attributed to Robert Peake the Elder *c* 1600 The doublet and trunk-hose were padded and stiffened to a fashionable shape. Knitted stockings were usual after the mid sixteenth century.

elegance in the arrangement of their hair, which was longer and curled more softly, and their clothes were lavishly coloured and decorated with embroidery, but above all, the fashion for short trunk-hose revealed the length of their legs to an almost unprecedented degree [22]. Women's dresses, on the other hand, were excessively stiff, supported by boned bodices and the wheel farthingale, which made them appear rather formidable.

The body line remained fairly rigid and unnatural until the second decade of the seventeenth century. Doublets were padded with horsehair and although the peascod belly disappeared in about 1600, the stiff, elongated, wasp-waisted effect remained. The skirt of the doublet consisted of a series of overlapping tabs (usually eight in number) and the peascod swelling at the centre front was replaced by two stiffened triangular 'belly-pieces' which formed a sharp point or lozenge-shape at the waist.[29] Doublets and hose were still richly embellished with embroidery in silks and metal threads and there is a stiff, icon-like impression about male portraits of this period. Long, baggy breeches or 'slops', however, replaced the round trunk-hose. They were voluminous and reached almost to the knee (at their most exaggerated in about 1613) [24].

During the second decade of the century men's dress took on a more informal note and a new image became apparent. The waistline rose to its natural position, the ruff or collar of the shirt was worn open at the neck, there was less use of embroidery and clothes in general seemed to be loosening up. The continuing Spanish influence on fashion encouraged a preference not only for darker colours but also for garments which were well but simply cut. This trend continued until the 1640's and increasingly greater attention was paid to the quality and cut of the fabric than to extravagant forms of decoration. Plainer cloths and more subdued colours were worn by the middle and lower classes.

By 1620, trunk-hose had been replaced almost entirely by breeches. The raised waistline, combined with longer breeches, focused attention on the legs, which were an important area of fashion. Stockings and shoes were elaborate and colourful, the feet and the knees were emphasized with decorative rosettes and the breeches displayed a mass of material in soft, full folds. During the 1620's breeches grew longer but slimmer-fitting and the waistline rose to a height just above its natural position [25]. As the body of the doublet grew shorter, the tabs of the skirt lengthened and were reduced in number (to six and later four) so that the garment began to resemble a kind of jacket [26]. At this period the breeches started to be attached to the inner side of the doublet by hooks and eyelet holes instead of ties or points; however, a series of tags or laces with metal tips (aiglets), relics of the tie-fastening, were often used to decorate the outer surface of the garment at the waist.

The long-legged look was taken a step further in the 1630's when the breeches were cut closer to the leg [56]. The high-waisted, deep-skirted doublet was surmounted by a broad lace collar (or falling-band) which spread across the shoulders and reached its maximum width by the middle

56 Lord Belasyss by Gilbert
Jackson 1636
The fashionable lace collar
spread over the shoulders
while the doublet and
breeches became longer and
straighter.

of the decade. A decorative effect was to slash or 'pane' the sleeves and body of the doublet to reveal the shirt beneath. White linen shirts looked particularly well against the darker colours now preferred, and an elegant combination of black and white was often worn. Men's dress now struck a plainer and more sophisticated note and an air of refinement emanated from the Court of Charles I. Men continued to look informal, but there was a more studied carelessness about their appearance with the increasing display of underlinen and a longer, curled haircut. The stiffness and padding of earlier decades was abandoned completely.

The fashionably romantic image, often thought to be the typical feature of 'cavalier' dress, reached its peak in the late 1630's and early 1640's [26]. The doublet was cut with a softer line and shorter sleeves which exposed more of the shirt. Colouring and texture were all-important, and there was a general liking for layers of shimmering satins, gauzy underlinen and creamy, cloudy lace. The hair was worn even longer, and was loosely curled, while large hats with broad brims were becoming more usual. There was a certain fussiness about the new look with all its slashing and lace trimming but, as we know from the portraits of Van Dyck, it had a distinct grace and charm.

During the next two decades, wars in England and throughout Europe had their effect on men's clothing. Fashions altered comparatively little and the influence of military dress was strongly felt [28]. Buff leather jackets and knee-boots were commonly worn and the baldrick or military sash, tied diagonally across the chest, was frequently seen. The long, vertical look continued to predominate, breeches were worn long and narrow and the doublet was rather short and straight [27]. Although there was no recognizable form of 'Puritan' dress in England during the Civil War and Commonwealth periods it may be said that clothes tended towards plainer, more sober fabrics and colours than hitherto, and garments of a simpler cut.

During the 1650's and early 1660's, however, men's fashions began to express some of the baroque spirit of the period [57]. The doublet revealed still more of the underwear and the shirt oozed out negligently from the sleeves and centre-front opening and at the waist. The effect was encouraged by a general shrinkage of the doublet; the sleeves and body were shortened and the lower buttons at the front were left undone – by the early 1660's the doublet was reduced almost to a bolero jacket.

As the doublet began to shorten in the mid 1640's, the breeches gradually widened to a squarer shape so that by 1650 they resembled a pair of modern 'shorts', rather full in the leg and reaching the knees.[30] By this date the breeches were no longer attached to the doublet but were fastened at the waist with a button or strap. This left a gap between the lower edge of the doublet and the waistband of the breeches; as the doublet diminished in size the space increased and allowed more of the shirt to be exposed. There was now a great liking for ribbon decoration which was attached in loops and bunches to the waistband, centre-front openings and legs of the breeches. An extravagant yardage of material also became characteristic of

57 Portrait of a Man in Black by G. ter Borch 1656 As the doublet shrank in size more of the shirt was exposed at the arms, waist and centre front. Petticoat-breeches were extremely wide and resembled a skirt.

68

fashionable male dress at this stage and the extreme to which it went after the Restoration of the monarchy in 1660 may perhaps be attributed to a reaction against the restrictions of the Commonwealth period. Breeches were cut with increasingly wide legs and by the end of the 1650's had become a virtual pair of culottes, or a very full, and gathered, divided skirt. The aptly-named 'petticoat breeches' were first seen in England in 1658 but were not universal until the early 1660's. In 1663 Anthony à Wood thought it was 'a strange effeminate age when men strive to imitate women in their apparell, viz long periwigs, patches in their faces, painting, short wide breeches like petticotes, muffs, and their clothes highly scented, bedecked with ribbons of all colours.'[33]

The small doublet and open-kneed breeches were a fairly short-lived fashion. The doublet, in fact, was nearing the end of its life. It had been the main body garment for men since the Middle Ages and was an essential feature of the male suit of clothes, with the hose or breeches and an upper tunic or mantle; but in the later 1660's changes took place which were to alter the composition of the suit. Doublets and cloaks were replaced by a waistcoat and coat while breeches returned to the narrower form, closed at the knee. By 1670 the transformation was complete. It did not represent an entirely new departure since the suit of three garments – breeches, tunic and upper tunic – was based on a long tradition; but its different composition heralded a new pattern for the future. After 1670 the three-piece suit was frequently modified, but its basic form was to remain unchanged for the next three centuries.

CHAPTER FOUR

The Suit II: 1670–1970

The modern version of the man's suit, consisting of a coat, waistcoat and breeches or trousers, is usually considered to have evolved by the last quarter of the seventeenth century. From the 1670's onwards there were variations in the cut and style of these three garments but the essential form of the suit did not change. The coat, for instance, was originally knee-length but shortened to become a jacket in the 'lounge suit' of the later nineteenth and twentieth centuries; the waistcoat or 'vest', also long at first, had become waist-length by the later eighteenth century and knee-breeches were generally replaced by trousers in the early nineteenth. At times the waistcoat has been discarded; the two-piece suit came into more general use during the Second World War, for example, when economy measures restricted the use of cloth; but the three-piece suit has remained the basis of the male wardrobe and continues to be fashionably worn by men of all ages.

The set of garments which made up the suit were intended to be worn together but they were not necessarily of the same colour and material. Until the later nineteenth century it was not uncommon for breeches or trousers and the waistcoat to differ from the coat in both shade and fabric [61]. In the eighteenth century, while coat and breeches often matched, the waistcoat might be similar in tone but decorated in a different manner [60]. Fancy waistcoats, embroidered or made in patterned fabrics, continued to be worn in the nineteenth century, and by the middle of the century patterned trousers, in checks or stripes, were also fashionable and were often worn with a plain coat [62]. It was not until the 1860's that lounge suits, for informal wear, began to be made of a piece – that is, with the coat, waistcoat and trousers all of the same material [63]. It has been customary for twentieth-century lounge suits to match, but variations continue to be possible: two-piece suits may still be worn with a coloured or fancy waistcoat, while plain black morning coats can be worn with striped or checked trousers [64].

The most usual materials for the male suit have been silk or wool although linen has also been used for cool, lightweight suits for the summer or hot climates. In the late seventeenth century and during the eighteenth century, silks of various types (plain, ribbed and brocaded, satins or velvets) were used, especially for formal or Court wear. Cloth suits were worn during the day, for travelling or for warmth and by those who could not afford silk (in 1617 Fynes Moryson remarked that merchants wore woollen and worsted cloth whereas gentlemen wore silk[1]); but fine quality cloth could be worn in the evening and was often embroidered in silk or gold and silver metal thread.

By the early nineteenth century, however, cloth began to be adopted for all but the most formal of men's suits (such as Court and official dress). English tailors had worked with woollen cloth for generations, but its qualities were now to be fully explored and appreciated. Cloth is more pliable than tightly-woven stiff silks, and can be more successfully moulded to the body, so far greater attention began to be paid to the cut and fit. The art of tailoring was developed to a high degree.

A second revolution in the use of suiting materials took place in the mid twentieth century, with the introduction of man-made fibres such as nylon, terylene, acrilan and tricel. These were mixed with natural fibres to produce a cheaper, lighter-weight cloth which was resilient, hard-wearing and resistant to stretching and creasing but could retain permanent creases. Man-made fibres have not proved as satisfactory as the natural fibres in the tailoring of either men's or women's clothes as they lack the elastic and draping qualities of wool and silk, but the advantages of modern fabrics probably, on balance, outweigh the disadvantages. With the increased mass production of clothing and the corresponding decrease in tailor-made garments the emphasis on cut and fit has, in any case, declined.

Colour and decoration, so noticeably absent from twentieth-century men's suits, were usual until the middle of the nineteenth century. Both silks and cloths in bright colours were worn by men in the seventeenth and eighteenth centuries and although black or dark-coloured cloth became fashionable at the beginning of the nineteenth century, shades of blue, green, red and white were still worn for evening wear for the first few decades. The second half of the nineteenth century saw day wear becoming uniformly sombre. By the early twentieth century, men's suits had settled into a convention of black, dark grey or dark blue cloth for formal day wear and patterned cloths or tweeds of brown or greenish hues for informal or country clothes. Brown was otherwise considered unsuitable and incorrect for town or formal wear. Julius Beerbohm, who maintained the standards of a dandy even on his deathbed in 1906, was offended to receive a visit from his brother wearing a reddish-brown suit: '"Ginger!" he said disgustedly, and turned his face to the wall.'[2]

Shades can be subtly varied by the use of patterned cloths such as checks, plaids or stripes but after the mid nineteenth century these were never striking. 'Loud' colours or patterns have, since then, almost always been condemned; the *Tailor and Cutter* invariably ascribed a taste for such clothes to the 'bounder', 'horsey individual', 'sporting publican' or other such characters. As a rule, the plainer and darker the cloth, the more formal was its purpose: dark blue or black for evening dress, a discreetly patterned, darkish cloth for formal day wear and a bolder, brighter pattern for an informal suit.

Texture has been another important feature of suiting materials. A heavyweight cloth with a rough or hairy texture, such as a tweed, has usually been considered the most suitable for overcoats and country suits which might be exposed to harder wear and rougher weather. Cloth of a smoother, finer grade was required for more formal suits, and in the nineteenth century cashmere wool was often used for evening dress. After the First World War lighter cloths began to be worn and by the 1950's, when efficient heating ensured constant temperatures in houses and offices and more people travelled by car, there was increasingly less need for weight and warmth.

During the late seventeenth and eighteenth centuries, decoration was applied to the surface of men's garments by means of embroidery, gold and silver lace or braid. It was usual for coats and waistcoats to be adorned in this way, even if they were already made of patterned silks or velvets, but breeches tended to be left plain, after the mid eighteenth century. A great number of finely embroidered silk coats and waistcoats survive from the eighteenth century and can be seen in almost any museum with a collection of costume, but these were formal garments rather than ordinary day wear. The custom of wearing a patterned or embroidered waistcoat continued well into the nineteenth century and had a brief revival in the 1890's. The coat, on the other hand, had become almost plain by the 1790's and during the nineteenth century more attention was paid to cut than to decoration, which was confined to minor, subtle details. Buttons continued to be decorative and when not covered in the fabric of the coat were made in silver or silver gilt, brass, cut steel, horn, wood and other materials in a variety of designs. The edges of the coat or waistcoat could be bound in silk ribbon, collars were made of velvet and lapels were faced with silk or satin. It was also customary to apply braid to the outer seams of trouser legs. Colour and decorative effects in the suit were gradually toned down and confined to the necktie or fancy waistcoat, and in 1894 Oscar Wilde was complaining: 'I find an ever-growing difficulty in expressing my originality through my choice of waistcoats and cravats.'[3] During the twentieth century the suit has remained sombre in colour and somewhat uniform in appearance, lightened by coloured and patterned shirts and ties; but since the late 1960's younger men have taken to suitings in less conventional shades and textures (such as cream or light green gabardine, black velvet and rust or olive-green corduroy) which produce a somewhat brighter and more varied impression.

During the period since 1670 the general character of the suit has been influenced by several different factors, the most significant of which have been the development of uniforms, the introduction of sports clothes and the manufacture of clothing by machine.

In the early part of this period military dress began to be standardized, and the policy of regulation continued throughout the eighteenth century. The styles were based on current fashion but once adopted did not change as rapidly as styles in civilian dress. Military uniforms have always tended to be conservative. They are also designed to set a standard and inspire confidence. Uniforms confer a sense of identity and responsibility on the wearer: a disciplined appearance is an expression of a disciplined force, and a smart or splendid-looking regiment not only presents an impressive façade to the enemy but fills its own members with a certain pride and courage.

The reasoning behind the development of uniforms in the eighteenth and nineteenth centuries led to the perfection of a form of dress within strictly defined limits. The quality, cut and fit of the garments and the ways in which they were worn and cared for were to reach the highest possible standard, and this tradition survived into the present century.

At times like the World Wars of the twentieth century, when men and women have served with the armed forces in great numbers, civilian dress for both sexes has undoubtedly been affected. The military greatcoat, for example, has come in and out of fashion many times. But some of the standards as well as the fashions of military and naval dress have infiltrated civilian clothes. Men who have been in the army or navy bear the mark in their deportment and in their minute attention to the condition of their clothes; they are usually noted for their smart or elegant appearance, even if it is conservative in style. Certainly at the close of the Second World War, after several years in the services, men disliked the loose, shapeless style and rather poor quality of the standard-issue Demob suit, and by 1950 a neater, closer-fitting and generally more elegant suit began to be worn.

In some ways, then, it is the uniforms that have encouraged the uniformity in men's civilian dress, but there have been other influences at work. Towards the close of the nineteenth century an increase in sporting activities of all kinds began to affect male fashions. The stiff, formal clothes of the day were found to be uncomfortable and impractical for audience as well as participants and alternatives were introduced. A soft-collared shirt, usually made of flannel, became usual for cricket or cycling, for example; enthusiasm for yachting brought in the reefer jacket; and for informal wear, the lounge suit with a shorter coat or jacket was adopted. Looser, softer clothes were greatly encouraged and eventually led to a softening of even the most formal types of dress, while many of the sporting or country styles were gradually taken up for ordinary day wear. This trend too has continued into the twentieth century.

The other major influence on the life of the suit has been the invention of the sewing machine. Until its widespread use after the 1850's, men's suits were made to measure, by hand. For those who could not afford to have a suit made to measure, there was a market in second-hand clothing. With the introduction of machinery, however, clothes could be mass-produced and suits of a reasonable quality and price became available to a large number of people. Towards the end of the century the production of ready-made garments steadily increased as machinery and manufacturing techniques improved, and a great boost was given to the industry by the Boer War and the 1914–1918 war, when there were large demands for uniforms. Suits continued to be made to measure but parts of that process too could be mechanized. At first tailors were reluctant to come to terms with the new invention, but by the last years of the century they were beginning to accept the existence of the sewing machine.

By the 1930's both ready-to-wear and made-to-measure suits were being produced in factories by large tailoring firms such as Montague Burton (who became known as the 'Fifty Shilling' tailor because that was the average price for suits and overcoats of an acceptable quality). Ready-made suits were brought out in increasing quantities but it was not until after the Second World War that they were worn by the majority. During the 1930's the ready-to-wear was still considered to be rather inferior to the suit made to measure. In 1937 Simpson's *Magazine for Men* was advocating 'the modern way of buying a suit' but in a somewhat defensive tone stressed how difficult it was to tell the difference between the two. 'As these unretouched snaps show – we can fit nine out of ten men in our ready to wear suits,' it said. 'One of these three men is wearing a made-to-measure suit, which is he?'

By the 1950's, with new developments in production and the invention of man-made fibres, a wider variety of good quality and well-priced garments came on the market. Fewer men either chose or could afford to have their suits made to measure and the ready-made began to be accepted in its own right, rather than as a second-rate imitation of a hand-made article. The quality of ready-made suits improved considerably after the war although in style and fabric they were neither exclusive nor individual, being made, on the whole, in 'safe' designs and materials – not that suits made to measure were any less conservative in style (if anything they were more so), but they were at least distinguished by cut, fit and the quality of the suiting. By the beginning of the 1960's the multiple tailors realized how urgent it was to inject new life into the clothes they were producing and they began to employ design consultants from the field of haute couture. In 1961, for instance, Hardy Amies joined the firm of Hepworths and by 1965 Pierre Cardin was working in the same capacity for the Associated Tailors (John Temple and Neville Reed). These innovations brought little radical change to the appearance of ready-made clothing ranges but it was apparent that most men were generally quite satisfied with what they were offered.

58 Etching by S. le Clerc 1670–80
An early version of the coat worn with a waistcoat and knee-breeches. The waistcoat has vertical pockets and grouped buttons.

The Development of the Suit

At the Court of Charles II, in the 1660's, several important developments took place in the form of men's dress, and by 1670 a three-piece suit, in the modern sense, had emerged. The significant factors in this process were the adoption of a knee-length coat, a long vest or waistcoat and closed breeches, ending at the knee.

As early as the 1620's a coat was worn for outdoor, practical wear such as hunting or riding;[4] it was a fairly long, loosely cut garment which had no part in fashionable formal dress until it began to be adopted by gentlemen for ordinary wear. By 1660, however, it is evident that a coat could be worn over the shirt in place of a doublet. On 3 February 1661, Pepys wrote in his diary: 'This day I first begun to go forth in my coate and sword, as the manner now among gentlemen is.' [58]

In 1666 we are told by Pepys, John Evelyn and other contemporary writers that Charles II introduced a new fashion, a garment called a vest. This was a long, straight, close-fitting type of coat which his courtiers described as 'oriental' (oriental clothes had been seen in London on visiting foreigners and were used in modified form in the theatre, for masquerades and amateur acting, and sometimes for romantic dress in portraits). Charles II's vest was a version of an Eastern European garment, but it was devised as a new form of English dress, an alternative to the French fashions so predominant in the country at the time. It was also intended to be a style of dress which need not be changed. England was then at war with France and Charles wished to break the slavish habit of copying French clothes; since dress had become so extravagant he declared this to be an economy measure. Within a few weeks the king and most of his Court were wearing the new style. The fashion was largely confined to the Court but by 1670 a version of the vest, or what can be called a waistcoat, had come into general use, worn with the coat [29]. Charles II's vest had at first been spurned by the French Court but the modified form was adopted all over Europe a few years later.

In the first half of the 1660's the French fashion for petticoat-breeches had been popular [57], but the voluminous legs were to prove inconvenient when worn with the long coat rather than a short doublet. The petticoat-breeches bulged below the hem of the coat to rather ungainly effect and were soon replaced by those of the narrower Spanish cut which were straight and close to the leg. When worn with the coat and waistcoat, they produced a longer, statelier line. The new style of dress, a simple, dignified outfit, soon became established and in the course of the next hundred years its essential form was gradually improved and refined.

When the coat first began to be worn in the 1660's it was cut with little shaping to the figure and hung loosely from the shoulders to just below the knee [58]. There were long vents from waist to hem at the sides and centre back, generally edged with buttons and buttonholes. The vents allowed the sword to be worn beneath the coat, the hilt emerging at one side and the point through the back. The coat had no collar, partly because men's hair was now worn over the shoulders and covered the neck; the sleeves were wide and turned back at the elbow to form a cuff. The centre front was buttoned from neck to hem, but by 1685 it had become customary to fasten the coat only at the waist, leaving it open above and below to reveal the waistcoat.

During the 1670's and 1680's the coat became closer-fitting with a slight shaping at the waist to produce a longer, narrower, more severe line. The sleeves were worn longer and tighter but still with cuffs. Trimmings in the form of sashes, ribbons and shoulder-knots continued to decorate the coat [29] (although the bunch of ribbons or looped cord worn on the right shoulder was shortly to pass out of fashion and be retained only for livery). The slim, straight line was emphasized by low-set vertical pockets, but in the late 1680's these were largely replaced by horizontal pockets which were later given flaps [30]. This coincided with a general movement away from the vertical emphasis, towards a fullness in the skirts of the coat. By the last decade of the century the coat was becoming noticeably more waisted with a curved centre-back seam and a kick out of the skirt tails at the back. Greater width was added by pleats in the vents which were headed by a button. The sleeves were also cut fuller with deep, wide cuffs. Pockets were still set near the hem but rose gradually in time.

The waistcoat was cut on similar lines but with little or no width in the skirts, and after 1690 it was a few inches shorter than the coat [31]. It had pockets but no collar and it buttoned from neck to hem (like the coat, however, most of its buttons and buttonholes were sham and only fastened at the waist). As early as the 1680's the back of the waistcoat, which was hidden, could be made of an inferior material; but some waistcoats were worn as an alternative to the coat indoors and many at this date had sleeves. Waistcoat sleeves were slightly longer and closer than the coat, and were turned back over the coat-cuff; when the waistcoat was of a patterned or embroidered material this provided a decorative contrast [33]. With the coat worn open to the waist a fair amount of the waistcoat was revealed; with the waistcoat itself left open at the top, to display a ruffled shirt-front and cravat, the suit could give the impression of several layers of different materials, colours and textures. The front of the waistcoat was always intended to be seen, it was not simply an extra garment for warmth. Charles II's vest, the prototype of the waistcoat, had been elaborately decorated and the coat was cut away to reveal it; Pepys records in 1666 that he was 'fearful of an ague' with his chest so inadequately covered.[5] The decorative function of the waistcoat was one of its features until well into the nineteenth century. In summer the waistcoat could be left off and the coat worn directly over the shirt.

Knee-breeches, though narrower in the leg that the wide petticoat-breeches fashionable in the 1660's, were still cut rather full in the seat and legs. They had a centre-front opening, fastened at the waist, and were worn without other support. The legs were gathered into a band above or below the knee, closing with ties, buttons or a buckle and strap. Stockings were drawn up over the knees and covered the lower edge of the breeches [137]. There was apparently a variety of different styles in breeches and Randle Holme described 'some few' of them in 1688. There were, for example, the 'Spanish' breeches cut straight and close to the thigh, 'buttoned up the sides from the knee with about ten or twelve buttons' (a seventeenth-century fashion mainly for the sake of ornament); the 'Sailors Breeches, full and gathered both in the waist and at the knees, standing full out'; open breeches (that is, not closed round the knees); 'pantiloon', 'trunk' and 'peticoat' breeches.[6] As a rule, breeches were made either of the same material as the coat or of black velvet. Linen drawers were worn beneath.

By the last years of the century there was an increased tendency towards grandeur and bulk, with the wide-skirted coats made from rich and heavy brocaded silks. France had taken the lead so far in the manufacture of dress silks, but after the revocation of the Edict of Nantes in 1685 many Huguenot silk weavers were forced to leave the country and take their skills elsewhere. By the early eighteenth century the English silk industry was well established and fine textiles were produced at Spitalfields in particular. Silks in the so-called 'bizarre' designs, influenced by the oriental taste, were popular for waistcoats, and further decoration was added to edges and seams by gold and silver lace or braid.

Buttons became larger in the 1690's and were placed not only at the centre-front opening of the coat or waistcoat, but on the sleeve-cuffs and at the apex of the side and back vents. The fanciful, extravagant style of dress in the Restoration period, with its yardage of material and ribbons and oozing out of shirts, gradually gave way to a more stately, sober and classic taste in clothing which was to be characteristic of the earlier eighteenth century; the narrow, long-bodied look was replaced by a squarer, more solid but shapelier line [31].

The first decades of the century saw a continuation of the trends set in the 1690's. The skirts of the coat remained wide and were stiffened by buckram, horsehair and other means to fan out over the hips, a silhouette which matched the swelling bell-shaped skirts of women's dresses. There could be from three to six pleats in the side vents to achieve this effect and the coat reached to just below the knee. The sleeve-cuffs, pocket-flaps and buttons were large and the weighty appearance of men's dress was completed by the long, curled, full-bottomed wig.

There were various styles in sleeve-cuffs. They could be either open or closed at the back and fastened with buttons [32]; some sleeves were made without cuffs, ending in a slit which exposed the shirt sleeve. Ruffles of lace or fine pleated linen were attached to the wristband of the shirt and extended well below the coat-cuff. Horizontal pockets were finished with flaps which were shaped or scalloped at the edge. Buttons were either covered in the material of the coat, over a wood base, and embroidered to match, or made of metal such as gold, silver, gilt, brass or steel or of stones and paste. There was still no collar on the formal coat and the top edge lay flat round the neck. Fashionable colours at this time were sharp blue and red.

The waistcoat remained slightly shorter and narrower than the coat but followed its general cut. The skirts were flared and stiffened but never pleated with extra fabric, so that the side vents widened to an acute angle at the hem. Sleeved waistcoats continued to be worn but the sleeves and back were often made of a cheaper material. There were buttons from the neck to the hem and two horizontal flapped pockets. The coat and waistcoat were usually made in contrasting materials, and fringed waistcoats were popular until the 1740's.

Knee-breeches were ample in the seat, cut on the cross-grain of the fabric, with a characteristically wide angle at the fork ('their legs springing apart like the open blades of a scissors' as one writer has described them[7]). They were gathered in to a waistband which could be adjusted by laces and the breeches hung on the hips. The legs were straight but not tight-fitting and fastened just below the knee in a band which was buttoned or buckled. Buttons rather than a fly or concealed fastening closed the centre front. Several pockets including a fob pocket were in the waistband.

During the 1730's and 1740's several changes were discernible in the appearance of the suit. The front edges of the coat, which previously had been cut straight, began to curve slightly towards the back to reveal more of the waistcoat and breeches. Closer attention was, as a result, paid to the cut of the breeches which generally became narrower and better-fitting, closing at the knee (over, rather than under, the rolled stockings), with an ornamental buckle. The centre-front closure was altered to a 'fall' or flap front, that is, a square flap covering the opening, buttoned up at the sides and to the waistband; a wider flap called a 'whole fall' fell from the side seams, otherwise a 'small fall' was used.

The waistcoat gradually began to shorten and by the late 1740's reached mid thigh. After this date sleeves were usually omitted. Both coat and waistcoat were becoming closer-fitting, and the coat sleeve was tighter, especially in the upper arm, although the cuffs remained wide and almost reached the elbow. Pockets were placed higher, at waist level. Colours were more subdued and murrey brown was particularly popular, but coats were often lined with an alternative colour. Gold and silver lace or braid were used to trim the front of the coat.

The formal coat, which was close-fitting and had no collar, was made of silk or cloth which could be trimmed or embroidered. Practical cloths such as camlet or frieze were used for ordinary wear and during the 1730's an alternative form of coat was adopted for informal occasions. The 'frock' was a looser-fitting coat distinguished by a turned-down collar and its plain appearance in cloth [59]. Originally worn by working men it was taken up by gentlemen for greater comfort and ease of movement and by the middle of the century had become ordinary wear, with the coat reserved for more formal dress. It was not until the end of the century that the term 'frock coat' came into use.

By the 1750's the fashionable silhouette had altered and the line of the suit was considerably pared down [34]. The width and stiffening in the coat-skirts was abandoned and there was a general impression of shrinkage, with the sides of the coat curving away from the front and the breeches becoming increasingly tighter. The preferred shape was long, slim and elegant.

The back of the coat was becoming steadily narrower and as the front skirts were cut away the side seams also curved backwards (while the buttons which headed the side vents moved towards the small of the back). After the 1760's the coat-skirts ceased to flare and there was little or no suppression at the waist. Sleeves were longer and close-fitting, to the wrist; the 'round' or closed cuff was the most usual, but cuffs in general were less conspicuous. Pockets were set just below the waist and the flaps were slightly narrower. During the 1760's a small, standing collar developed at the neck of the coat which increased in height during the next few decades [60]. Coats and waistcoats for formal or court wear continued to be lavishly decorated with silk embroidery which often incorporated spangles, mirror-glass and lace insertion to give a lighter, more delicate and sparkling effect. The taste for elaborate trimming was diminishing and day

59 Lord Willoughby de Broke by Zoffany *c* 1762 (det of 35)
The 'frock' was a looser-fitting coat distinguished by a turned down collar.

wear became generally rather plainer. Fabrics and colours tended to be more sober and after the mid 1750's wrist-ruffles became less extravagantly laced. By the early 1770's suits of one colour were worn, and 'drab' (a light brown) was a particularly popular shade [**36**].

The waistcoat continued to be the focal point of decoration in the male wardrobe but it became both shorter and straighter in the second half of the century. By the early 1780's the lower edge of the waistcoat finally reached the level of the waist and a double-breasted fastening was becoming popular [**36**]. Striped patterns also began to be worn and tended to emphasize the slender cut of the suit. Following the line of the coat, in the 1760's the waistcoat too was given a narrow 'stand' collar which rose similarly.

Stripes were also fashionable on the legs in the later 1760's and 1770's when striped stockings were worn with the tighter knee-breeches. In the last quarter of the century breeches were usually known as 'small clothes'. John Wilkes, writing to his daughter from Bath in April 1778 said : 'dear sweet Polly. I have a new coat and it is all blue and it has a fine edging, and I have a fine silk waistcoat and it is all ribbed and is blue and has likewise a gold edging. And I have small clothes all blue, and fine mother of pearl buttons in every one of which you might see your pretty face. I am undoubtedly the greatest fop in Bath.'[8] Breeches usually fastened at the knee with a buckle; this was a small square or oval which became a little larger in the 1770's [**1**]. In the 1780's breeches became even tighter and rather longer, sometimes tied rather than buckled at the knee.

During the last two decades of the century a new style in men's clothes was emerging. It reflected to some extent the changes in the social, political and artistic climate. The increasing mood of romanticism encouraged a way of dress that was softer and more informal than that of the first half of the century. Sir Brooke Boothby [**36**], reclining in a wood with a volume of Rousseau in his hand (an unthinkable pose in the stiff silks and heavy coat of forty years earlier), illustrated the new enthusiasm for the ideal of the essential goodness of man and a return to the natural life; a simpler, countrified look was affected by the upper classes and formality was no longer fashionable. The vogue for more practical country and sporting wear accelerated after the outbreak of the French Revolution in 1789, and all that appeared aristocratic or ostentatious was unpopular. English fashion adapted itself to the new social changes by taking up aspects of lower-class dress, and in a wave of Anglomania the French copied these clothes with fervour. The English riding coat was transferred to the height of fashion in Paris [**37**].

The frock was replacing the coat for normal wear, cloth was more generally preferred to silks, simpler styles and forms of decoration were in use and laced wrist-ruffles were abandoned altogether. In the 1790's most men discarded wigs and hair powder in favour of their own hair worn short and in its natural state. Such decoration as there was, was light and delicate; small spots and stripes were popular.

The fashionable suit of the 1790's was essentially a smartened version of

60 English Court Suit
c 1780. Victoria and Albert
Museum
Coat and breeches of striped
silk embroidered with floral
sprays; covered buttons to
match. White, embroidered
waistcoat. The coat has a
small standing collar and is
cut away at the sides.

61 Thomas, 9th Earl of
Haddington by Henry
Edridge 1802
The fashionable suit was a
smartened version of country
clothes: riding coat, breeches
and boots.

country clothes [37]. The swallow-tailed coat with a standing collar remained in use for Court occasions and only the most formal wear, while the frock, or some version of sporting or country dress, was adopted for day and town wear. For riding, the front of the coat was cut away sharply from the waist to improve the fall of the skirt tails; by the 1790's it was either curved or cut in horizontally across the waist. The squarer cut could be balanced by a double-breasted fastening and collars and lapels had become a feature. During the last quarter of the century the stand and turned-down collars had increased in height; the top buttons of the coat were often left unfastened and the front edges fell back to form lapels or revers (that is, exposing the reverse side of the garment) [36]. Dark or sober-coloured cloth was fashionable and was frequently worn with buttons of silver gilt, brass or another metal. The single- or double-breasted coat with narrow skirt tails was slightly shorter. The shorter waistcoat could also have the double-breasted fastening with collar and lapels although this was still generally confined to informal wear. Under-waistcoats of flannel or other material were sometimes worn for additional warmth but were not particularly fashionable. Marianne Dashwood, one of the heroines of *Sense and Sensibility* (written in 1797), had a poor opinion of men who 'sought the constitutional safeguard of a flannel waistcoat', which she 'invariably connected with aches, cramps, rheumatisms, and every species of ailment that can afflict the old and feeble'.[9]

Breeches, which had usually matched the material of the coat, tended to be made in different colours and fabrics towards the end of the century. The increasingly tight fit required an even firmer and more pliable material than cloth, so buckskin or doeskin of a light colour came into widespread use [61]. For riding and country wear, breeches were worn with boots and were therefore made longer to reach just below the knee. In the 1790's pantaloons also began to be worn. Like breeches they were close-fitting and were shaped to the leg; they were often made of an elastic jersey-weave material, such as stockinet, cut on the cross-grain. They extended well below the knees to the calves or ankle and fastened with drawstring ties. Pantaloons were also fashionable with boots and often appear almost indistinguishable from the tight breeches of this period; but they were still considered unsuitable for formal or Court wear and knee-breeches (worn with shoes) were to remain compulsory for Court dress until well into the twentieth century [90].

The 1790's were essentially a transitional period for both male and female dress. Whereas eighteenth-century clothing had for the most part been rigidly formal, original in design and sure of its taste, the dress of the 1790's was not; confidence and direction began to waver and this uncertainty gave rise to romantic or unrealistic forms of dress. At the turn of the century women's dress imitated the soft draperies of ancient Greek statues while men indulged in a different form of dressing-up. The adoption of sporting or country clothes for fashionable wear was not just a practical or comfortable innovation, it was the cultivation of a new image. Men's clothes were intended to be classless and casual and the stable-boy appearance of some young men had an almost thuggish air. At the same time, men were not unaffected by the prevailing mood of neo-classicism; although their costume might seem far from the idea of the antique, the hair was cropped short in styles reminiscent of ancient Greece and Rome (à la 'Brutus', 'Titus' or 'Apollo') [61]. Skin-tight breeches and pantaloons which traced the natural shape of the leg suggested an air of nudity not unlike the late-fifteenth century fashion of closely fitting doublet and hose, and was undoubtedly influenced by a revived interest in classical art.

The romantic appearance of men's dress was intensified during the early years of the nineteenth century by colour rather than shape. Black began to be worn to great dramatic effect against a stark white shirt and neckcloth; there was an air of simplicity and refinement in men's clothes with every detail made perfect [39]. Coats were superbly tailored and cravats carefully arranged, although the final impression was intended to appear the reverse – careless and unassuming. The way in which clothes were worn was equally dramatic; coats and cloaks were negligently thrown over the shoulder, and hair looked windswept. In an atmosphere conjured by Goethe's *Sorrows of Young Werther*, Sir Walter Scott's novels, Byron's poems and the painting of John Martin, young men began to look suitably pale and intense. Many writers, including Stendhal and Alfred de Musset, saw the increasing blackness as the symbol of a century in mourning. A less romantic view is that the sombre colouring heralded a new, more sober and more practical dress in the coming industrial age. Certainly, nineteenth-century men began to adopt what had been the dress of the professional classes in the eighteenth century [1], and it was the businessman rather than the aristocrat who was to dominate the new society. The dress of the first three decades was, in fact, a curious blend of romanticism and utility and in the future it was to become increasingly stylized and functional.[10]

By the beginning of the nineteenth century the three garments which comprised the suit rarely matched in colour or material [61]. Alternatives to the knee-breeches had been introduced and in time trousers were to replace both breeches and pantaloons for ordinary day and evening wear. Various forms of the suit were differentiated by the cut of the coat and were worn according to the time of day or occasion. All but the most formal coats, worn at court (and still made of silk or velvet), were tailored in cloth without ornamentation. Fastenings could be single- or double-breasted; there was always a collar but not necessarily with lapels. The so-called 'shawl' collar, without lapels, rolled away from the neck with no break or notch in the facing on the chest. The 'step' collar had a V- or an M-shaped notch between collar and lapel which allowed it to lie flat [61, 62]. The double-breasted lapel tended to be slightly broader than the single-breasted and the rever pointed upwards to join the collar at an acute angle. Collars were often faced with velvet and buttons could be decorative.

The three most usual styles of coat were the dress coat, morning coat and frock coat. The dress coat was cut squarely across the waistline and the tails hung straight down at the back. Single- and double-breasted fastenings were used. It was worn for all dress occasions, both day and evening, but as

62 *The World of Fashion* 1841
Fashion plates illustrated the fashionable silhouette: a 'pouter pigeon' chest, sloping shoulders, small waist and tiny feet.

63 *The Tailor and Cutter* 1870
Portraits of famous men were often used for fashion plates. Charles Dickens wears a short, double-breasted frock coat, single-breasted waistcoat, light trousers and top hat; Benjamin Disraeli models a less formal single-breasted lounge suit and soft hat.

the century progressed, was gradually confined to evening and the most formal functions.

The morning coat, similar to its modern equivalent [64], was originally a riding coat (for morning wear). The front edges sloped back in a curve, in contrast to the horizontal cut of the dress coat. The riding coat was taken up for informal wear but increasingly replaced the dress coat in the daytime and eventually became a formal coat.

The frock coat did not appear until after 1815, and its distinctive feature lay in the front edges which were cut straight and fell vertically to the knee. The term had been applied to the cut-in tail coat of the late eighteenth century (which derived from the frock) but it was now used to refer to the full-skirted coat [63]. It was similar in shape to a greatcoat but was more fitted to the body. In the early part of the nineteenth century this was an informal garment but like the other two coats it became increasingly more formal. In the second half of the century it was the predominant coat for daytime wear.

Waistcoats continued to be worn short, with or without a collar and lapel, single- or double-breasted. Materials in contrasting colours to the coat were used and were ornamented by woven or embroidered patterns.

Breeches, pantaloons and trousers were all worn in the early years of the century, and did not usually match the coat or waistcoat. Breeches were worn with tail coats for the first decades, after which they were retained only for unfashionable wear, court dress or sports and country pursuits.

MEN'S WEAR SECTION
Distinguished Tailoring in Clothes Ready for Wearing

Harrods Ready-to-Wear Clothes have attained such a degree of perfection that many men always choose suits which can be worn right away. They know that whatever their type of figure there will be a size and fitting which will ensure a perfectly made suit at prices which are consistently moderate

SUITS FOR BUSINESS AND FORMAL WEAR

BLACK MORNING COAT

Pantaloons, which were longer and tighter than breeches, replaced them for formal wear but were in turn ousted by trousers which made their fashionable appearance in England about 1807. Trousers had their origins in the long loose garment worn by working men and sailors and were strictly informal when first introduced, being worn, for example, for the summer at seaside resorts such as Brighton. In their early form they were close-fitting and short, barely reaching the ankle, but by 1817 they had reached the shoe and until the middle of the century were generally worn with straps which passed under the foot [39]. Wider trousers, known as 'Cossacks', which were gathered into the waistband and ankles, were fashionable after 1814 for a number of years. As trousers became higher-waisted they were supported by braces. By 1825 trousers had come into general use but pantaloons continued to be correct wear for evening until about 1850; the two garments were at times almost indistinguishable and the terms tended to be used indiscriminately. In America the shortened form of pantaloons – 'pants' – was more generally used than 'trousers', but both names now refer to the same piece of clothing.[11]

In the 1820's much of the intensity and studied carelessness of male clothes was abandoned. The fashionable silhouette for both men and women exaggerated the natural contours of the figure: waists were tightened, and shoulders and hips were enlarged by wider sleeves and skirts [78]. Men's coats were padded in the chest, and gathered at the head of the sleeve while trousers were baggy in the leg. The shoulder line was also

64 Harrods 1929
Black jacket and striped trousers with black bowler and rolled umbrella for business wear; morning coat and striped trousers with top hat and walking stick for formal occasions. Double- and single-breasted lounge suits.

dropped slightly to achieve the fashionable curve in the upper part of the body, and the coat was often unbuttoned and thrown back to show an expanse of snowy shirt front beneath a coloured waistcoat. In the mid 1820's a seam had been introduced at the waist of the coat; without one a crease usually formed when the coat was tightly buttoned, and by removing a slice of material and inserting a seam the tailors could achieve a better fit. The frock coat was becoming popular for day wear but was worn short, to about mid-thigh. Waistcoats with softly curving shawl collars were frequently worn, and were highly patterned. Trouser braces were also decorative; they were often made of canvas and could be embroidered in coloured silks or wool.

By the 1840's the shape of men's clothes was less exaggerated by padding and gathering but their colouring was more flamboyant [40, 62]. Brighter colours and lustrous textiles were popular, especially in the form of satin cravats and waistcoats of brocaded or embroidered silks, which lightened the matt effect of sombre shades of cloth. There was a much more worldly air about most men's appearance, expressive of the rising businessman and the increasingly prosperous middle classes. Some clothes appear to have been in questionable taste. Charles Dickens, for example, took a number of brightly coloured and richly embroidered waistcoats on his American tour in 1842 and they were stigmatized in the press as 'somewhat in the flash order' (although G. A. Sala considered Dickens to be 'next to Count d'Orsay, the choicest and most tastefully dressed dandy in London'[12]). In his early career, Disraeli was another who drew attention to himself by the flamboyance of his clothing and although his taste was far more extreme than that of the average man it is interesting to find that it was possible to wear, for instance, a black velvet, satin-lined coat, purple trousers with a band of gold braid at the seams, a figured scarlet waistcoat, lace ruffles falling to the tips of his fingers, a profusion of jewels and chains and long black ringlets.[13]

In addition to the popularity of fancy waistcoats in the 1840's and 1850's, bold patterns for trousers were fashionable, in a variety of striped, checked or plaid tweeds and worsteds for informal wear [79]. Plainer trousers were embellished with fancy braid along the outer leg seams. During the 1840's the trouser strap under the instep was disappearing and the fly-fastening generally replaced the fall or flap front. Trousers continued to be cut rather tight but wider 'peg-top' trousers came into fashion in the later 1850's. These were cut full at the waist and tapered towards the ankle to give their distinctive shape (after the introduction of the crinoline petticoat in 1856, jokes appeared in *Punch* advocating miniature versions to support the fuller legs for men); but this never became a universal fashion and peg-top trousers were not worn in the evening.

The frock coat was the most usual coat for day wear and by this date a closer fit was achieved by the introduction of 'side bodies': in addition to the three back seams an extra piece of material was inserted in the underarm seams above the waist, bringing the total to five seams. The waist was fairly long but the skirts were short and full (in sympathy with the swelling shape of women's skirts), and the sleeves fitted closely to the arm. The fastening could be either single- or double-breasted but rose a little higher as the lapels were shorter. The M-shaped double-notched lapel was no longer used after about 1850. The frock coat was worn throughout the century but lost its dominant position in the 1850's when the morning coat was preferred.

A variety of new coats for morning and sports wear appeared in the 1840's and 1850's and amongst these the jacket was a popular innovation. This was a short-skirted coat and unlike the frock coat or morning coat had visible pockets. It was an informal garment but by the late 1860's became acceptable for ordinary daytime wear.

The dress coat could still be worn for formal day wear in the 1840's but it was more usually restricted to evening dress and by the 1860's was worn for nothing else.

There was a gradual trend towards greater uniformity in men's clothes during the later 1850's – although they were still reasonably colourful – which culminated in a generally different character in the 1860's. There was a noticeable lack of imagination and liveliness in men's approach to dress by this date and both styles and colour became restrained and unchanging. Trousers, for example, were cut straight, without interesting curves (and were aptly described as 'tubes' a decade later) [41, 42]; suits had a crumpled, sack-like appearance and were often made of thicker, clumsier materials. At the same time, however, an increasing informality in dress was encouraged and looser, more comfortable clothes were permitted. The lounge suit, in particular, became popular for spectator sports and informal wear with its easier fitting, three-seamed jacket and a low turned-down shirt collar. Lounge jackets were usually worn with matching trousers and waistcoat [63]. Other forms of informal jacket such as the reefer and the Norfolk jacket also came into general use [97]. In the following decades the lounge suit became acceptable for day wear and by the 1890's had been adopted for all informal occasions.

With the introduction of more sombre colouring, and the custom of making suits of one piece, the fancy waistcoat began to decline in favour but did not pass altogether out of use. Wilkie Collins' unpleasant villain, Count Fosco, in *The Woman in White* (1859–60) had a fondness for fancy waistcoats, and on such a large man these effeminate touches seemed to emphasize his sinister character: 'He is as fond of fine clothes as the veriest fool in existence, and has appeared in four magnificent waistcoats already – all of light garish colours, and all immensely large even for him.' The most magnificent 'was made of pale sea-green silk, and delicately trimmed with fine silver braid.'[14]

During the 1860's the coat was made to button up higher on the chest [41] and by the late 1870's the waistcoat was completely concealed. Until the fancy waistcoat was briefly revived in the 1890's the coat eclipsed this garment and there was relatively little variety in design or decoration.

By the last quarter of the century the frock coat had become 'the hallmark of Victorian respectability',[15] [63] the correct though somewhat dull wear of the upper, middle and professional classes. With the top hat, the frock coat was worn in the West End of London, the City, the Law Courts, for paying social calls and for other formal occasions where the lounge suit would have been inappropriate. The sobriety of the frock coat was emphasized by its black, dark grey or dark blue cloth and its longer, straighter appearance with little definition at the waist. As a rule the frock coat had tended to be double-breasted but the high-buttoning, single-breasted style became more usual at the end of the 1870's. Lapels were faced with silk. In the 1890's the appearance of the frock coat was generally smarter (it was well cut to fit the body with longer and fuller skirts), but it was rivalled by the morning coat. 'Despite the popularity of the Lounge and the dressiness of the Frock,' reported the *Tailor and Cutter* in 1897, 'there are a very large section who desire a garment between the two, something that shall be dressy without being formal; stylish without being stiff. These features are found in the Morning Coat.'[16] [**93**] The morning coat was usually single-breasted with three or four buttons and an outside breast-pocket.

Lounge suits gained in popularity. The lower edges of the single-breasted jacket were rounded, it fastened with three or four buttons and had four outside pockets (including a ticket pocket). In the late 1890's a reporter for the *Tailor and Cutter* stationed himself near Charing Cross and observed that 'there were nearly two Lounges to one Morning Coat, and quite three Lounges to one Frock Coat, the proportions per thousand working out as follows: Lounges 530, Morning Coats 320, and Frock Coats 150.'[17] Knickerbockers were worn for the country and for sports such as cycling and golf, which were becoming immensely popular. They were often made to match the material of a Norfolk jacket and were worn together as an informal tweed suit.

In the 1870's trousers were cut straight in the leg with the fly front-fastening but without a waistband. The legs remained fairly narrow until the later 1870's when they tended to be fuller in the knee. An average of about eighteen inches in the knee and at the bottom was a general measurement in the 1870's and 1880's. Trousers were occasionally turned up at the hem as early as the 1860's but this was not a fashionable practice before the later 1890's. The custom had a practical origin – the hems were turned up temporarily in wet or muddy conditions to keep them clean and dry or for games such as tennis to prevent them from being caught by the feet. It was also not the fashion to wear a centre crease in the trouser legs until the 1890's when the trouser press was invented and came into general use. The problem of trousers bagging at the knees was evidently one which troubled both tailors and customers. Prince Friedrich Leopold, reported the *Tailor and Cutter* in 1898, took the matter so seriously that 'on a railway journey he passes the greater part of the time on his feet for fear that his trousers may possibly during the journey get baggy at the knees. With the exception of this weakness, the Prince has few faults.'[18]

Baggy trousers apart, men's suits towards the end of the century especially in contemporary photographs, have an unmistakably creased and crumpled look. This is partly accentuated by comparison with modern suit materials in man-made fibres which are crease-resistant and permanently pressed, but the Victorians themselves seem to have been aware of it. Well-dressed men such as the Prince of Wales [93] looked immaculate but many others did not. Beatrix Potter was surprised to see Gladstone really looking 'as if he had been put in a clothes-bag and sat upon. I never saw a person so creased. He was dressed entirely in rusty black, like a typical clergyman or a Dissenting Minister or Dominie, and has a wrinkled appearance of not filling his clothes.'[19]

The first decade of the twentieth century, or more precisely the reign of Edward VII from 1901-10, is often regarded as a high point in the history of men's fashions, a period of considerable style and refinement. In comparison with the years which followed, the Edwardian era seems to have been in almost every way a time of great opulence, gaiety and frivolity, inspired and encouraged by the monarch himself. From the point of view of men's dress, Edward VII was undoubtedly a revered and influential figure; he was passionately interested in clothes and was to a certain extent something of an innovator. His father considered that as a young man 'he took no interest in anything but clothes, and that even out shooting he was more concerned with his trousers than with the game.'[20] It has also been recorded that 'the Prince did not in the least mind changing his dress half a dozen times a day. He loved clothes and . . . had so many he could never travel with less than two valets; and two more valets were left at home cleaning, brushing and pressing his vast wardrobe.'[21] His clothes and appearance were closely watched and copied by the men of his generation and a contemporary remarked that 'there are in society several gentlemen who bear an extraordinary resemblance to him, and who take some pride in dressing and moving exactly like him so that it is often very difficult to identify him as he passes in the street on foot or in a hansom cab.'[21]

In some ways the Edwardian period appears to have reacted against the strait-laced atmosphere of the Victorian age but strict social conventions hardly relaxed before the outbreak of the First World War and clothes remained formal, governed by clearly-defined rules of etiquette. Edward VII occasionally wore a lounge suit instead of a frock coat but the frock coat was still correct for formal day wear and a lounge suit could not be worn at an office in the City. A morning coat with striped trousers and a top hat was worn for work and most men changed in the evening. Mass-produced clothing had not yet reached a wide market and, for any man with the least pretension to gentlemanliness, cut was all important (the idea that 'the apparel oft proclaims the man' still held good). Matthew Peel-Swynnerton in Arnold Bennett's *Old Wives' Tale* (1908) was a pottery manufacturer but he was taken by a cabman for a young duke because he wore a suit admirably cut and nearly new.[22] Edward VII once told Sir John Fisher 'That is a very old suit you are wearing.' 'Yes, Sir,' replied the Admiral brightly, 'but you've always told me that nothing really matters but the cut.'[23]

The frock coat was nearing the end of its fashionable life and even in 1900 it tended to be worn by elderly rather than young men [43]. By this date it was usually double-breasted with four or six buttons, generally worn open; it was black or sometimes grey and was accompanied by either matching, striped or checked trousers.

For morning or business wear the morning coat was usual but the lounge suit was a less formal alternative. The morning suit could take two forms, either it consisted of the black morning coat with striped or check trousers and contrasting waistcoat, or it was a matching suit – coat, waistcoat and trousers all being of the same material (often checked tweed). Unlike the frock coat it was almost always single-breasted, fastening with three or four buttons, and was several inches shorter than the frock coat. The front edges curved back from the waist and the tails had a centre-back vent and pleats headed by two hip buttons. The correct waistcoat was also single-breasted. Edward VII is popularly thought to have originated the fashion for wearing the lowest button of the waistcoat undone, having dressed hurriedly one day and omitted to fasten it, but in view of the king's attitude to clothes this is most unlikely. The habit was noted by the *Tailor and Cutter* in 1908, but it has a much earlier history. Many eighteenth century waistcoats were only fastened at the waist, the lower buttons and buttonholes being either sham or left unfastened. A vestige of this custom remained in nineteenth century men's suits and from at least the 1820's onwards waistcoats with the lowest button undone can be seen [39].

The lounge jacket could be single- or double-breasted; it was fairly long but had short lapels. The sleeves were slit at the cuff with a button-fastening and there were four pockets: two flapped pockets at the hips, an outside breast-pocket and a ticket pocket. As a rule the front edges of the single-breasted jacket were rounded at the bottom; the lapels and other points of the double-breasted jacket were sharply cut. Waistcoats and trousers usually matched the jacket.

Trousers in the early years of the century were rather narrow (the bottoms measuring an average of seventeen inches) and short, and were often turned up. Creases were not invariable but were sharp and neat when present [98].

The general impression of men's dress in the years just before the outbreak of war was very neat and stark, in keeping with the new, column-like silhouette of women's dresses with their straight, plain skirts and decreased emphasis on ornament. Between 1914 and 1918 men's clothes altered very little and the man who went into the war came out of it looking very much the same. In the long term however, the war and the subsequent economic and social upheaval, had a profound effect on both male and female dress.

The 1920's saw an increased tendency towards informality in men's dress, due in part to a lessening of rigid social etiquette, the influence of American fashions and an even greater interest in sport. After the war the frock coat failed to be revived, while the morning coat, although still correct for formal day or business wear, was gradually taking the place of the frock coat and becoming confined to ceremonial or gala occasions, for the races or weddings [64]. The lounge suit was rapidly assuming all the respectability of the Victorian frock coat and could be worn for most daytime functions [44], while it was replaced for informal occasions by the sports jacket and flannel trousers [98]. In the evening the dress coat was still worn but the less formal dinner jacket was becoming more popular and starched shirts, collars and cuffs began to be abandoned. In the second half of the decade, there was generally more comfort and ease in men's clothes, especially when trousers were cut wider and jackets looser, but many younger men felt them to be lacking in interest and colour. The Prince of Wales (later the Duke of Windsor) made frequent attempts to enliven male dress and, like his grandfather, made several fashions popular [45]. He was particularly impressed by America, its people and their way of life and tried to introduce some of their informality in dress and social habits to Britain. His influence over male dress in the 1920's was considerable although his taste was not always thought to be entirely reliable. He had a liking for flamboyant, colourful clothes and caused a sensation in 1924 when he arrived in America dressed in a grey double-breasted suit with wide lapels and tan suede shoes, both of which were generally considered little short of caddish at the time. As an elderly man, in the South of France, he used to wear, in the garden, crimson trousers with a light blue shirt and red and white shoes, or bright blue trousers with a canary-yellow shirt.[24] Max Beerbohm questioned his fitness for office after hearing rumours that the Prince appeared at Sunday lunch in an Italian hotel dressed in shorts; he thought the Prince should have realized that the Italians would not approve of such a costume on such an occasion. 'I'm sadly doubtful of the future effects of Edward VIII. But of course he *may* turn out all right.'[25]

Probably the most significant change in the appearance of men's dress in the 1920's was the longer, wider trousers which became known, in 1925, as 'Oxford Bags'. There is more than one theory about the origin of this fashion and title, although it is agreed that the trousers were popularized by Oxford undergraduates. It has been suggested that the origin lay in the ample trousers made of towelling worn by undergraduate oarsmen over their shorts,[26] but Harold Acton, in his memoirs, claimed entire credit for the new fashion. Acton and his friends had, at that time, an unusual interest in the nineteenth century:

> as an outward manifestation of my attitude I filled my rooms with Early Victorian objects, I bought a grey bowler, wore a stock and let my side-whiskers flourish. Instead of the wasp-waisted suits with pagoda shoulders and tight trousers affected by the dandies, I wore jackets with broad lapels and broad pleated trousers. The latter got broader and broader. Eventually they were imitated elsewhere and were generally referred to as "Oxford Bags".[27]

This may be true, but like so many fashions they probably had no such specific origin; there may have been a general move away from the narrow trousers of the early 1920's to a wider cut and it was natural for young men to take this trend to its extreme (at their widest, trousers were about twenty-four inches round the bottom). Waistbands for trousers had become popular after 1912 when a pleated, peg-top shape was re-introduced from America. Pleating allowed greater width in the leg and after 1924 they were no longer tapered at the ankle. Trousers were worn with or without turn-ups but cuffs were the more fashionable.

To balance the widening trousers, jackets were cut slightly shorter and fuller, with less definition at the waist and with broader shoulders [64]. The square-cut jacket looked better with the double-breasted fastening and by the 1930's this was more usual than the single-breasted version. At its most extreme, in the later 1920's, this fashion was severe and comparatively short-lived, but the general features were carried on into the 1930's. By 1935 the *Tailor and Cutter*, which may be taken to represent conservative opinion, had accepted wide trousers. With the larger, squarer appearance of men's suits, cloth in bolder, checked patterns became acceptable and added a certain amount of variety and colour.

The general shape of the suit in the later 1920's reflected the silhouette of women's clothes, especially the loose, shapeless, virtually rectangular chemise dress which obliterated the natural contours of the bust and waist, to emphasize the slimness of the hips. The square shoulders of men's jackets made the hips appear narrower despite the increased width of the trousers [2].

During the 1930's the trend towards more ease and informality in men's suits continued. Two-piece suits were more often worn and the waistcoat could be replaced by a pull-over [46]. Professional and business wear still required formal clothing but in the 1920's and 1930's a black jacket and waistcoat with striped trousers was an alternative to the frock or morning coat [64]. A dark lounge suit was also becoming acceptable [133]; in 1938 a Simpsons catalogue remarked that 'the double-breasted blue suit, plain or pin-striped, is probably the most useful business suit a man can have.' At weekends, for the country, sport or general casual wear more informal clothes were worn, especially flannel trousers and sports jackets or a tweed lounge suit.

Trousers remained wide in the leg and were almost always turned up at the hem. The zip fastener for the fly front-opening was introduced in 1935 but took time to replace buttons altogether. Jackets were made with well-padded and squared shoulders to give the impression of breadth in the chest and upper arm. To accommodate the extra width a 'draped' cut was adopted in 1936; the drape soon passed to America and later, in the 1940's, was re-introduced to Britain from there in a more exaggerated form. The cut was popular until the Second World War but was abandoned in Britain by 1950 and in America a few years later.

By the end of the 1930's men's suits had a less exaggerated cut and with the outbreak of war in 1939 fashion stood virtually at a standstill for the next six years. Relatively few new suits were made since so many men were in the services, and most made do with pre-war clothing. In June 1941 the rationing of cloth and clothing was introduced, and it lasted in some form or other until the beginning of 1949. Rationing included a number of utility regulations which governed the making of suits. Utility cloth was of a lower quality and the wool was often mixed with cotton, while only three colours were available – brown, navy or grey – and there were no fancy cloths. Every feature of the suit was reduced to the minimum to save materials: the waistcoat was omitted, the jacket had no drape or shoulder padding, it was single-breasted with two or three buttons, there was only one breast-pocket (either inside or out) and the cuffs were no longer trimmed with buttons. Trousers had no pleats, turn-ups or back pockets and if a customer had a suit made in his own cloth the regulations had still to be observed. 'These innovations,' observed Anthony Powell, 'always gave the wearer, even if a thin man, the air of being too large for his clothes.'[28] Good cloth was sometimes to be obtained on the black market and several of the regulations were evaded. A tailor was often asked, for example, to cut the trousers longer than necessary and the customer made his own turn-ups. At the end of the war the de-mobilized forces were issued with mass-produced suits cut on similar utility lines. 'Demob suits' seemed almost another kind of uniform and were not considered very smart as they were, on the whole, ill-fitting and shapeless. By the late 1940's, when Britain started to recover from the war and men began to buy new suits again, there was a renewed interest in fashion amongst younger men and different styles were adopted.

By 1950 a new image in men's suits had emerged which might be compared with the sensational 'New Look' which Christian Dior presented for women's clothes in 1947. Both were the result of a reaction against the dreariness of wartime dress, a certain nostalgia for the fashions of the past and an attempt to introduce new life into the clothes of the present. In men's clothes this took the form of a new elegance, pioneered by affluent young men in the West End of London. In the April 1950 issue of *Vogue*, an article appeared on men's fashions entitled 'Back to Formality', and this was the keynote of the new style. Very dark suits were worn with white shirts, hair was slightly longer and the cut of men's clothes was narrower [47]; 'there's a new, almost Edwardian formality in men's London clothes, which is reminiscent of the pre-1914 period, and is in direct contrast to the studied sloppiness which was characteristic of men's fashions between the wars,' said *Vogue*.[29] The 'Edwardian' idea was eagerly seized and used to describe almost all the innovations which appeared – coats with velvet collars and cuffs, longer, narrower single-breasted overcoats, tighter sleeves and narrower trousers – but the sheer dreariness of utility and demob suits was also partly responsible. A Sackville Street tailor maintained that when men came out of the army they had become so used to close-fitting tunics that they found their old suits square and baggy and they welcomed a slimmer, more natural-looking line.[30] The dress of the neo-Edwardians contained a number of gimmicks but in the new line, formality and elegance were quickly imitated and retained long after the more 'Edwardian' features had passed out of fashion.

At the lower end of the social scale the Edwardian fashion was adopted and transformed into a distinctive new style for young working-class men in the East End of London – who became known as Teddy Boys. In their hands the look was adapted and exaggerated; they grew their hair and side-whiskers longer, wore knee-length, single-breasted jackets with padded shoulders, the draped cut and velvet collars, fancy waistcoats, very tight, straight trousers, brightly coloured socks, narrow bootlace ties and crepe-soled shoes. The Teddy Boy style was in time copied by other young men, including the sons of Sir Alfred and Lady Wincham in Nancy Mitford's novel, *Don't tell Alfred* (1960). Basil had 'side whiskers, heavy fringe, trousers apparently moulded to the legs, surmounted by a garment ... performing the function both of coat and of shirt'. The two youngest sons (still at Eton) dressed as Teddy Boys 'with their slouching, insouciant gait, dead-fish hands depending from, rather than forming part of, long loose-jointed arms, slightly open mouths and appearance of shivering as if their clothes, rather too small in every dimension, had no warmth in them.'[31]

Teddy Boys took the 'Edwardian look' to an extreme but during the 1950's men's clothes in general were to exhibit characteristics of both styles in a modified form. The changing shape of trousers was probably the most significant shift in emphasis. The narrow line required a different cut, to curve and show the shape of the leg while abandoning the turned-up hem. Jackets were correspondingly reduced in length and width and shoulders were less pronounced. Sleeves, lapels, collars, ties and shoes were all narrowed, lighter suiting fabrics were worn and two-piece suits were becoming more usual. In the second half of the decade the predominant influence in men's clothes was the 'Italian look' which refined the line still further. The look, mainly inspired by the designer Brioni, encouraged a lighter, skimpier effect: trousers were tighter and shorter (without turn-ups) and were worn with narrow pointed shoes; jackets were shorter, closer-fitting but fairly square in shape with a boxy effect. It was a less extreme style than the Teddy Boy look and remained popular for some time. A young British designer, John Michael, took it up, removed its exaggerations and produced ready-to-wear suits in new, young, more interesting and colourful designs which were considerably less conservative than the ready-made suits manufactured by the multiple tailors.[32]

The manufacture of both men's and women's clothing expanded and developed to an unprecedented extent after the end of the Second World War. Improved techniques, a wider range of cloths and patterns, and a greater variety in designs appreciably raised the standard of the ready-made suit and with increasing costs the established tailors began to decline. More and more men bought off-the-peg suits which gradually proved to be a perfectly acceptable, respectable and satisfactory alternative to the tailor-made garment. At the same time man-made fibres which were cheaper and more practical came into widespread use and by the mid 1950's terylene trousers were available from every chain store in Britain. Lighter cloths –frequently a mixture of natural and man-made fibres such as terylene and acrilan – were also being adopted and a twelve-ounce rather than a twenty-ounce cloth could now be used for an everyday suit. The increasing popularity of the two-piece suit helped to promote the lighter, slimmer look.

Suits manufactured by the multiple tailors were conservative and restrained in style with few, if any, startling innovations although designs were constantly improved and refined [65]. The lead in men's fashions, however, no longer came from above, from the upper and middle classes, but rather emanated from below, from the young, from the Mecca dance hall and not the Savile Row tailor.

In the late 1950's and early 1960's young designers began to produce clothes exclusively for young men and women, cheaper, more colourful and more varied than those generally available. These were sold in small shops or 'boutiques' and the best-known group of shops in London was concentrated in Carnaby Street. Many of the clothes were little more than fashionable fancy dress[33] or stage costumes for pop singers and

65 Man's suit by Simpsons and woman's suit by Lachasse (both in silk tweed) 1964 Two-piece lounge suit with snap-brim hat and casual slip-on shoes. The small shirt collar, narrow tie and short hair were also fashionable.

entertainers, but the new movement injected life, colour and amusement into the process of buying and wearing clothes, especially for young men, and was to have far-reaching effects on the clothing industry. In an interview with *Vogue* in 1965, Cecil Beaton – who was not a young man – remarked that 'in the old days there had to be some justification for being eccentric, nowadays everyone is.' He condemned the unchanging Savile Row image which turned out types like P. G. Wodehouse characters and approved of Carnaby Street (with some reservations): 'I love the flamboyance, colour and excitement. Some ways of dressing I still find embarrassing: Regency ruffles for instance.'[34]

Experiments were made with shapes and designs and at the level of haute couture Pierre Cardin's ideas were probably the most influential. His collarless jacket was made immediately famous when it was worn by the Beatles. In general there was also a bolder use of bright colours and patterns in shirts and ties, suits and linings. On the whole, Carnaby Street and other designers were trying to break away from the formal convention of the two- or three-piece suit so that the emphasis was on alternative, more informal garments, but the ordinary suit was itself affected by these trends by the end of the decade. The formality of the dark suit and white shirt worn with short, neatly cut hair, which was the new, elegant image in 1950, seemed uniform and dull ten years later and by 1970 it had become possible to break away from that image altogether [**48**]. Although the suit of the late 1960's had not altered radically in shape or form, men in general felt more freedom in the choice of the colour, patterns and textures of suiting materials and accessories.

By 1961 *The Ambassador* export magazine believed that the skimpy, tubular cut was being rejected and that there was a return to 'a more natural adult appearance' consisting of a gently indicated waist, soft natural shoulders and wider, more shapely lapels on jackets.[35] Trousers continued to be slim-fitting but in 1962 flared hems were introduced and, once established, made a longer length necessary [**48**]. The long, straight trouser leg continued to be fashionable and 'cigarette shaped trousers' were praised by *Vogue* in 1966. Cardin advocated the long, slim look with longer jackets buttoning high in front with long vents at the back. By 1965 the influence of Ted Lapidus was also being felt in men's clothes, while in London, the new tailoring firm, Blades, brought style and fresh ideas to tailored garments, to combine the old order and the new. In 1969 a Blades' suit for the summer could be made in pale brown gabardine with wide lapels and a one-button fastening, worn with a pink cotton shirt and plump kipper tie.[36]

In the main, however, most men's requirements were modest. Aquascutum summed them up in a 1960's sales catalogue: 'men like suits which are simple but well-tailored, elegant but not fancy, perfectly fitting without exaggeration.'

CHAPTER FIVE

The Shirt

The shirt is probably the oldest and most basic garment in a man's wardrobe. Since very early periods it has been usual for men to wear a tunic with long or short sleeves, of wool or linen, next to the skin and beneath the normal outer clothing. This garment has continued to be worn, without a break, until the present day and although its cut and construction have altered over the centuries it has retained the essential features of its original form. It is still the principal undergarment to cover the upper part of the body, and still basically tunic-shaped with a front opening, sleeves and some form of neckband or collar.

Until the middle of the nineteenth century the shirt was always worn next to the skin; even when an undershirt or vest was later worn beneath it its main purpose continued as a protective layer between the skin and its outer clothing. The shirt helped to prevent the overgarments from being soiled by direct contact with the body and could be changed and washed frequently to ensure an acceptable standard of hygiene. In periods when the main body garments were made of heavy silks or woollen cloths which were not cleaned easily or often, this was important, and even now one of the shirt's main requirements is that it should wash well. The shirt also protected the skin from the outer clothes, which being of a heavier or coarser texture might rub or irritate it (especially in the mediaeval period when linings were made of fur face-inwards). The shirt always extended a little beyond the edge of the garment at the neck and wrists, where chafing most often occurred [19]. An equivalent undergarment was worn by women until the early twentieth century, in the form of the chemise or shift.[1]

For most of its history, the shirt has played a dual role as both a useful and a fashionable garment. Apart from its basic function as an undergarment it could be worn without top covering as a type of informal dress for working out of doors, especially in warm weather. Illustrations from the mediaeval period, in particular, show workers in the fields clad only in shirts and this was standard for many kinds of manual labour which required cool, comfortable and easy clothing. In the Renaissance period it was also customary for the shirt or chemise to be worn as part of theatrical dress to represent on stage the loose, draped garments of ancient Greece or Rome.[2] In the warmer climate of Italy and southern Europe it appears to have been acceptable for both men and women to wear only a shirt or chemise for comfort and ease in the home, or out of doors. This was less usual in the north but, particularly during the eighteenth century, it was possible for men in 'déshabillé' to wear a shirt with a loose covering such as a nightgown or dressing-gown.

At the same time, however, the idea has persisted that a man in shirt sleeves is still in his underwear and improperly dressed, or at best only informally clothed. In Henry Fielding's novel, *Tom Jones* (1749), for example, Mrs Deborah Wilkinson, 'tho' in the 52nd year of her age, vowed she had never beheld a man without his coat'.[3] That was over 200 years ago but it is still the rule, at least for formal dress, that a shirt should be covered. Even in the second half of the twentieth century it has not been considered perfectly correct or polite to remove the suit jacket in public.

Nevertheless, the shirt, unlike most other underwear, has always been partly visible since the end of the Middle Ages. The areas at the neck, centre front and wrists were not only permitted to show but were regarded as a decorative feature of fashionable male dress, setting off or complementing the main body garments. The shirt could be a luxurious garment, and was sometimes worn to deliberately erotic effect. At more than one period, but particularly in the later fifteenth and seventeenth centuries [17, 28], a great deal of soft, voluminous shirt was exposed to view and must have appeared casual and provocative, the masculine equivalent of that 'sweet disorder in the dress' which the poet Herrick thought 'kindles in clothes a wantonness'.[4]

The use of rich or delicate embroidery and lace also proved to be a popular form of enhancement at the neck and wrists. Long sleeves or ruffles falling over the hands have been another favourite feature and although laced wrist-ruffles disappeared at the end of the eighteenth century, shirt-cuffs have usually been allowed to show at the edge of the coat-sleeve. In 1935 Max Beerbohm was seen wearing long cuffs which came right over his wrists, emphasizing 'the exquisite gestures of his trim deliberate hands'[5] (which no doubt explains why the fashion was successful). Small touches of white or an expanse of shirt-front and sleeves have frequently been effective in showing off the material or cut of the main garments, whether rich or sombre. In the nineteenth and twentieth centuries coloured shirts have also been worn to lighten a dull suit [81].

Perhaps more than any other garment in the male wardrobe, the shirt has served to underline distinctions in wealth and social status. The finest, softest and whitest linens are the most expensive to buy and need careful laundering, especially when frilled or embroidered. White linen also shows up dirt almost immediately, so the man with immaculate collar and cuffs clearly does not need to work with his hands and can afford to change his shirt once or twice a day, or even more.[6]

It is apparent that, from the earliest periods, shirts were changed and washed frequently. It was usual for a gentleman to have several dozen in his wardrobe and even Parson Woodforde, as a young student with little means, took nine shirts with him to Oxford in 1762.[7] In the nineteenth century cleanliness became an even more important element in fashionable dress and a certain confirmation of gentility, possibly because the Industrial

Revolution widened the gulf between the manual worker and the gentleman. The nineteenth-century dandy, whose dress had to be as perfect as possible, paid particular attention to fresh, white and beautifully laundered linen ('fine linen, plenty of it, and country washing' was Beau Brummell's maxim[8]). Even at the turn of this century, Julius Beerbohm, was sending his shirts from London to Paris every week to be specially washed.[9] Few men went to these lengths but it set a standard and the novelist R. T. Surtees considered that a gentleman needed two clean shirts a day.[10] Sometimes a false front, or dickey, was put on over a soiled or tumbled shirt to give a neat appearance; 'they are, however, seldom used, it being much better to put on a clean shirt at once', said *The Workwoman's Guide*.[11]

During the nineteenth century, separate, starched collars came into fashion. A degree of gentility was attached to the stiff white collar and it became almost a badge of the upper, middle and professional classes. Working men and those with little means tended to go collarless except for special occasions. As late as the early 1950's a distinction was made in British army uniforms between officers, who wore a collar and tie beneath their battledress jackets, and the other ranks who wore neither with their shirts. No equivalent garment in the female wardrobe has been used to emphasize social status in quite this way.

Although the shirt has at times been made of all four of the natural fibres – wool, linen, cotton and silk – linen, until quite recently, proved to be by far the most suitable. It is the oldest material to have been used for undergarments and the word became synonymous with a man's underwear. The advantage of linen is that it washes well and is hard-wearing; with its cool, smooth and absorbent texture it is also a pleasant and comfortable cloth to wear next to the skin. It is evident that the ancient Egyptians, whose standard of hygiene was high, made widespread use of linen for these reasons.

It was general practice, until the present century, for men of all social classes to wear a linen shirt, although the texture and weight of the material varied a great deal. The quality of the fabric was, in fact, rather more important than the fashionable shape of the garment. The best quality linens such as cambric, fine holland cloth, lawn or muslin were almost transparent, while the least expensive cloths were the coarsest and thickest, such as hemp, Scotch cloth and other stout linens. Apart from being cheap these were practical for heavy manual work and were worn by the poorer classes. A shirt of inferior cloth tended to be cut on less generous lines than the fashionable shirt, both for the sake of economy and to prevent too thick a layer beneath closely fitting garments. The finer and softer the linen, the more voluminous the shirt could be without being bulky and uncomfortable; and fashionably tight-fitting garments usually indicate fine texture in the linen beneath [17].

Some of the earliest shirts were made of wool, especially in the colder climate of northern Europe. Fine wools or flannel continued to be worn for extra warmth or sporting activities until the twentieth century, but such

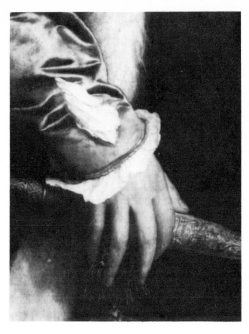

66   Detail of a fresco by
Pietro Lorenzetti, early
fourteenth century
A young man removes his
tunic to reveal a long linen
shirt.

67   The French
Ambassadors by Holbein
1533 (det of 19)
Doublets were decorated
with small splits or slashes
through which the shirt could
be pulled in small puffs.

material is less suitable for warm weather or for wearing next to the skin
and does not wash as well as linen. (It used to be believed that wool was
more likely than silk or linen to harbour lice.[12]) Until the second half of the
nineteenth century it was not usual in cold weather to wear shirts of a
warmer fibre, or additional garments next to the skin; instead, more layers
were added to the outer clothing.

Shirts were occasionally made of silk but such a delicate and expensive
material was generally impractical for underwear. Cotton has several of the
qualities of linen but has only been in general use for underclothes since a
comparatively recent date. In the mediaeval period cotton was used for
padding and stuffing but for little else and it was not until the later
seventeenth century that garments were made of this fibre in any quantity.
In the nineteenth century it was considered a socially inferior material for
shirts. The *Workwoman's Guide* lists shirts for labouring men as made of
calico with linen collars and wrist bands, whereas gentlemen's shirts were
to be made altogether of fine Irish linen. After 1850, however, striped
cotton shirts could be worn for sporting or country pursuits, and cotton
became acceptable and even popular as a shirting fabric in the present
century. It is still preferred by some in spite of the various man-made fibres
available which tend to be cheaper and are much easier to look after.

Spun rayon shirts began to be produced in the late 1930's but not in great
number until after the Second World War. In the 1950's man-made fibres
were developed on a large scale and the first terylene and nylon shirts were
brought out. They were quick-drying with a special finish which required
little or no ironing. Shirts made of a mixture of terylene and cotton had the
appearance and feel of cotton but were much easier to care for.

Starch has been used intermittently since the sixteenth century as a stiffening agent for shirts. It gives a crisp, almost sparkling effect to linen and came to be associated with an air of formality. It began to be used widely in the reign of Elizabeth I and was essential to the success of the pleated ruffs or collars then fashionable. It was used again, almost universally, in the second half of the nineteenth century when the collar, cuffs and centre-front panel of the shirt were stiffened [69]. Soft shirts and collars tended to be worn only for sports or casual wear and starched shirts were obligatory for formal and respectable dress. By the 1920's, however, men began to rebel against the discomfort and inflexibility of the stiff shirt, and the starched front was gradually abandoned for all but the most formal occasions. Stiffened collars and cuffs continued to be worn but starching was replaced by built-in stiffeners. By the 1960's soft collars had become standard wear.

Until the last years of the nineteenth century the shirt was almost invariably either white or pale-coloured, the standard for undergarments. Cotton or calico shirts with coloured stripes could be worn, and in the 1850's some shirtings had a small pattern, but coloured shirts did not become acceptable for more formal day wear until late 1890's and they were usually worn with a white collar. In the late nineteenth and early twentieth centuries, the coloured shirt with coloured collar was associated with labouring men and the white shirt and collar with the professional and middle classes – hence the terms 'white-collar worker' and 'blue-collar worker', which came into use to distinguish clerical from manual labour. In the first few decades of the present century, however, the striped shirt with a stiff white collar was considered perfectly correct and it was not until the early 1950's that the plain white shirt (worn with a dark suit) was re-established.

Coloured shirts were revived in the early 1960's and were even considered fashionable for evening dress wear, with a dinner jacket; but the traditional preference for white died hard and in 1965 Harrods' catalogue claimed that 'the shirt of the year has the crisply-laundered look of a conventional stiff-collared shirt and is in "Bri-nylon" – with collar attached. Needs no ironing. White only.'

The Development of the Shirt

Although the modern shirt is quite different from its mediaeval counterpart the basic shape and construction have altered comparatively slowly. It is a characteristic of undergarments, which are rarely exposed to full view, that they change far less quickly than the fashionable upper garments and often retain very old features of cut. For most of its history the shirt has been basically rectangular and not fitted to the body [66, 68] (closely fitting shirts are a recent development of the 1960's). Until the mid nineteenth century, because they did not require expert tailoring, shirts were made by hand, and as a rule at home, by the women or servants of the family.

The earliest shirts were simple T-shaped tunics. They were designed to be made from cloth straight from the loom, with the minimum amount of cutting and wastage, and were easy to sew. There is evidence that some shirts could be woven in one piece on a wide loom (with the sleeves and neck-opening woven in[13]), but as a rule the front and back pieces were joined by seams at each side and often a seam straight across the shoulders. Until the fourteenth century the shirt was usually cut long (at least to mid-calf) and full, with an opening at the neck and long sleeves.

The original neck-opening was a slit or hole large enough to pass over the head; it had no neckband or collar so did not fit closely to the neck. The opening could be reinforced and decorated by embroidery but it was not until the beginning of the fourteenth century that a separate neckband began to appear. This was a flat strip of fabric attached to the opening which encircled the neck and could fit quite closely round it. To allow enough room to pull on the shirt the opening was extended part of the way down the centre front and it was closed at the neck by strings or ribbons. Buttons were sometimes used but not as a rule until after the mid seventeenth century. The height of the neckband varied with fashion and it could be worn as a small standing collar. By the fifteenth century there was considerable variation in the neckline of the shirt and there appears to have been no particular, universal style. Shirts continued to be made without neckbands, with wide and unshaped openings; some were cut to the base of the neck or slightly higher, others quite low and finely gathered on to a band. The opening was usually at the front but some shirts were fastened at the back.

The sleeves could either be cut in one with the garment (in the kimono shape) or set in separately. When the sleeve was gathered into the armhole neither was shaped. In the mediaeval and Renaissance periods, sleeves were cut long, to the wrist, and were wide and straight, with no cuff. An important development in the construction of the shirt was the insertion of a gusset under the arm to allow more freedom of movement. This was a square inset folded diagonally and set into the right-angled seam beneath the armpit (so that in profile the gusset appeared triangular). Until men's garments grew shorter the shirt was worn long [66]. After the mid fourteenth century it was generally slightly shorter than the present-day length but it was full at the hem. The bottom was cut straight across and did not dip at the back. Some shirts had side vents, that is the side seams were opened at the hem to allow ease of movement at the hips. Side vents were usually found in the narrower shirts worn by the poorer classes. After the sixteenth century, however, they became a usual feature of the shirt [68].

In the second half of the fifteenth century it was fashionable to expose more of the shirt at the neck and shoulders, centre front and sleeves. The body and sleeves of the doublet were reduced in various ways or split and laced across, allowing the shirt to ooze out [17]. The fuller the shirt, the more effective this was, but clearly the linen had to be very fine to produce a mass of soft folds without being thick and clumsy. The fashion for exposing the shirt continued well into the sixteenth century when it was customary to decorate the doublet with small slits or slashes through which the shirt could be pulled in small puffs [67].

By the beginning of the sixteenth century the neck of the doublet was cut fairly low and square and the shirt was visible above it, being finely gathered on to a narrow band at the base of the neck. The sleeves, which were still long and wide, could also be gathered into a band at the wrists. The neck and wrist bands were frequently decorated with embroidery in coloured silks or gold and silver thread, but the most popular form of embroidery was blackwork [20]. Apart from its decorative effect the embroidery strengthened these exposed areas and helped to disguise inevitable soiling.

In the first half of the sixteenth century the neckband grew in height and importance to become a standing, circular collar, which could be surmounted with a small, decorative frill [21]. This was the fore-runner of the ruff [22]. As the frill became larger it was arranged into formal folds or pleats; eventually it had to be detached from the shirt, although it was still closed by ties at the centre front. The radiating pleats, which looked like organ pipes, were formed over a heated wooden stick and stiffened with starch. They were often several layers deep. The pleats could be arranged in a number of different styles, according to the fashion. The starch was blue at first and later yellow, so that collars were probably less purely white than they appear in pictures of the time. By 1580 the ruff had reached an enormous size and was quite rigid, resembling a cartwheel. It could be decorated with an edging of fine, spiky lace or embroidered in silk. The wrists were similarly adorned by small frills or cuffs of lawn or lace. Lace began to appear after about 1540. Lace-making was a relatively new skill and it soon became extremely popular. Once the ruff became fashionable, embroidered neck and wrist bands gradually disappeared. The ruff was fashionable between about 1550 and 1625; after 1620 it collapsed into a drooping circular collar and continued to be worn only by the more old-fashioned and with official dress.

An alternative type of collar which began to replace the ruff in the 1580's and was fashionable for the first two decades of the seventeenth century was the standing neckband [24]. 'Band' is a general term for a collar and the turned-down collar (usually attached to the shirt) was first known as a 'falling-band'. In the late sixteenth century the band could be stiffened and worn erect at the back of the head to frame the face; it was semi-circular and open at the front. This was known as the 'standing-band' or 'golilla' and was worn with a fine wired frame (called a 'supportasse', 'underpropper' or 'pickadil') to support it. Like the ruff, it was made of fine, almost transparent linen often trimmed with lace or embroidery. It too, after reaching a climax of width and stiffening, gradually softened and collapsed, falling and spreading on to the shoulders after the 1620's [25]. The falling-band continued to be edged with lace but of a different character. Instead of the sharp, delicate needle lace, a softer, heavier bobbin lace began to be worn. The English lace industry was established by the early seventeenth century but the best bobbin lace was imported from Flanders.

By the 1630's the lace-edged collar had spread to its maximum width across the shoulders [56]; at the same time its shape began to be altered by

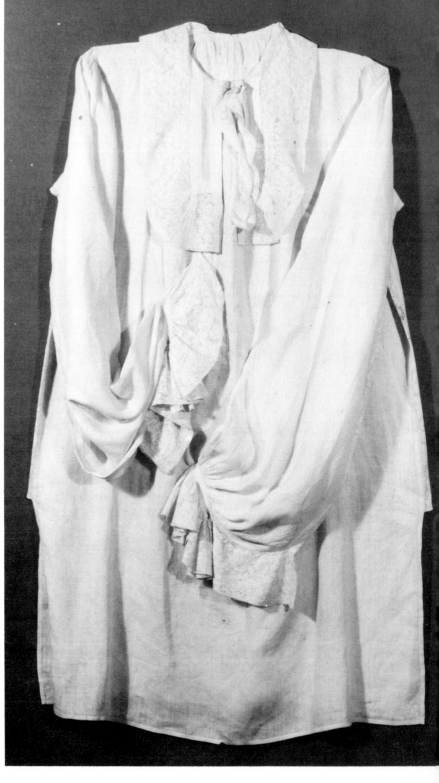

68 White linen shirt
1660–80. Museum of London
The collar, front opening and
sleeve ruffles are trimmed
with bobbin lace.

the increasing length of men's hair. The weight of the hair on the shoulders
pushed the collar towards the front of the doublet so that it hung in folds
[28, 57]. By 1638 it was possible to tie up the collar by a ribbon at the neck
and at this stage the cravat began to be adopted. An alternative was the
deep, bib-like collar which no longer spread at the sides but lay flat at the
centre front [68], but by the 1640's a new, small collar was more
fashionable. By about 1650 this collar had stiffened slightly and was tied
with tasselled strings while the lace collar lost favour and had almost
disappeared by the late 1670's. Once the separate neckcloth or cravat began
to be worn, attention was concentrated on this item and it became the
fashionable form of neckwear.

Other parts of the shirt were prominent features during the seventeenth
century. By the middle of the century the shirt was displayed to an almost
startling extent [28, 57]. The doublet was slashed or paned at back and front
and in the sleeves, leaving a kind of lattice-work revealing the shirt
beneath. It also began to shrink: it gaped at the waist, was shorter in the
sleeve and was worn unbuttoned at the front. The shirt sleeves were cut full
and caught in at the wrists (sometimes also at the elbow) with ribbon ties.
The wristband was decorated with a frill or ruffle which by the 1660's was
made of lace and fell over the hands. The shirt on the funeral effigy of
Charles II (who died in 1685), for example, has wrist-ruffles of Venetian *gros
point* lace mounted on linen strips and wristbands (which have four
buttonholes).[14] If ruffles were not worn, the shortened coat sleeve could

69 'Mariage de Convenance
– After!' by Sir W. Q.
Orchardson 1886
A stiffly-starched shirt-front
'of intense rigidity, which
stood out before him like the
chest of a pouter pigeon.'

reveal a full shirt sleeve puffed out below and ending in a plain buttoned wristband. Elaborate wrist-ruffles were more usual wear for Court or formal occasions and the fashion continued until the end of the eighteenth century.

By the later seventeenth century, the centre-front opening of the shirt was edged with a narrow gathered or pleated ruffle of linen or lace [68] but for the most part this was concealed by the cravat. During the eighteenth century, when the hanging cravat passed out of fashion, the ruffle was more prominent and showed just above the top of the waistcoat [34]. This served both to conceal the shirt-front opening and to decorate it; it was attached to the shirt and was not a separate accessory.

The basic shape of the shirt changed very little in the eighteenth century. The hem was still cut square but the back was slightly longer and there were side vents. The body and the sleeves were still amply cut. The material of the shirt was gathered into a deep neckband over which the neckcloth was worn. It was closed by two or three linen thread-covered buttons. The fullness of the sleeves was often carefully pleated along the outer side and then gathered into a narrow wristband which fastened with a button. The plain shirt sleeve tended to be worn for more informal dress, otherwise a sleeve-ruffle was attached. The ruffles were smaller in the second half of the century and were abandoned in the 1790's. By the end of the century the shirt was used far less for extravagant display but there was still considerable emphasis on the quality of the linen and laces worn. A lighter, more delicate lace became fashionable in the early eighteenth century. After the 1750's creamy and lustrous silk laces (called 'blonde') became very popular but they were not often worn by men.

The eighteenth-century form of the shirt continued to be worn for part of the nineteenth century, but by the beginning of the present century it had changed quite considerably in general appearance. Several modifications were made in cut and fit, in particular at the shoulders and neck. During the eighteenth century a gusset had been introduced on each shoulder, to ensure a better fit and to ease the collar, since the body of the shirt was still gathered on to the neckband. After about 1840 it was customary to make shirts with a yoke at the back which gave a smooth fit over the shoulders while allowing fullness lower down the back. This eliminated the bulky, round-shouldered effect of gathering all the fullness into the neck. The nineteenth-century shirt was cut with longer tails at the back and had side vents; after 1850 the corners at the hem were rounded rather than left square. The most usual form of opening was at the centre front although shirts occasionally fastened at the back or the side if the front was elaborately frilled or embroidered.[15]

After the 1830's there were alterations to the centre-front opening. Until this time the frilled opening had been worn [78]; now it was relegated to evening dress, and by the middle of the century it was passing out of fashion altogether. The frill was replaced (from the 1820's onwards) by a front panel with vertical pleats or tucks. The edges of the opening overlapped slightly and in time it became usual to fasten the shirt-front with two or three buttons or studs [91]. Studs were used more generally once the shirt-front began to be starched, after about 1850 [141]. By the 1870's the shirt-front had become quite plain but it was stiffened and then fastened by decorative studs. There was a clearer distinction during this century between shirts for day and evening wear, and dress shirts were usually more decorative. Possibly this was the result of increasing industrialization and the tendency to wear more utilitarian and less colourful clothes during the daytime. A certain amount of shirt-front was exposed above the waistcoat, and in the evenings or in summer the waistcoat was cut a little lower for this purpose.

For most of the eighteenth century the neckband of the shirt had been concealed by a neckcloth and in the first decades of the nineteenth century it was still scarcely visible, although it increased in height. The neckband was attached to the shirt to form a deep, standing collar, the tips of which could just be seen above the neckcloth wrapped round the throat. At its highest, the corners of the stiffened collar overlapped the cheeks [38]. It was not usual to wear the collar turned down over the cravat until the middle of the century. In the 1820's the separate collar appeared and this was at first attached to the shirt by a button at the front and strings at the back; later the collar was closed at the front by a button or a stud and was fastened in the same way to the shirt at the back. The collar continued to be starched and was worn upright. There were variations in its shape: the points could be wide apart, or almost meet, or overlap, or bend over at the corners (to form the wing or butterfly collar) [70]. The turned-down, or double, collar was worn for more informal occasions; when not starched it was considered even more informal [41]. After the middle of the century the double collar was more generally worn but only in the daytime; the single collar remained the more formal and was always worn with evening dress [69].

By the 1860's, the collar was worn much lower and it was only in the 1880's that it began to rise again. By the 1890's it reached its maximum height (at the most extreme, three inches high) [80]. This type of collar was indispensable for formal dress, low collars being only permissible for very young men and for sportswear.

Shirt-cuffs have usually kept pace with changes in the collar and during the nineteenth century they shared many of its features. They were rectangular and, after 1850, stiffly starched. The cuff was allowed to hang about half an inch below the coat sleeve (which in the early decades was often left unbuttoned at the side). Like the collar, the cuff could be single or double, but it was the double cuff that came to be thought of as the more formal. Links to fasten the cuff were not usual until the 1840's and for some time afterwards they were described as 'buttons'. It was possible to obtain separate cuffs (which could be reversed when one edge was soiled) and cuff-protectors to slip over for office work but these were never considered socially acceptable. There were, in fact, a number of rigid conventions attached to the types of collars and cuffs worn for different occasions or times of day.

Towards the end of the century coloured shirts came into more general

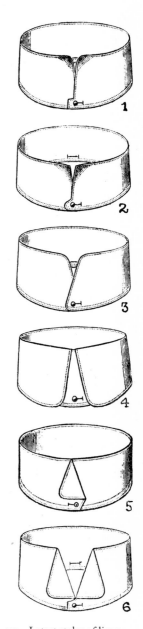

70 Latest styles of linen collars from *The Tailor and Cutter* 1900
The double collar (4) was less formal than a single, winged or butterfly collar (6).

use but it was not until the last years of the 1890's that they could be worn with formal day clothes. Coloured shirts had been worn by working men for some time, and on occasions by the unconventional. William Morris, for example, was recorded in 1892 as wearing his usual 'dark blue serge suit – a little untidy . . . a linen shirt dyed indigo in his own vats' and no tie.[16]

Several innovations originated from America and it was partly due to American influence that in the last years of the century there was a move towards less formal, less uncomfortable dress. A significant development was the introduction of the 'coat' shirt which buttoned all the way down the front and did not need to be pulled over the head; but it was some time before this was generally adopted.

Although the starched shirt and collar reached the height of their popularity in the last years of the nineteenth century [70], new fashions were already beginning to take hold [71]. Collars were gradually lowered, coloured shirts were worn by day and in 1906 a soft-fronted shirt for business men appeared. The rule of starch was slowly undermined, although it held good until the outbreak of the Second World War.

The 'boiled shirt', made of white linen (rather than flannel or striped cotton), had a stiffly starched front panel and was so called because it needed to be boiled to remove the starch; it was worn with the single, wing collar and was correct with formal day dress until the 1920's and essential to evening clothes [69]. After the First World War younger, forward-looking men such as the Prince of Wales condemned the boiled shirt (although his father, George V, and men of that generation, continued to wear it with a frock coat by day in London[17]) and the striped shirt with a stiff, white collar (double or winged) was general for formal occasions. Sporting or more informal shirts were still cut in the tunic style, with a soft front and soft, turned-down collar [72].

The distinction between day and evening shirts was preserved. At the end of the 1920's it became possible to wear a soft-fronted shirt with a dinner jacket but a stiff, dress shirt was always worn with the tailcoat. Usual fronts for dress shirts in this decade were made of plain or indent marcella or piqué and some were pleated. By the early 1930's soft, double collars could be worn with the dinner jacket.

Dorothy L. Sayers' novel, *Gaudy Night*, reflects some of the variety in men's dress shirts in the mid 1930's. Harriet Vane and the Dean 'had begun to collect shirt-fronts': there was the young man, 'extremely tall and thin and rather hollow-chested', who, by way of emphasizing this defect, always wore a soft, pleated dress shirt which made him look 'like the scooped-out rind of a melon'; in contrast, there had been an eminent and ample professor of chemistry 'who had turned up in a front of intense rigidity, which stood out before him like the chest of a pouter pigeon, bulging out of all control and displaying a large area of parent shirt at either side [69]. A third variety of shirt fairly common among the learned was that which escaped from the centre stud and gaped in the middle.' Yet another was the lecturer whose every gesticulation caused his waistcoat to leap in the air, 'allowing a line of shirt, adorned with a little tab, to peep out, rabbit-like,

7003—Men's or Boys' Shirt.

5799—Men's or Boys' Shirt.

71 Butterick patterns for clothing the troops 1914 Shirts were made in the tunic and coat styles and had separate collars. Collar points could be buttoned down. Cuffs were double.

over the waistline of the confining trouser'. Lastly, Dr Threep's shirt-front 'popped' or 'exploded with a merry little report like the opening of ginger-beer'. Lord Peter Wimsey explained that the sound:

> is produced when the shirt-front is slightly too long for the wearer. The stiff edges, being forced slightly apart by the inclination of the body come back into contact with a sharp click, similar to that emitted by the elytra of certain beetles ... it may be obviated by an increased care in selection, or, in extreme cases, by having the garment made to measure.[18]

Separate collars continued to be worn but by the 1930's they were often attached to the shirt. Both types were in use until the late 1960's although collar-attached shirts gradually became the more common form. The changes in laundering methods with the use of washing machines in the home probably encouraged this trend but the separate collar was also threatened by the growing informality in men's dress, especially during the 1960's (it is almost impossible to wear an open-necked shirt with a separate, stiffened collar).

Soft collars were not usually starched but stiffened, either with celluloid tab insertions or by a patent process called trubenizing, by which the outer

72 Jaeger clothes for men
c 1934
Striped shirt with matching collar and tennis shirt in the tunic style.

73 Party shirts by Michael Fish and Barry Sainsbury 1968
Shirts in daring new colours, patterns and shapes were produced in the 1960's. Regency ruffles might be worn in the evening.

fabric and inner lining of the collar were fused into a semi-stiff whole which required no further dressing or starch (and could be laundered at home).

Collar shapes and styles have continued to alter, even if only subtly in the course of the present century [81]. The points of the turned-down collar could be short, fairly long and narrow, rounded or even buttoned down to the shirt. Cuffs also changed; the starched ones were gradually abandoned except for evening dress and there was only light stiffening on ordinary shirts. The more practical single cuff which fastened with a button became more usual than the double cuff with links after the 1950's.

A Simpson's catalogue of 1937 declared that all their shirts were coat style and that most men found them more comfortable. By this date shirts could be bought ready-made [72] and after the Second World War fewer men had their shirts made to measure, although Harrods, in 1955, maintained that 'many men prefer their shirts made to their own measurements finding that the craftsman can produce a garment which fits the most difficult combination of neck and arm exactly.'

By the 1930's popular shirting fabrics included cottons and poplins as well as linens [81], but in the mid 1950's these were being replaced by nylon and other man-made fibres. In the mid 1960's fashionable shirt materials were highly colourful, patterned and fanciful. Flower-patterned shirts appeared in 1964 and the Jermyn Street shirt makers, Turnbull and Asser, produced shirts designed by Michael Fish in daring new colours, patterns and shapes, decorated with ruffles, beads and embroidery[19] [73]. In 1969, *Vogue* magazine was describing shirts such as a 'Rainbow Art Deco print voile', 'a narrow and floppy collared sky blue and white embroidered Swiss voile made by Peter Golding' or a shirt by Deborah and Claire of 'deep collared ivory silk printed with spinach green insects and ivy'.[20] These were mostly worn by the adventurous and hardly became a general fashion, but they affected even the most conventional forms of dress and by the end of the 1960's men were wearing coloured shirts and patterned ties to the office, which ten years earlier had been unthinkable. Fancy, tucked fronts for dress shirts were revived with enthusiasm in the 1960's and they could be made, for example, of hand-stitched voile with guipure lace edging.

There were attempts to introduce alternatives to the traditional shape and cut of the shirt, for instance a polo-necked shirt for evening wear with a dinner jacket; another innovation was a loose-fitting garment or informal shirt in the coat style, worn outside and not inside the trousers; but these were subsidiary fashions and the general appearance of the shirt altered very little.

CHAPTER SIX

The Necktie

The necktie entered the male wardrobe shortly before the three-piece suit began to evolve. By 1670 a separate neckcloth had replaced the spreading, lace-edged collar attached to the shirt; it became an important dress accessory which is still a usual feature of modern costume. The neckcloth and, later, the necktie were worn over the neckband or collar of the shirt and were virtually inseparable from it; it was not until well into the twentieth century that it became respectable for a shirt to be worn open at the neck and the shirt collar continued to be specifically designed to be turned down over a necktie. Before the second half of the seventeenth century collars were not always attached to the shirt and were large and elaborate enough to be considered as a separate item (the ruff is one example). Separate collars were also worn in the nineteenth and twentieth centuries but essentially they were an extension of the shirt and not an accessory to it.

The various words used to describe types of neckwear can be confusing. From the late seventeenth to the early nineteenth century 'neckcloth' was the general term; literally, a cloth worn round the neck, it could take two forms – the cravat and the stock. A cravat was a long strip of fabric wound around the neck and tied in front with a knot or bow [77]. A stock was a band of material which passed round the neck to fasten at the back with a tie, buckle or hook-and-eye; it was often stiffened and gave the appearance of a circular, upright collar [76]. The stock was in general use during the eighteenth century but by the beginning of the nineteenth century it had been replaced by the cravat.

The term 'necktie' was not usual until the nineteenth century when, after about 1830, the cravat was wound once round the neck and tied in front with a larger bow or knot [79]. Neckpieces were known by a number of different names, usually referring to the way in which they were arranged: the 'Ascot' for example was a cravat, folded scarf-like over the front of the shirt and fixed by a pin; the 'four-in-hand' was knotted at the throat with the long ends left to hang loose (as the tie is now normally worn) and the bow tie, of course, explained itself. By the early twentieth century most people used only the long knotted tie and the bow tie.

Different materials have been used for men's neckwear but the most usual were linen and silk. Cravats and stocks in the later seventeenth and the eighteenth century were made of fine linen, usually white. In the nineteenth century silk was worn (in white, black and other colours) and became customary for daytime wear, but linen and cotton were correct for the white tie with evening dress. Wool has been worn, but, as a rule, only with informal or sporting dress. After the Second World War man-made fibres such as rayon, imitating silk, came into widespread use for ties.

Unlike the shirt, the neckcloth or necktie does not appear to fulfil any useful function; it is the collar which provides necessary protection and warmth for the neck and prevents the soiling of outer garments. Rather, the purpose of a neckpiece is decorative and aesthetic, as an accessory to complete and embellish the costume. In the later seventeenth century, for instance, the cravat was a means of displaying fine linen and expensive lace; in the later nineteenth century it could provide a touch of lightness and colour to relieve the generally sombre uniformity of the suit, and indeed the necktie has remained one of the few means left to men to express individual taste and style in dress. For example, Count Robert de Montesquiou, renowned for his elegance in France in the 1880's, dressed himself as a work of art: 'the sobriety of his colour-scheme was mitigated by the coquetry of his lilac perfume and pastel-hued cravats'.[1] John Ruskin was described in 1887 as having: 'the bluest of blue eyes. Their colour was repeated with a difference in his large blue neckties.'[2] Neckties were undoubtedly chosen with care. *The Tailor and Cutter* reported in 1898 that a leading tie manufacturer spent more time and thought on the production of ties for winter wear than for the spring when 'men are hopeful and are easily pleased'.[3] The tie played a more important role once the two-piece suit became more generally worn, for when the coat was unbuttoned the tie was revealed in its entirety; during the 1960's it grew larger, more brightly coloured and highly patterned and was used to enliven an otherwise dull formal suit (with the increasing mass production of clothing, ready-made suits could not always rely on first-rate cut and fit for a striking effect).

After its introduction the neckcloth or necktie became an essential feature of the male costume and no formal dress was either complete or correct without it. The convention of white or black neckwear for evening dress was established during the nineteenth century and by the present century a reference to the tie alone could identify the exact form of dress. 'Black tie' on an invitation to an evening function indicated not only a black bow tie but also a dinner jacket, whereas the white tie was always worn with a wing collar, stiff shirt and tail coat [**91, 92**]. Coloured ties with evening dress were not permissible until the 1960's when a dark red, green or blue bow – and often a matching cummerbund—might be worn with a dinner jacket. 'Black tie' has another important use, of course, indicating the black four-in-hand tie for a funeral.

The idea that a man without a tie is improperly or incorrectly dressed has persisted well into the present century. During the 1960's there was an increased informality in both male and female dress and the tie was worn far less by younger men [**48**], but a formal, two- or three-piece suit still required a tie to complete it and many hotels, restaurants, clubs and other institutions continued to refuse entry to men without one.

The neckcloth, like the shirt, could quite clearly indicate the man's social or financial status, according to not only the whiteness and fineness of the linen but also the quality and quantity of lace displayed with it. Both lace and fine linen were expensive, delicate and required careful laundering. An immaculately clean and well-arranged stock or cravat denoted a gentleman and man of fashion. In 1676 a man could marvel 'that a man's excellency should lie in Neatly tying of a Ribbond, or a Cravat!'[4] and by the beginning of the nineteenth century the neckcloth was one of the most important considerations of the dandy's dress. Several manuals were written on the art of tying it correctly and Beau Brummell's reputation rested, in part, on his perfection of the skill.

During the nineteenth century there was a marked preference for a self-tying rather than a made-up bow; ready-made bow ties were patented and became readily available but, although undoubtedly much easier to use, they were considered inferior and incorrect until at least the second half of the present century. Mr Pooter in *The Diary of a Nobody* (1892) illustrated the point – to the reader's rather than his own amusement – when he went to the theatre with friends:

> I was leaning out of the box, when my tie – a little black bow which fastened on to the stud by means of a new patent – fell into the pit below. A clumsy man, not noticing it, had his foot on it for ever so long before he discovered it. He then picked it up and eventually flung it under the next seat in disgust . . . I felt quite miserable. Mr. James, of Sutton, was very good. He said: "Don't worry – no one will notice it with your beard. That is the only advantage of growing one that I can see" . . . To hide the absence of the tie I had to keep my chin down the rest of the evening, which caused a pain at the back of my neck.[5]

If made-up bows were not, as Mr Woodhouse remarked of Frank Churchill, 'quite the thing',[6] neither were loud colours. Many nineteenth-century neckties appear to have been quite highly coloured and patterned (the 'willow pattern' necktie, for example, was a popular novelty of 1897 and was not, according to the *Tailor and Cutter*, 'confined to the orthodox and familiar blue shade in which it has for such a long time been produced upon our dinner plates' – 'it looks particularly smart and dressy in some tones of browns and greens'[7]), but a necktie in red, crimson or 'other sanguinary hues' was more risky and never worn in the best circles. 'How is it,' asked the same journal in 1898, 'that if anyone describes a man wearing a red necktie, nothing further need be said, you imagine a horsey individual, or a sporting publican with a suit of loud checks, a loud voice, and much jewellery.'[8] (Red ties have still been frowned upon at times during the twentieth century, although the colour came to be associated more with communist than caddish tendencies). A man's reputation could clearly be damaged by wearing a made-up tie or a colour thought to be too loud. The correct necktie for the time of day or occasion remained an important consideration and it was said that Edward VII could have his whole evening spoiled if one of his guests wore the wrong tie.[9]

The symbolic character of the necktie is probably its most significant feature; apart from indicating social status or savoir faire it could proclaim a man's education, profession, aspirations or allegiance. Certain types of neckwear were connected with particular people; in the nineteenth century, for instance, a loosely knotted, flowing necktie was associated with artists and poets. In the last years of the century, neckties sporting the colours, badges, devices or crests of public schools, universities, regiments or clubs began to be worn and have remained popular in the present century. Almost every kind of organization has adopted a tie to be worn as a badge of membership or allegiance; the pattern of the tie has come to have a distinct meaning and its symbols or colours may be recognized and read by other men. Such ties confer a sense of belonging and exclusivity, they can even impart an air of respectability. 'The old school tie' (that is, a public school tie) par excellence implies a certain outlook and standard of behaviour, and above all ensures a certain standing in society. In the case of schools, colleges or regiments, the relevant tie is obviously only worn by those entitled to it through membership, but some club ties – especially sporting clubs and teams – can be presented to a non-member, with the right to wear it, as a gesture of friendliness.

It is interesting to note that the necktie is a feature of male dress which has no equivalent in the female wardrobe.

The Development of the Neckcloth

The neckcloth, or cravat, evolved in England during the 1630's. At this date the fashionable male doublet was accompanied by a broad linen shirt-collar, edged with lace, which spread over the chest and shoulders [56]. As men's hair was worn longer, however, the lace began to be obscured and the weight of the hair tended to push the collar towards the centre front where it fell in loose folds [28, 57]. It became the practice to tie the ends of the collar together with a ribbon and before long the collar itself was replaced by a separate length of linen and lace which could be tied or knotted at the throat [29]. With a mass of hair falling over the shoulders this had, at first, been a practical measure but it also allowed the lace, previously hidden, to be more prominently displayed, hanging down rather than spread across the chest [74].

Lace was expensive and valued highly (James II, for example, ordered a Venetian lace cravat costing £36. 10s. for his coronation in 1685[10]) both as a form of decoration and as a distinctive mark of social standing. Only the visible parts of the cravat – the ends – were trimmed with lace, and the main part, surrounding the neck, was made of linen. By the 1660's the most fashionable lace was the Venetian 'gros point' (immortalized in the unique wooden carvings of Grinling Gibbons) [74] which was too heavy to tie in a knot; instead, the ends of the cravat were caught together with a ribbon. One or more ribbons could be used and they were often coloured. In the 1680's the ribbon, or cravat-string, was tied in a wide, stiff bow which was worn beneath the fall of the cravat [58].

In the last decades of the seventeenth century the cravat grew much longer (the one on the effigy of Charles II in Westminster Abbey, dating from about 1685, was 86.32cm (thirty-four inches) long and 15.23cm (six inches wide)[11]). Lighter, more delicate laces such as Mechlin also became fashionable so that the cravat could be self-tied, in a knot, twist or fold. Some cravat ends were edged with fringes or knots and ohers were quite plain.

The derivation of the word 'cravat' is not altogether clear. A popular theory is that it comes from 'Croat' and that French soldiers fighting with Croatian mercenaries in the Swedish army during the Thirty Years War adopted their fashion. It appears, however, that neckcloths were already worn by the western military by that time and were not exclusive to the Croats. It seems more likely that the name originated from the French term 'rabat' or 'crabbat', meaning a lace collar. Randle Holme described the 'cravatt' in 1688 as a kind of 'adornment for the neck being nothing else but a long Towel put about the Collar, and so tyed before with a Bow knot, this is the Original of all such Wearing; but now by the Art and Invention of the Seamsters, there is so many new ways of making them, that it would be a Task to name them, much more to describe them.'[12]

In the last years of the seventeenth century one of the most popular forms of the cravat was the Steinkirk [75]. The name refers to the distinctive way in which it was arranged: it was passed round the neck and folded over, with the long ends hanging in front; the ends were then twisted together and one of them was passed through a buttonhole of the coat to keep it in place. It was popularly believed that the style was created

74 Lace cravat carved in limewood by Grinling Gibbons, late seventeenth century
Venetian 'gros point' lace was fashionable but expensive – James II paid £36. 10s. for a cravat to wear at his coronation in 1685.

75 Portrait of a Man, attributed to Sir Godfrey Kneller c 1710
A cravat arranged in the distinctive manner 'à la Steinkirk'. The long ends were twisted together and one end passed through a buttonhole of the coat.

76 'The Marriage Contract' by William Hogarth *c* 1743 (det of 33)
The 'solitaire' necktie was a black silk ribbon attached to the draw-string of the wig bag, it encircled the neck and tied in front with a bow.

77 Sir Brooke Boothby by Wright of Derby 1781 (det of 36)
The cravat of lawn or muslin was folded into a band and wrapped round the throat with a knot or bow tie at the front.

during the battle of Steinkirk in 1692 when French soldiers, caught unawares, had no time to do more than twist their neckcloths carelessly round their throats; but there is little if any evidence to support this theory and it cannot be taken too seriously (the practice of giving to a new style the name of a recent, noteworthy event occurs throughout the history of fashion). The cravat 'à la Steinkirk' replaced the shorter, beribboned neckcloth of the 1680's and was worn well into the next century, although from the 1730's to the 1770's only by older men or those of more conservative habits. In the early decades the cravat could also be worn informally tied round the neck to hang end over end, straight down the chest [32].

By 1740 the stock had become much more popular than the cravat [76]. The stock was essentially a made-up neckcloth: a long piece of fine lawn or muslin was gathered or pleated into a slightly stiffened band which fastened at the back of the neck. It was fashionable for most of the eighteenth century and during the second half of the period it steadily increased in height, often stiffened with pasteboard. The stock was generally white, but black was worn with military dress and sometimes for sporting wear.

Both the cravat and the stock were worn over the shirt collar, which was a deep standing neckband attached to the shirt. Whereas the hanging cravat had concealed the front opening of the shirt, the stock left it uncovered and provided further scope for the display of fine lace. The edge of the opening was trimmed with a gathered frill of linen or lace, which showed just above the top of the waistcoat [76]. Stock-buckles were often decorative although they were not visible beneath the longer style of wig; they could be made of silver and set with stones or paste.

A necktie or ribbon might also be worn over the stock [76]. The so-called 'solitaire' became fashionable in the 1730's and it was almost always worn with a bag wig. A length of black silk ribbon attached to the draw-string of the wig bag encircled the neck and was tied in front with a bow. The bow was quite stiff and sometimes very large (but this was not considered to be in the best of taste). Mr Simpkin, the hero of Christopher Anstey's satirical poem, *The New Bath Guide* (1766), pleased with his fashionable new appearance recently acquired at Bath, wrote to his mother:

> But what with my Nivernois hat can compare,
> Bag-wig and lac'd ruffles, and black solitaire?
> And what can a man of true fashion denote
> Like an ell of good ribbon tied under the throat?[13]

Although the stock was more common than the cravat (in 1762, Parson Woodforde listed nine shirts, nine stocks but only two cravats in his wardrobe[14]), the cravat returned to fashionable wear in the 1780's [77]. The cravat of the late eighteenth and early nineteenth centuries was a large square of lawn or muslin folded scarf-like into a triangle and then into a band which could be passed round the throat, and knotted or tied in a bow. Its general effect was similar to the stock and it was worn equally high but it did not require such heavy stiffening, and was only lightly starched [38]. Cravats were, as a rule, made at home by a man's family. Jane Austen made her brothers' cravats,[15] as did the heroine of *Northanger Abbey* (1818) when she found time: her mother complained to Catherine that she did not 'know when poor Richard's cravats would be done, if he had no friend but you'.[16]

In the early years of the nineteenth century men's dress looked dramatic and romantic with its stark combination of black and white. The black or dark-coloured garments were thrown into relief by a sparkling white collar and neckcloth [39] (or sometimes the white collar and shirt-front were contrasted with a black silk cravat). The points of the shirt-collar – which was deep and worn upright – showed just above the top edge of the cravat and almost encased the lower part of the jaw. The neck was entirely swathed in the neckcloth, which must have been considerably restricting. Mr Turveydrop, in Charles Dickens' *Bleak House* (1853), conveys some idea of the discomfort: 'He had such a neckcloth on (puffing his very eyes out of their natural shape) and his chin and even his ears so sunk into it, that it seemed as though he must inevitably double up, if it were cast loose ... As he bowed to me in that tight state, I almost believe I saw creases come into the whites of his eyes.'[17] Mr Turveydrop, 'celebrated everywhere for his Deportment', greatly admired the Prince Regent with whom this style of neckcloth is often associated, but it was George Brummell who made it famous. He could apparently spoil several cravats each time he dressed, before achieving a satisfactory arrangement of folds and creases, (this was probably not remarkable for a perfectionist – a hundred years or so later, men of less exacting standards might still be obliged to use more than one fresh white tie before managing an acceptable bow for evening dress). One of the early manuals on the art of tying the cravat to be published in England was H. le Blanc's book of 1828, which included thirty-two methods, each with its own name, and the author warned the man aspiring to elegance and fashion that he would attract less attention to his coat than to the set of his cravat: 'should this unfortunately not be correctly and elegantly put on –no further notice will be taken of him.'[18]

The stock did not pass immediately out of use and was worn by old-fashioned men until the 1850's. It was lined and stiffened with horsehair, pig's bristle or whalebone to form a deep, curved band; it could be made of silk (often black), and decorated with a ready-made bow attached to the front. A style called the Royal George (after George IV) was made of black velvet with a satin bow. By the early nineteenth century the stock was no longer worn with full dress and the cravat was usual for formal or evening wear. After the mid nineteenth century the stock was confined to sports-wear and, in particular, hunting.

The Necktie

The cravat continued to be fashionable during the nineteenth and twentieth centuries but during this period its shape and appearance altered. After about 1840 the term 'necktie' began to be more generally used and the different ways in which it was tied or worn were given individual names.

By the end of the 1820's men had begun to shed the dramatic intensity of their dress, with its strong contrasts of black and white [78], although white was retained for evening dress. In the 1840's coloured silk neckties were usual with ordinary clothes and contributed to the general air of flamboyance and colour then fashionable [40]. Changes also occurred in the shape of the cravat, there was less emphasis on the swathing round the neck and increased attention to the bow, which became the focal point and grew considerably larger. During the late 1840's the bow was both large and loud and could be worn with boldly checked or patterned trousers and florid waistcoats [79]. A bow tie was by this date the correct form for evening dress and it was worn with a decorative shirt-front.

The cravat tied in a bow was not, however, the only fashionable arrangement. A variety of knots were possible and it could also be simply folded end over end or across the shirt-front, with a stick-pin to secure it in place. There was a general trend towards loosening up and the cravat appeared much softer and fuller. The broad ends could, in the 1840's, entirely cover the shirt-front above the waistcoat opening and by that stage it was often referred to as a scarf rather than a cravat [40].

In the early years of the nineteenth century it had been fashionable for some young men to wear a cravat or scarf loosely knotted about the neck with the ends hanging free to give a casual, romantic effect. This style came to be popularly associated with Lord Byron and with all those with poetic aspirations (the dress of poets, distracted by their thoughts, was by tradition supposed to be careless[19]). As late as the 1930's Harold Acton described Lady Ottoline Morell's husband as looking like 'a country squire with poetic leanings' because he wore riding breeches, 'his hair was long and he had a flowing tie'.[20] This form of tie was also popular with artists in the later nineteenth century; Millais, for example, was known to wear a

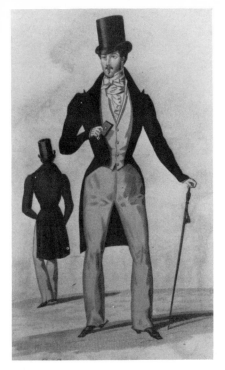

A MOST ALARMING SWELLING!

hanging necktie knotted through a ring. More than one style of cravat was called after Byron and in the 1840's a narrow, shoe-string tie was still known by his name.

The moderately broad necktie tied in a flat bow in front continued to be worn during the 1850's. It was about this time that American magazines began to reproduce new styles in men's neckwear, whereas before this date American fashions had been based on English and French fashion periodicals.

In the second half of the century the cravat had become a long, shaped band, wider at each end than at the centre (the part which covered the back of the neck). By the 1860's the necktie had changed its general character and was altered to fit the new, lower shirt-collar. The cravat was cut narrower and tied in a small flat bow or knotted and fixed with a pin. More informal shirt-collars were turned down over the necktie [41]. The knotted tie, then called the four-in-hand (and resembling the modern tie) became popular, probably because it stayed tidy. Neckties continued to be narrow while the collar was low and during the 1870's and 1880's their importance was further diminished by a fashion for buttoning the coat and waistcoat high to the neck. The so-called 'once-round' tie with a small flat bow over an upright, stiffened collar was usually worn by professional men.

The shirt-collar rose during the late 1880's and 1890's and attention was again focused on the neck area with a variety of different neckwear styles [80]. The stricter rules of etiquette were beginning to relax, owing in part to the influence of the United States, and there appeared to be more freedom of choice in the arrangements available. Neckties were worn in

78 *Modes de Paris* 1830
White cravat tied with a bow. The ruffle concealing the shirt front opening can be seen above the waistcoat.

79 *Punch* cartoon 1849
Cravat bows became very large in the late 1840's and were worn with boldly-patterned waistcoats and trousers.

80 Photograph of five young men 1901 Starched collars reached a maximum height in the 1890's. By 1900 the bow and knotted cravat were the most popular forms of necktie.

varying widths and the most popular versions were the bow tie, the four-in-hand and the wrapped or folded cravat called the ascot [42]. In the late 1890's the bow tie was the most fashionable shape, worn quite small [43]. Stripes (in two colours only) were the favourite design. Another style was the Sailor's knot, a long necktie with a reef knot. It was worn in the early years of the present century but was discontinued after the First World War.

A white bow tie remained correct for evening dress; it was small and neat and altered comparatively little. The *Tailor and Cutter* reported in September 1897 that 'the attempt which has been made for the past two or three seasons to introduce embroidered silk bows for evening wear, has not met with much success. They are hardly even being shown by the best tie houses. The small white plain cambric bow continues to be the correct thing for evening wear.'[21] The journal also reported that primary colours were generally only demanded for the low-class trade and tartan neckties did not sell well. Black bow ties could be worn with evening dress but after the

First World War it was customary to wear one only with a dinner jacket.

In the first two decades of the twentieth century the established styles remained in fashion [**44, 98**]. During the 1914–18 war, however, many rules of etiquette and outmoded traditions were swept away for good. In the 1920's the ascot cravat tended to be worn only with formal morning dress and the most usual ties for day wear were the bow and the long, knotted tie (which became the standard form of tie in following years). The bow and long ties were made of silks in various colours and patterns. Diagonal stripes were popular especially in school, regimental or club colours, as introduced during the 1890's. Spots were also worn, and the *Tailor and Cutter*, reviewing the blue and white spotted necktie in 1900, thought that 'taken on the whole, it is the necktie in which the average Englishman looks best'; blue and white, in spots or stripes, and combinations of red and green were thought never to go out of fashion.[22] The bow tie continued to be worn with the wing collar, by day and for evening dress; when black, it was made of silk or satin, while the white tie was made of cambric or cotton piqué.

In the first half of the century the necktie was still an important accessory to dress but altered very little in general appearance [**81**]. Minor variations were introduced in the size of the knot or the shape of the blade or in the materials and patterns worn. A Simpson's catalogue of 1938 thought, for example, that 'a good thing to remember about ties is that younger men like them plain, while older men go for checks and stripes'. Silk was the principal fabric (and Macclesfield silk considered one of the best) but by the 1940's artificial silk (rayon), wool, linen and poplin were frequently used. Woollen ties were more informal and as a rule worn in the country where they were thought suitable because less likely to spoil in the rain. By the 1930's the tie was being expertly cut (on the cross grain of the fabric) and lined to ensure a satisfactory fit and appearance.

A certain amount of significance was still attached to styles in men's neckwear despite the apparent increase in uniformity. In the 1930's intellectuals and eccentrics were bold enough to walk about London in open-necked shirts but it continued to be regarded as extremely 'casual' to abandon a tie and loosen the shirt-collar. John Braine's novel, *Queen of the Distant Country* (1972), describes distinctions in the dress of young men in the late 1940's and early 1950's; the narrator notices that the 'intellectuals' of a provincial seaside town in the north of England: 'were wearing clothes like mine – coloured shirts, woollen ties, tweed jackets, flannels in the case of Ted and blue corduroys in the case of Ralph. This was at that time the intellectual uniform, together with brown (always brown) brogues, occasionally in suede. Polo-neck sweaters and crew-neck sweaters were sometimes worn, but always in heavy wool for warmth [thus abandoning the tie altogether].' Maurice, the narrator's cousin, was a school teacher and not strictly 'intellectual'; he wore 'a tweed jacket and flannels and brown brogues, it is true. But his hair was short and his shirt was white with a separate collar and his tie was patterned rayon. And he had a white handkerchief in his breast pocket, folded into two symmetrical triangles.'[23]

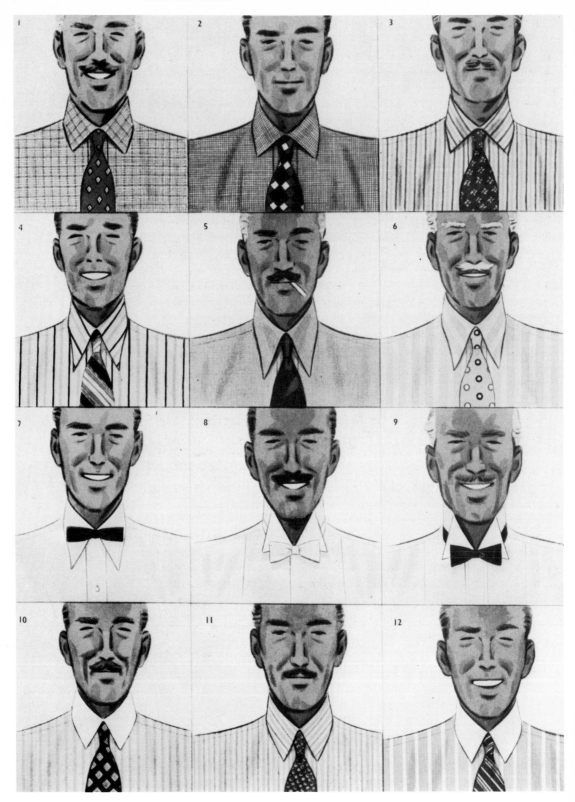

After the 1930's America devised many of its own styles and patterns for neckties instead of following those produced in Europe and, in time, England began to imitate some of the American fashions. In the 1940's colourful, patterned ties, many of them hand-painted, were popular and these were introduced into England by Cecil Gee in 1946. With his 'American Look' clothes he sold ties painted with cowboys and Indians and other devices. Ten years later another American fashion was revived, the white tie worn with a black shirt which was originally associated with American gangsters of the 1920's.[24]

The general mood in British men's fashions in the 1950's was conservative and understated, but by the late 1950's the tie was worn much narrower and a thin, knitted tie with square-ended blades was fashionable. Teddy Boys wore extremely narrow, bootlace ties. In 1961 the British export magazine, *The Ambassador*, ran a feature on men's ties and one authority complained that the tie was 'a dreary bit of rag tied round the neck, the wrong size and the wrong shape to give any real emphasis – emphasis which should be as logical and effective as the punctuation in a sentence.' But another replied that, on the contrary, 'the tie of today can be a thing of beauty, unlimited in range of colour and design. It is acknowledged by both sexes as an article of apparel which expresses the character and taste of the wearer.'[25] In the course of the next few years the tie was in fact to become a much more colourful and highly patterned dress accessory.

The kipper-shaped tie with a broad, pointed blade as much as five or six inches wide was introduced in the mid 1960's in a striking range of new designs and bold colours. Some of the most flamboyant were designed by Michael Fish for the Jermyn Street shirtmakers, Turnbull and Asser. Floral patterns, in particular, became popular and were soon added to general stock ranges. It was also fashionable to wear a shirt and tie of matching patterned fabric, often in black or navy and white 'op art' designs.

By the end of the 1960's men's ties had, in general, moved away from conventional patterns of spots and stripes in club colours. Shirts and ties together burst into colour, creating a dazzling new effect which confirmed the tie in its position as an important item of male dress. At the same time, however, a counter-trend during the decade was discouraging the use of the tie at all. Many younger men preferred to wear an open-necked shirt or a polo-necked sweater for all informal occasions [48], and an attempt was even made to remove the bow tie from evening dress. During the later 1960's a white polo-necked shirt was introduced for evening wear with a dinner jacket; it had a small following, but the fashion was largely unsuccessful and was never generally accepted. The tie was perhaps less generally worn than previously but it remained a necessary and accepted feature of formal dress. A collar and tie were required uniform for most men working in offices or professions and the absence of a tie continued to be only really permissible with informal clothes.

81 'Twelve collar schemes' by Simpson (Piccadilly) Ltd 1938
Spotted, striped or small figured silks were fashionable for men's ties between the wars. A wing collar continued to be worn with white and black bow ties for evening dress.

CHAPTER SEVEN

Mantles and Overcoats

The male wardrobe has always included at least one outer garment which can be worn over the rest of the clothes for extra protection and warmth. This has usually taken the form of a mantle or an overcoat. The mantle is one of the earliest forms of clothing, and has been in constant use by both men and women until the present century, but the overcoat has been a practical and popular alternative since at least the seventeenth century. In general terms, mantle means an unshaped, sleeveless covering which can be hung or draped about the body, such as a cloak (which is usually long) or a cape (which is shorter). A coat has come to mean a fitted garment with sleeves and a centre-front closure.

The mantle and overcoat are garments designed primarily to be worn out of doors, especially for travelling. Their function is to provide a protective outer layer to guard the body and clothes from the weather (wind, damp, cold, dirt and dust), so their shape and material are their most important features.

In order to cover the other garments, mantles and overcoats are usually slightly larger and longer than these, with an easier cut, but they also vary in design amongst themselves to suit the occasion. For some forms of travel or sitting, when the legs need as much protection as the upper part of the body, the overgarment has been wide enough and long enough to be wrapped around the figure; but for active pursuits such as riding or walking, when freedom of movement is required, it is usually shorter and less voluminous. Because of this variation in use, more than one style can be in fashion at a time.

Essentially the mantle or overcoat is a utilitarian garment. A very early piece of clothing was the rectangular Irish or Scottish plaid, which doubled as a garment by day (draped and fixed on the body) and as a groundsheet or blanket by night. Whether rectangular or semi-circular, the mantle has always been particularly useful in this respect and has a long tradition of association with the dress of travellers and soldiers [82]. Its unshaped and sleeveless form allows it to be all-enveloping and to cover almost the whole of the body, including the hands. The overcoat can perform the same function but the openings at the neck, wrists and centre front do not entirely seal it as an outer covering. The advantage of the coat over the mantle is to leave the arms (and usually the legs) completely free to move, unencumbered by folds of material which shift and slip. The coat can also, with the addition of pockets, act as a kind of travelling bag. Dr Johnson, for instance, wore a 'very wide brown cloth greatcoat' on his tour to the Hebrides in 1773, and according to Boswell it 'might have almost held the two volumes of his folio dictionary'.[1] In 1870, the Reverend Francis Kilvert 'set of to walk over the hills to Colva, taking my luncheon in my pocket, half a dozen biscuits, two apples and a small flask of wine. Took also a pocket book and opera glasses'.[2]

To provide a warm, durable layer through which water or dust cannot easily penetrate, wool has been the material most frequently used. A heavy-weight woollen cloth with a rough or closely woven texture proved to be the warmest and most hard-wearing of the natural fibres for this purpose. Wool, however, does not repel water unless specially treated, and one of the earliest methods was to oil it. Repeated experiments were made to find a thoroughly effective means of waterproofing and in the early nineteenth century Charles Macintosh patented his 'India rubber cloth', but with only partial success. Rubberized cloth has a particularly unpleasant smell and any non-porous materials are uncomfortable because they fail to provide ventilation inside the garment. When leather is used, or certain man-made materials which also keep out the rain, they usually need to be punched with small ventilation holes. It was not until the early twentieth century that proofing techniques reached a relatively high standard, for example with the coats produced by the firm of Burberry [88].

Not all outer garments need to be water-proofed, however, and those which are required mainly for extra warmth can be made of skin or fur, or cloth with a fur lining. On the other hand, raincoats or capes which are worn in both hot and cold weather are often required to be light and cool; cotton or a lighter woollen cloth such as gabardine are preferred, and these materials can be successfully proofed. When motor cars were first introduced, passengers travelled without cover and needed large coats both for warmth and for protection from the dust; for the summer they wore a lighter-weight version.

Apart from their protective function, mantles and overcoats have been put to decorative, fashionable and ceremonial use, and can, in these circumstances be made in fine, ornamental textiles. The mantle was often a decorative rather than a functional feature of male costume, and in the sixteenth and seventeenth centuries in particular a cloak or cape could be made *en suite* with the doublet and hose or breeches, decorated with embroidery, gold and silver lace or braid, with linings of a contrasting colour. In the nineteenth century cloaks and overcoats were ornamented with braid or frogging and fur, velvet or silk collars and lapels.

The shape of the overgarment could sometimes be as decorative as the materials. The draping qualities of the mantle, for example, have long been appreciated especially at times when it was fashionable to imitate the drapery of the ancient Greeks and Romans. In the late fifteenth century in Italy, during the revival of interest in classical art, young men wore mantles draped over tightly fitting doublets and hose; and again, in the neo-classical early years of the nineteenth century, huge cloaks could be flung over the shoulders to achieve a similar effect.

Methods of fastening, whether functional or decorative, have been a significant feature. Mantles can be closed in more than one way: apart from draping the cloth around the neck or shoulders, it can be fastened either at the centre front [5], beneath the chin, or at the side on one shoulder [4] – in either case, with a cord, a tie or knot, a clasp, brooch, pin or button. Both methods were used in early periods; the fastening beneath the chin ensured that both arms were covered and when closed gave maximum protection to the body, but if the opening was at one side it left an arm completely free to handle a weapon and was therefore practical in a different way. One-sided mantles seem from an early time to have been a mark of royalty; they occur repeatedly in pictorial records, from at least the sixth century A.D. [4]. It is possible that the mantle worn in this way is a late survival of the Roman toga; its basic shape – a rectangle with rounded edges – is certainly similar. The fastenings themselves could be rich and decorative, made of precious stones and metals (a tradition which has survived in church vestments with the 'morse' fastening of the cope). Buttons on overcoats in later periods could be similarly ornamental.

The Development of the Mantle

Ecclesiastical vestments were originally the ordinary dress of the laity when the Christian Church came into existence and two versions of the cloak have survived to this day in the form of the chasuble and the cope.

The chasuble is the most sacred vestment of the Western Church and its origins lie in the *casula* which appeared in late Roman history. It was a closed mantle (with only an opening for the face) which was put on over the head. As an outer garment it gave maximum protection and was usually worn by working men before becoming adopted for general use.

The cope, when first used by the clergy, was a functional outer wrap and it was put on for travelling in processions or from the vestry into the sanctuary (artists sometimes depict the Archangel Gabriel in a cope as he travels to earth from heaven). It lost its practical character when it came to be made of the finest brocaded or embroidered silks and damasks – the cope then became exclusively a processional vestment.

Another early form of the mantle was the *paenula*, a semi-circular cloak made of weatherproof material such as leather or wool (it is likely that a felted cloth was used). When the Romans settled in Northern Europe they found it necessary to wear protective garments for the colder climate and they took up the paenula in the provinces. Semi-circular or rectangular mantles were worn by the Roman army as travelling garments and were also used as blankets. As early as the fifth century A.D. the mantle was recognized as the distinctive dress of a knight; the legendary hero, the Thracian Knight, for example, is always depicted in a short tunic with a flying mantle.

The mantle was worn by both sexes and was common to all classes, although the poor could probably afford little more than a hooded cape in contrast to the long, flowing cloak of the nobility [82]. Illustrations of the

story of St Martin and the Beggar often appear in mediaeval paintings and manuscript illuminations; they show St Martin as a rich young man dividing his large, and no doubt fine, mantle in half with the beggar. The shape of the mantle can usually be seen to be a large rectangle, although semi-circular cloaks and capes were also worn and both could be fastened at the side or at the front. A mantle could sometimes be placed on the head and fixed under the chin to make a temporary hood, but by the late eleventh century separate hoods were being attached to mantles for travelling or outdoor work. In the twelfth century mantles were commonly fastened by a cord or band at the centre front; this band lay across the chest and often had to be held by two fingers to prevent it slipping backwards (an unconscious but characteristic gesture in male and female dress of the Middle Ages). It is evident that mantles were also worn in the form of closed, poncho-like garments to slip over the head.

The surcoat, a sleeveless upper garment, was worn by knights over chain armour. The patterned fabric of the surcoat served as a means of identification in battle and it is thought that it may have prevented strong sunlight reflecting off the metal which would have strained the eyes and alerted enemies. Surcoats were made of hemp or coarse linen cloth with painted or embroidered decoration and fringed or serrated edging.

By the thirteenth century fur linings and hoods were increasingly common (one of the late thirteenth century carved figures on Naumburg cathedral wears a cloak with a rolled collar at the neck). There was considerable variety in types of outer garment at this date, ranging from very short hooded capes to long cloaks with or without the addition of fur, and it seems probable that some forms were particular to rank or profession. The quality of the material as much as the shape of the garment denoted social

82 Stone carving representing St George and the Dragon
The mantle is one of the earliest forms of clothing. It was often used by soldiers and travellers as a blanket at night.

or financial status; the poorer men who worked out of doors usually wore coarse wraps and inexpensive skins while those with greater means could afford finer woollen cloths and more expensive furs.

There are references in fourteenth-century literature to the quality of the outer clothes worn by various characters. In Italy, in Boccaccio's *Decameron*, for example, 'a pair of shabby old woollen capes' are borrowed from a peasant.[3] Both Boccaccio and Chaucer deplore the way in which contemporary friars dress in 'elegantly tailored and finely woven habits'. Saint Dominic and Saint Francis, says Boccaccio, did not have 'four cloaks apiece' but 'clad themselves in coarse woollen garments of a natural colour, made to keep out the cold'.[4] Of the Friar in the Prologue to the *Canterbury Tales*, Chaucer says:

> Of double worsted was the semi-cope
> Upon his shoulders, and the swelling fold
> About him, like a bell about its mould
> When it is casting, rounded out his dress.[5]

Other poems such as *Sir Gawain and the Green Knight, Ywaine and Gawain*, and *Sir Launfal* mention fine furred mantles of silk and velvet, embroidered and bordered with gold.

By this time there was a clear differentiation between the types of furs used for linings by the various social groups: sable and ermine were the finest luxury furs and usually reserved for royalty; squirrel and beaver were the next most expensive and were worn by the upper classes; lamb, coney, cat and fox catered for a middle range; and lambskin or budge were relatively cheap. The standard of measurement for furs in the Middle Ages was the 'fur' or 'mantle', because the skins were sewn together in strips or tiers and then joined to make a rectangular piece big enough to line a mantle.

The open-fronted mantle in various forms was an important item in the mediaeval male wardrobe although in the later years of the fourteenth century it was made superfluous by the long, closed and fur-lined gown. Mantles continued to be indispensable for travelling but by the turn of the century contemporary pictures show few if any being worn with ordinary fashionable dress. During the International Gothic period (*c* 1390–1420) the 'houppelande' was worn both indoors and out and it is not until the last quarter of the fifteenth century that the mantle reasserts itself. Van Eyck's portrait of Giovanni Arnolfini (1434) shows an alternative form of outer garment, the tabard (that is, a sleeveless, open-sided gown), which is lined with fur [83].

Towards the end of the fifteenth century the male gown or tunic became short once again and reached the mid or upper thigh. A small cape, of a corresponding length, could be worn over it (fastened on one shoulder) [15] but by the last decade of the century young men tended to discard the upper garments altogether and go about in skin-tight doublets and hose[17]. This appears to have been a deliberate imitation of nudity at a time when works of classical antiquity were admired and the image was

83 The Marriage of Giovanni Arnolfini and Giovanna Cenami by Jan van Eyck 1434
The tabard, a sleeveless open-sided gown, lined with fur was an alternative to the mantle. The hat is of finely-plaited black straw.

now quite out); but he being gone to church, I could not get one.' Pepys mentions his cloaks several times: there was a 'fine Camlott cloak, with gold buttons' in 1660, one lined with velvet in 1663 and one which in 1668 he lent the Duke of York when it began to rain in St James's Park. The black velvet cloak was made in October 1663 for mourning, although Pepys was reluctant to have it until he was sure it was needed: 'This morning, hearing that the Queene grows worse again, I sent to stop the making of my velvett cloak, till I see whether she lives or dies.' But the cloak was finished and he was wearing it the following month.[6]

By the later 1660's the coat was increasingly worn in place of the doublet, over the vest or waistcoat, while the cloak, as an indoor upper garment began to pass out of fashion. Pepys noted in August 1668 that M. Colbert, the French Ambassador, was 'a comely man' but wore 'a black suit and cloak of silk; which is a strange fashion now, it hath been so long left off'.[7]

By the beginning of the eighteenth century, the cloak was being replaced by the coat even for travelling and outdoor wear although it was never discarded altogether. Garsault's *Art du Tailleur* of 1769 describes the *manteau* as 'the old circular cloak which is now out of fashion but may come in again as it gives good protection against cold when worn on foot or horseback'.[8] Another version of the cloak which was popular for a time

84 Cromwell dissolving the 'Long' Parliament (det), Dutch engraving 1653 Knee-length cloaks were worn both indoors and out; in the earlier seventeenth century a square, flat collar was added to the neck.

was the 'roquelaure': it was ample in cut and reached the knee, it fastened at the front with buttons and had a cape collar. It was distinguished from the ordinary cloak by being shaped rather than gathered at the neck and it was usually made in four pieces or panels. Eighteenth-century cloaks were generally made of cloth and were lined, with a back vent. As an unfashionable garment the cloak was mainly confined to funeral wear, the learned professions and the army, for which it was still practical and comfortable.

In the nineteenth century the overcoat was generally preferred to the cloak, but cloaks were worn for travelling, country pursuits and with evening dress. The first time Jane Eyre met Mr Rochester, for example, she noted that 'his figure was enveloped in a riding cloak, fur collared and steel clasped.'[9] Some overcoats of the time effected a compromise with the cloak by the addition of deep collars with shoulder-capes which gave warmth and protection to the shoulders and arms without restricting their movement. The Inverness cape, in particular, was a coat with wide sleeves and an added cape. By the middle of the century cloaks and caped coats were being made in textured or patterned tweeds and sometimes waterproofed cloth. Cloaks for day wear often had velvet collars and could be made with slits at each side for the arms to pass through. Evening (or 'opera') cloaks were fashionable during the first half of the century and were usually dark blue or black cloth with a silk lining, but overcoats were becoming more usual than cloaks for evening dress too by the 1840's.

In the later nineteenth and the twentieth centuries cloaks were worn less, by day or night, and in time came to be regarded as a rather theatrical or 'artistic' form of dress. Sir Hall Caine affected a black sombrero and cloak (which reminded Harold Acton of 'a vanished school of actors') and the writer Lytton Strachey wore a similar kind of dress during his 'Augustus John' period.[10] In the 1960's the cape had a brief revival in the general vogue for fancy dress when young men were buying old clothes, uniforms and government surplus items (such as policemen's capes). In 1964 Hardy Amies produced a range of capes for Hepworths but the fashion did not become widespread.

The Development of the Overcoat

Although the mantle was one of the most practical and popular kinds of outer covering, the overcoat in some form has been worn in most periods. From the seventeenth century onwards it became the principal outer garment. In early periods additional gowns or tunics could be put on for warmth, especially if they were fur-lined; but overgowns, and such garments as the houppelande [12] cannot strictly be termed as overcoats although they performed much the same function.

Cloaks with sleeves and cloaks which could be adapted into coats were worn in the sixteenth century. The mandilion or casaque, for instance, was a short cloak cut in such a way that it could be worn as a coat. It had front, back and shoulder pieces each in two parts which could be buttoned together to form a semi-circular cape or a sleeved jacket. It was worn mainly for travelling and by the military. Horsemen and hunters also wore a loose overcoat with wide sleeves. The seventeenth-century buff coat was another military garment [28]. In shape it was somewhat similar to the doublet – close-fitting with a fairly high waist – but it had deep skirts which made it much longer. It had no collar and could be laced, tied or buttoned to fasten at the front as far as the waist. The buff coat was originally made of buffalo leather but other cheaper leathers such as deerskin were used to similar effect. Buff had been used for jerkins during the previous century (the leather often slashed for greater comfort and pliability). Leather was practical for military clothing because it was tough, hard-wearing and resistant to blows, sword cuts and bullets; the buff coat came into widespread use with the Thirty Years' War on the continent and the Civil War in England, during the first half of the seventeenth century. After the Restoration in England, however, buff coats passed out of use. (There are several examples of this garment at the Museum of London.[11])

Many fashionable clothes originate from working or sporting dress. The coat began life quite low on the social scale, but it became the height of fashion in the course of the seventeenth century. From at least the 1620's a long loose coat was being worn for riding or military dress in a purely functional capacity. It was usually cut with two front panels and two back, with straight side seams left open below the waist to allow the sword to pass through; and it had wide, cuffed sleeves. It had little shaping or ornamentation. By 1664, John Evelyn was reporting that 'the loose Riding Coat' is 'now the *Mode*'.[12] In the intervening period the coat had begun to be adopted by gentlemen for ordinary wear and in the last quarter of the century it was worn fashionably over a waistcoat or vest and knee-breeches, its shape and cut having been improved and refined [58].

A similar case in the next century was the frock, a loose, easy overgarment worn by working men. In the 1730's it was taken up by gentlemen as an informal, comfortable alternative to the coat and by the end of the century it had risen to the level of fashionable and formal wear [35, 36].

Although the seventeenth century riding coat had been absorbed into ordinary men's wear, a form of overcoat, over and above the fashionable coat, continued to be worn to the end of that century and throughout the next. The greatcoat or surtout was cut on similar lines to the coat but was larger and longer, reaching to below the knees with ample skirts. It was cut with two side seams and a centre-back vent which was essential for riding. The sleeves were wide with a turned-back cuff. The front fastening could be single- or double-breasted and it has a broad, cape-like collar with a smaller, inner collar (either turned down or a narrow standing band) which could be fastened up round the neck. Occasionally these coats were belted.

In the 1780's and 1790's the greatcoat often had one or more deep overlapping collars or shoulder-capes in a fashionable imitation of the coachman's coat. When Catherine Morland, in Jane Austen's *Northanger*

85 'Mise d'un Elégant' in *Costume Parisien* 1799–1800 The greatcoat often had one or more deep overlapping collars or shoulder-capes; the topmost collar could be faced with velvet.

Abbey (1818), was driven out in a curricle by Henry Tilney, she thought that 'the innumerable capes of his greatcoat looked so becomingly important!'[13] [**85**]. It was made of stout woollen cloth and the topmost collar could be faced with velvet; the buttons were usually metal. The greatcoat continued to be made long and loose and, although practical for travelling, must have been heavy and cumbersome. Mr Allen in *Northanger Abbey* did not seem to enjoy wearing his, and his wife complained: 'I hope Mr. Allen will put on his great-coat when he goes, but I dare say he will not, for he had rather do anything in the world than walk out in a great-coat; I wonder he should dislike it, it must be so comfortable.'[14]

In the early years of the nineteenth century greatcoats with an Eastern European appearance were popular. These 'Polish', 'Hungarian' and 'Russian' coats were lined or trimmed with fur, loop or frog fastenings and braid decoration. Greatcoats were a fashionable item of dress and were worn long and in town regardless of the weather. In the 1820's and 1830's the overcoat was a little shorter and rather more shaped with a close-fitting waist and a full chest, accentuated by a deep roll collar; the sleeves were slightly swelled at the shoulder. In 1830 a cavalry officer wrote in *The Whole Art of Dress*:

> Surtout-coats, which are almost all made double-breasted, are nearly the only, or at least the chief undress wear of fashionables westward and eastward. The attention should be most directed in the make of these (which I think, only look well buttoned up close to the throat) to the sit of the skirts, which should be made proportionally full to the closeness of the fit round the waist. This kind of coat should always, to look well, be rather thickly and tastefully padded in front. A velvet collar, too, is becoming; black, blue, and olive are I think, nearly the only colours worn.[15]

After the 1830's there was a great variety of coats for different kinds of sporting and travelling activities. The 1840's and 1850's were a particularly inventive period which produced an assortment of long and short coats for both formal and informal occasions [**86**]. During the remainder of the century overcoat styles continued to be produced with a bewildering number of names, some of which it is no longer possible to identify with accuracy. There were, however, a few main types and most other overcoats were variations on these themes. The best known coats were the Paletot, Chesterfield, Inverness, Ulster, Raglan and Covert coat.

The shorter, wider and more informal coats of the mid nineteenth century were derived from the Paletot, which was originally a 'short greatcoat' but came to be a general term for any kind of loose outer garment. Its easy cut lay in the absence of a waist seam and it could be worn both as an overcoat and as an informal jacket indoors. The hero of Charlotte Brontë's *Villette* (1853), the Belgian school teacher, Paul Emanuel, habitually wore a 'soot-dark paletot' whose 'vague folds, sinister and conspirator-like ... obscured the outlines of his person'.[16] In this case it seems to have been a suitably dignified but practical garment for teaching, lying somewhere between an academic gown and a formal frock coat.

One of the best known styles of overcoat is the Chesterfield which has survived into the twentieth century [87, 89]. It was originally a variation of the frock coat worn as an overcoat, but differed from it in several points. It was not shaped at the waist, it could be single- or double-breasted, and from the 1850's the concealed or fly front-fastening was also used. The Chesterfield was probably the most generally fashionable overcoat and the most formal, intended for smart rather than casual wear. It reached to well below the knee in the later nineteenth century.

The Inverness appeared in the middle of the century and was a combined cloak and coat, chiefly designed for travelling. It was a loose, knee-length overcoat with wide sleeves and the addition of a deep shoulder-cape which was its distinctive feature; it was usually made of tweed.

'No gentleman's wardrobe is complete without an Ulster,' said the *Tailor and Cutter* in 1897; 'it is very useful for travelling etc. It should be made from a good Scotch tweed, and looks well either single- or double-breasted.'[17] The Ulster was another popular travelling garment which was in general use by the 1870's. It was introduced by J.G. M'Gee and Co. of Belfast in 1867. Heavy woollen cloth for overcoats was manufactured in Belfast and Londonderry and it is probably from this that the Ulster derived

86 'The Last of England' by Ford Madox Brown 1852 The emigrant wears a heavy, brown, double-breasted overcoat with a plaid lining and his brown wideawake hat is attached by a cord to one of the buttons.

87 W. Graham Robertson
by J. S. Sargent 1894
The Chesterfield was cut on
similar lines to the frock coat
and was the most formal and
generally fashionable
overcoat of the later
nineteenth century.

its name. It was a long coat worn with a belt (in the 1890's a half belt was worn at the back) and a detachable hood. It could sometimes have an additional shoulder-cape and a fur lining.

In the late 1850's coats began to be cut with the Raglan sleeve, that is, without a shoulder-seam; the sleeve was cut to a point at the neckband (rather than rounded to fit into an armhole). The Raglan overcoat became very popular again in the 1890's although the *Tailor and Cutter* thought it was 'a somewhat difficult garment to cut, and at best it produces but a very indifferent shoulder'. Explaining its popularity, the journal said:

> it serves the double purpose of an overcoat and a waterproof. As a general rule the Raglan is made from Covert coating or other thin material which undergoes a process of waterproofing. It is cut very loose and easy fitting and is unlined, one of the chief points in its favour being its lightness and general adaptability to wear in all kinds of weather.[18]

The increasing interest in sport in the later nineteenth century encouraged the development of suitable garments such as the Covert coat of the 1880's and 1890's. This was a short Chesterfield or Raglan with a concealed fastening and it was particularly useful in the paddock or hunting field; 'the shortness and nattiness' of these coats gave them 'those qualities of smartness and ease in walking, which commends them to all who engage in active exercise and yet find it necessary to wear an over-garment'.[19]

Nineteenth-century tailors were greatly taxed by the question of effective waterproofing. Macintosh patented his 'India rubber cloth' in 1823 and by the 1830's cloaks and capes were being made of this new material. It appeared to be effective, but unfortunately it felt rather hard and smelled very unpleasant. There were also recipes for home-made waterproofing methods and the *Workwoman's Guide* of 1838 recommended a mixture of isinglass, alum and white soap boiled in water, to be brushed on to the cloth. There were other complicated means which involved boiling and soaking the cloth in mixtures of soap, alum and oil for a number of hours. Despite the difficulties, waterproof cloth gained in popularity during the century and there was a steady demand for garments of this nature [88]. Otherwise, the usual materials for cloaks and overcoats were the heavier milled cloths such as melton, worsted, cheviot and tweeds. The cloth was usually heavy enough for the hems to be left 'raw'; it was only stitched at the side edge to prevent ravelling. During unusually hard winters overcoats tended to be made longer, with fur linings.

In the first decade of the present century the previously popular styles of overcoat continued to be worn with only slight variations. A new type of overgarment was produced for motoring (in open cars) which required a warm, weatherproof and dustproof covering. Motoring coats and dust coats were generally full-length and large, but often belted to prevent the garment billowing out when the motorcar got up speed. These voluminous coats gave the wearer a curious aspect, somewhat larger than life, and it is easy to imagine how Mr Toad, in *The Wind in the Willows* (1908) must have looked, 'arrayed in goggles, cap, gaiters and enormous overcoat' as he

88 Advertisement for Burberry raincoat 1904 Proofing techniques reached a relatively high standard by the early twentieth century.

came 'swaggering down the steps, drawing on his gauntleted gloves'.[20] Zuleika Dobson and the exquisite Duke of Dorset in Max Beerbohm's novel (1911) disliked motoring for this reason: '"I never go in motors,"' said Zuleika. "They make one look like nothing on earth, and like everybody else." "I myself," said the Duke, "use them little for that very reason."'[21]

Motoring coats were often made of leather which was effective against the wind and cold, but cloth with a fur or leather lining was also used. 'It has been found that when travelling at a high rate of speed, the ordinary cloth is not sufficient protection for the chest,' said the *Tailor and Cutter* in 1900, 'so that it is desirable to either put a leather inter-lining or lining over that part.'[22] Duster coats, especially for summer or dry weather were made of light-coloured gabardine, twill or duck.

The First World War had its effect upon the cut and appearance of men's overcoats, since fighting conditions dictated specially adapted garments. The so-called 'British Warm', for example, was a short, double-breasted coat of melton cloth cut on easy lines which replaced the standard officer's greatcoat and was more suitable for the trenches. After the war it was adapted for civilian use (usually in camel or fawn wool) and was a popular style. During the war Thomas Burberry devised a practical weatherproof coat for trench warfare made of a fine twilled cotton gabardine which was chemically processed to repel water but allowed the fabric to remain porous and ensure adequate ventilation. The trench coat was not entirely waterproof but it was water-repellent and effective under normal weather conditions. It was officially adopted for the forces but subsequently turned to civilian use and remained a fashionable raincoat manufactured by the firms of both Burberry and Aquascutum.

In the 1920's the most popular styles in overcoats were the Chesterfield and the Raglan [89]. The Chesterfield was still the more formal of the two, close-fitting with set-in sleeves and cut in a dark cloth. It could be single- or double-breasted or have a concealed fastening and was suitable for town or business wear. The Raglan was a looser, single-breasted coat often made of tweed (a herringbone pattern was fashionable in the 1920's) and for less formal wear or the country it was a comfortable alternative to the Chesterfield. Raincoats of proofed tweed or gabardine were also worn and some were reversible.

By the 1930's a new conception of the motoring coat had emerged. What was now required was a shorter, lighter, less cumbersome coat which was easy to put on but not hampering at the wheel. The looser fit of the raglan sleeve was the most suitable; turned-back cuffs which could catch on door handles were avoided. Leather coats, often fleece-lined, continued to be worn for motoring but once saloon cars became more general there was less need for extra warmth and protection.

With the fashion for broader shoulders and fuller chests in the 1930's, men's overcoats correspondingly altered in shape. Loose-fitting, square-shouldered coats were worn with tie or buckled belts and larger checked or patterned tweeds were used. Ulsters were popular for a time and there was a fashion for 'Teddy Bear' coats of fawn camel fleece. On the continent and in the United States, Austrian loden cloth was found to be particularly suitable for overcoats; it had a warm texture, and was high in natural oil content. The fitted Chesterfield overcoat in plain dark blue, grey or black cloth remained fashionable for formal wear, but the double-breasted fastening was the most usual in this decade. Coats continued to be cut to well below the knee.

During the Second World War a new type of overcoat came into prominence and was to become a very popular informal coat in subsequent decades. The duffle coat was originally a practical, working garment worn by the Navy but it was popularized during the war by Field-Marshal Montgomery. Numbers of these coats were sold as government surplus at the end of the war and the style was brought out commercially in 1951; being inexpensive and practical they were quickly adopted by students and young people. The hooded duffle coat was made of thick, hard-wearing woollen cloth and fastened with leather or cord loops and wooden toggles.

With the slimmer-fitting, more natural suit of the early 1950's, men's

overcoats were a little shorter and less bulky. There was, however, no noticeable change in the general styles of the Chesterfield and the Raglan although there was a return to the single-breasted and fly front-fastenings. By the end of the 1950's the overcoat was knee-length or a little shorter and the raglan style, especially for raincoats, was fashionable. With the invention of man-made fibres and new materials, raincoats were continually improved and beside the usual proofed wool and cotton gabardines and poplins there was nylon and terylene. 'Gannex' waterproof cloth which claimed to be virtually weatherproof was generally available by 1956 and was to become popularly associated with the Labour Prime Minister, Harold Wilson.

Raincoats and overcoats altered comparatively little in the 1960's but were narrower and shorter. The most usual styles were raglan or set-in sleeves, double- or single-breasted fastenings or the fly-front. There was an increasing number of alternative informal outer garments, however, and jackets were popular. As various methods of transport had improved and car heaters became usual overcoats were considerably reduced in weight and length. Short car coats, sheepskin jackets, anoraks or windcheaters (originally worn for golf) and safari and battledress jackets were preferred by younger men to the formal overcoat and were worn by most people for informal or active pursuits. Simulated fur made in nylon fabric was an innovation in the mid 1960's when the price of natural fur was becoming prohibitive for coats and motor coats, and a large range was designed by Hardy Amies for the ready-to-wear market. At the end of the 1960's a longer length of coat was fashionable and there was a revival of the traditional trenchcoat style.

CHAPTER EIGHT

Dress and Undress

At every period in the history of dress distinctions have been made amongst the clothes of men and women to indicate their rank, occupation or aspirations. It has also been the custom to adopt different forms of clothing for various occasions or times of the day, ranging from the very formal and ceremonial to the casual and extremely informal. The terms used in the past to refer to these forms were 'Dress' (or 'Full Dress') and 'Undress' (or 'common dress').

It has been usual for men to adopt a reasonably practical or comfortable form of dress for working, sports and leisure pursuits or ordinary day wear, which can be exchanged for neater, more elaborate clothes for formal day or evening occasions, special functions or attendance at Court. Some garments have been specifically designed for these purposes and are unmistakable, but at times the difference between 'dress' and 'undress' was only slight and 'undress' wear could mean little more than not being dressed for Court. At other times there have been degrees of formality and informality within the categories of dress and undress. During the first half of the present century, for example, evening dress took two forms: the white tie and tail coat, or black tie and dinner jacket, which were worn according to the nature of the function; a loose smoking jacket or dressing gown could be put on as an alternative in the evening when relaxing at home.

The distinctions between formal and informal dress have, as a rule, been carefully observed. Sometimes they have been regulated by a rigid form of etiquette, the finer details of which are lost or incomprehensible to succeeding generations. Arnold Bennett noted in his journal of 1904 an incident which illustrated how important were the rules of both convention and good manners to his contemporaries:

> Davray gave me a new instance of politeness. At some English house a foreigner (nationality obscure, I forget, something small) wearing what looked like an overcoat. The hostess urged him to take it off; said it was the custom etc. He took it off, and appeared in his shirt-sleeves. Consternation of the hostess, especially as other guests were expected. Presently Laurence Housman came in and was advised privately of the situation. Housman took off his coat, and sat down also in his shirt-sleeves; then complained of the cold, and demanded from his hostess permission to resume his coat; the foreigner followed his example. "C'etait très fin", commented Davray.[1]

To wear the correct or suitable dress for the occasion has always been a matter of concern, although the rules rarely remain static. What might be thought an informal, undress garment at one date can be transformed in the course of a few decades into a formal or even ceremonial piece of clothing; in fact most formal 'dress' wear was in origin quite the reverse. The twentieth-century dress or tail coat for evening wear was, at the end of the eighteenth century, an Englishman's riding coat with the tails cut in horizontally across the waist to allow the coat to fall better on horseback [37]. The lounge suit when first adopted in the 1860's was strictly informal, literally for lounging, but a hundred years later had assumed the formality and respectability of the Victorian frock coat. From the time when the coat came into general use in the seventeenth century until the present day there has been a constantly changing order of formality with coat variations moving up or down the scale, as social patterns have shifted.

The Victorians developed the idea of wearing different clothes for different occasions to an almost unprecedented degree and a man might be obliged to change his clothes several times a day. In earlier periods it is not always easy to distinguish formal or informal garments in the fashionable dress of the time, especially when the cut and construction are almost identical, but other features such as material, colour or decoration may differentiate them.

Formal dress is almost always made of fine quality fabrics, such as silks of all kinds – satin, velvet, damask, brocaded or figured silks, cloth of gold or silver – or fine woollen cloths, cashmere, kerseymere, vicuna, superfine or worsteds. For sports clothes, working dress or informal garments, which need to withstand hard wear and rough weather rather than look aesthetically striking, more serviceable textiles tend to be used: woollen cloth (often of a heavy, rough variety, such as tweed), stout cottons, twills, corduroys and leather are some of the most usual. It should be added, however, that this is not the invariable rule. Men's nightgowns of the seventeenth and eighteenth century, although strictly for informal wear, were frequently made of expensive silks, while cloth was being used for both formal and informal dress.

Textiles have in many cases been distinguished by additional decoration. Functional or informal clothes are not generally decorated or encumbered with accessories (such as stiff, heavy embroidery) which might make them impractical or uncomfortable. Such decoration as these garments have is usually of a practical nature – slashing or smocking, for example, to allow expansion for ease of movement, or embroidery and topstitching to strengthen seams or exposed areas. Formal clothes, on the other hand, whose purpose is decorative rather than utilitarian, may be ornamented with woven or embroidered designs, applied lace or braid of gold and silver, stones, spangles, or buttons of stones and metals, and can be lined or trimmed with fur [60].

The emphasis on colour and decoration diminished considerably in the nineteenth and twentieth centuries and ceased to be a prerequisite of formal dress. It was said in 1865 that 'a gentleman of the present nineteenth century, attired for the gayest evening party, could, apart from his jewellery, be equally presentable at the most sorrowful funeral.'[2] By the second half of the nineteenth century, evening dress was almost universally black with white accessories and formal day clothes were sombre (happy occasions such as weddings and christenings might merit a light grey). Formal clothes were not entirely without decoration but the details were subtle: lapels were faced with silk and collars with velvet, the outside seams of the trouser legs had one or two bands of braid, and a certain amount of jewellery – tie pins, cuff links and dress studs – could be worn. It was an image of extreme refinement and the dramatic but masterly understatement of men's evening dress since the mid nineteenth century has, in its way, been as effective as any dress clothes before that date.

Colour played an early part in the distinction of different forms of dress. The most expensive of ancient dyes was purple, which was produced only in small quantities; its use was limited to those who could afford it and those who merited it. True purple became an imperial colour and purple garments were restricted to certain ranks or officials (or confined to the stripes in the Roman citizen's toga and tunic). Scarlet cloth, too, was for centuries the most expensive and most highly prized, and both these colours have continued to be associated with ceremonial dress. White is another colour used for ceremonial wear (it is the liturgical colour for festivals) and was a feature of Court dress (very often worn with gold). In the nineteenth and early twentieth centuries, for example, it was customary for men to have white breeches, silk stockings and waistcoats for attendance at Court. In the nineteenth century white silk embroidered waistcoats were worn for weddings and white piqué waistcoats have, of course, been usual with formal evening dress since then; by the early twentieth century a white bow tie was always worn with a dress coat. White was also one of the mourning colours of the Romans and is still used by the Indians for this purpose.

Black and white are probably the two colours most usually associated with formal dress although this is a tradition which has come about largely since the second half of the nineteenth century with the establishment of black (or a very dark blue which appears to be black in artificial light) as the correct colour for evening. Black was, however, a popular colour at other periods, apart from being the accepted wear for funerals or mourning; it was fashionable in particular at the fifteenth-century Burgundian court and the Spanish court of the sixteenth century. It has also been the traditional garb for professional men – churchmen, lawyers, doctors – since at least the sixteenth century. A dark lounge suit is still considered to be correct for business or formal wear.

In most periods the cut of formal and informal garments tends to follow the general lines of fashionable dress but there are some features which distinguish the lines of the two. It is in the nature of informal dress to be comfortable and practical, so the cut tends to be easier, to prevent undue restriction around the neck, in the sleeves and armholes, and about the waist and legs. Garments for relaxation or physical exercise are most often made of a fairly light and soft material which is cool and absorbent, although more stout and serviceable fabrics are sometimes necessary. In formal dress, materials can sometimes be stiff and uncomfortable, especially when decorated with embroidery or gold and silver lace as in the eighteenth century. In Samuel Richardson's novel, *Pamela* (1740), Mr B. had a waistcoat for one of the Court Birthdays which 'stood on end with silver lace'.[3] In the later nineteenth century, heavily starched collars and shirt fronts underlined the feeling of stiffness and discomfort in formal dress. Ceremonial and official clothes have often also weighed a great deal, partly because they were made of richly brocaded silks, velvets or fine cloths lined with fur and partly because they were bulky and long. Since the fourteenth-century fashion for short tunics, long garments have been retained for official and dignified dress, and in the early fifteenth century width and bulk were considered to add a mark of authority. These features naturally encourage a more formal bearing but sweeping trains, trailing sleeves and long, weighty gowns carry the additional suggestion that the wearer need not work with his hands and so tend to be a general sign of rank or office.

A man's deportment and gestures are very much conditioned by the nature of his clothes and if formal dress induces a certain amount of restraint the reverse is true of informal clothing. Easy fitting garments allow freedom of movement and encourage a relaxed posture [48]. In a paper of instruction 'for the guidance of gentlemen appointed to attend on the Prince of Wales', Prince Albert emphasized the view that behaviour and dress were interdependent:

> A gentleman does not indulge in careless, self-indulgent, lounging ways, such as lolling in arm chairs, or on sofas, slouching in his gait, or placing himself in unbecoming attitudes, with his hands in his pockets, or in any position in which he appears to consult more the idle ease of the moment than the maintenance of the decorum which is characteristic of a polished gentleman. In dress, with scrupulous attention to neatness and good taste, he will never give in to the unfortunately loose and slang style which predominates at the present day. He will borrow nothing from the fashions of the groom or gamekeeper, and whilst avoiding the frivolity and foolish vanity of dandyism, will take care that his clothes are of the best quality, well-made, and suitable to his rank and position.[4]

(Prince Albert, however, was not generally admired by English gentlemen. He was always considered a foreigner and had been known to smoke in the street which was thought to be a vulgar habit.)

There is a distinction between purely ceremonial and ordinary formal dress. Ceremonial clothing is rarely very fashionable; it is usually divorced from the levity of high fashion to preserve an aura of dignity and authority. The garments are often based on the styles of earlier fashions which have become fossilized, or they follow fashion at an austere distance.

Dress Wear

It is evident from pictorial and documentary evidence that dress in the early and mediaeval periods was of a hierarchical nature. Men dressed according to rank, to their official, social or financial position, and certain forms of dress were required for occasions and festivities. In the fourteenth century, for example, at the English Court of Edward III, members of the royal household were issued with cloth for new garments once a year and for special events such as the coronation and royal births. Persons of different ranks were given cloth in appropriate amounts and colours.

The colour, decoration and quality of materials used, the shape of the clothes and the way in which they were worn, were all significant. In particular, the mantle was to be worn on one shoulder by ruling monarchs and high-ranking officials (see, for example, the mosaics at Ravenna of the Emperor Justinian and his court in the sixth century A.D., and later the Bayeux Tapestry of c 1080). Royal garments often appear to be wrapped or draped in a complicated manner possibly influenced by the Roman toga. Early illustrations also include details of decoration on garments – braid or embroidery on hems or neck and sleeve edges – indicating rank or special standing [4]. In the late thirteenth century, buttons came into use and were used as a means of ornament; but they were soon restricted to the dress of officials or men of status.

Sumptuary laws, regulating the exact forms of dress which might be worn, were frequently enacted in an attempt to preserve the social order. The laws were intended to restrict social mobility and prevent the lower orders from dressing too finely; at the same time, some men were obliged to appear more splendid than they might have chosen (this was often the case with doctors at the mediaeval Italian universities, for example).

By the fifteenth century it appears that long rather than short gowns were usual for official forms of dress and that at Court the finest materials were the rule. The best quality woollen cloth cost as much, if not more, than silk and both could be lined with luxury furs. Full-length overgowns, lined or trimmed with fur, continued in use for official dress during the next two centuries and were worn over the fashionable doublet and hose or breeches [19].

Compared with the sombre colours and plainer cloths of the nineteenth and twentieth centuries, formal clothes in the seventeenth and eighteenth centuries appear strikingly decorative, fragile and impractical. Pepys, for example, had in 1660 a 'white suit with silver lace coat', a 'fine Camlott cloak, with gold buttons – and a silk suit' (which he adds, 'cost me much money, and I pray God to make me able to pay for it') and a 'velvet coat and cap the first that ever I made'. The following year, he describes the scene before Charles II's coronation when the King went from the Tower to White Hall:

> it is impossible to relate the glory of this day – expressed in the clothes of them
> that rid – and their horses and horse-cloths. Among others, my Lord
> Sandwich. Imbroidery and diamonds were ordinary among them ... the
> King, in a most rich imbroidered suit and cloak, looked most nobly. Wadlow
> the vintner, at the Devil in Fleetstreet, did lead a fine company of soldiers, all
> young comely men, in white doublets ... So glorious was the show with gold

and silver, that we were not able to look at it – our eyes at last being so much
overcome with it . . . I spoke with my Lord. He talked with me about his suit,
which was made in France, and cost him 200l. and very rich it is with
imbroidery.

Pepys wore his velvet coat, made the previous year, for this occasion.[5]

If anything, formal and Court dress in the eighteenth century was even
more splendid. At Court, dress was required to be more than usually fine
and although many of the eighteenth-century silks were richly patterned
they were not considered grand enough unless further ornamented. Cloth
was always embroidered for Court clothes and most suits were decorated
with gold and silver lace. Fancy buttons were added for dress wear and
were enamelled or set with stones. Mary Delany's descriptions give some
idea of the splendour of these garments. At the Princess Royal's wedding in
1734, for example, 'the Prince of Orange was in gold stuff embroidered
with silver; it looked rich but not showy. The king was in a gold stuff
which made more show, with diamond buttons to his coat; his star and
George shone most gloriously . . . The Prince of Wales was fine, as you may
suppose . . . Lord Crawford was in white damask laced with gold.' In 1740
Lord Baltimore was seen in 'light brown and silver, his coat lined *quite
throughout* with ermine'.[6] Sometimes the bounds of good taste were passed
and she did not hesitate to condemn this. As she wrote in 1773:

> The chief topick of conversation yesterday was Lord Villier's appearance in the
> morning at Court, in a pale purple velvet coat, turned up with lemon-colour,
> and embroidered all over with SS's of pearl as big as pease and in all the spaces
> little medallions in beaten gold, *real solid*, in various figures of *Cupids* . . . at best
> it was only a fool's coat, and so I leave it to tell you something better worth
> your attention.

Richardson's Pamela, too, disapproved of Lady Daver's nephew when he
was 'laced all over': 'I gave him a most contemptuous look. "Tinsell'd
boy!" said I.'[7]

Towards the end of the eighteenth century full dress of this kind was
restricted almost entirely to Court wear and dress coats gradually became
less elaborate. Much of the previous splendour of full dress was to survive
only in the decoration of the waistcoat in the following century. At this
time the correct dress for formal wear was the close-fitting coat which
sloped back at the sides and had no collar but a small standing neckband
[60]. It was the coat which had been worn fashionably in the earlier part of
the century but was replaced for ordinary day wear by the frock (a coat of
easier cut with a turned-down collar).

Court dress in the next century consisted of a dress coat (often velvet), a
white waistcoat and knee-breeches worn with silk stockings and pumps.
Knee-breeches passed out of general fashion after the first decade but were
retained for court wear as a very formal garment [90]. Baron Stockmar was
the only man at Queen Victoria's court in the mid nineteenth century to be
exempt from rigid etiquette – because of his rheumatism he was 'permitted
to wear long wool trousers instead of the prescribed stockings and knee-

breeches'. Later, Edward VII was to find that Americans could never understand the difference between breeches and trousers, frock coats and morning coats. 'Once when Lord Rosebery arrived at Windsor Castle wearing plain trousers instead of the silk stockings and breeches he had been commanded to appear in, the King bowed to him and said acidly: "I presume you have come in the suite of the American Ambassador." '[8] Levée dress was worn in England until the end of the Second World War.

During the nineteenth century, dress for formal and informal wear continued to be marked by the kind of coat worn. The three main variations – the dress or tail coat, the morning coat and the frock coat – were distinguished by differences in cut, but hardly at all in material and decoration since plain cloth had become almost universal (silk and velvet for coats was restricted to court and ceremonial wear). In the early decades coloured coats were worn for full dress or evening wear but dark shades were preferred and the convention for wearing black was gradually established.

Until the 1830's the dress coat – that is, the tail coat cut in across the waist, with a single- or double-breasted fastening, collar and revers [38] – was worn for daytime as well as evening wear but after this date it was more usual at night. By the 1860's it was only ever worn as evening dress and it has remained the most formal version of the coat since then. The dress coat had long lapels to reveal the waistcoat and dress shirt front beneath; it was usually made in a fine milled cloth finished with silk or vel-

90 Queen Victoria and Prince Albert with their children by Winterhalter 1846 Knee breeches were retained for court wear after they passed out of fashion. They were worn with silk stockings and low-cut shoes.

91 Early form of the dinner jacket, *Tailor and Cutter* 1889–90
An evening version of the lounge jacket was introduced for less formal wear. It was usually combined with a black bow tie.

92 Fred Astaire and Ginger Rogers in *Top Hat* 1935
Formal evening dress was a familiar sight on the stage and screen of the 1920's and 1930's.

vet collar and facings. Black, white or coloured waistcoats could be worn with the dress coat but in the second half of the century white or black were the most usual and white was required for full evening dress with a white necktie (it was not until after the First World War that black waistcoats became unfamiliar with dress coats). Trousers did not replace breeches for evening wear until the 1830's but by the 1840's they were generally black. In the later decades, dress trousers were cut closer than those for day wear and the outside leg seam was finished by one or two rows of black braid.

In the 1880's an alternative form of evening dress was introduced [**91**], essentially an evening version of the lounge suit for less formal wear. The dress lounge, as it was called at first, later became known as the dinner jacket. According to the *Tailor and Cutter* in 1900:

> The Americans call this garment "the Tuxedo" and they make it up in quite a variety of styles, even going so far as to make them from white flannel and serges. In England they are invariably made from the same black material as the Dress Coat. Occasionally velvet is used for this purpose, and there is no disputing the fact that the Dress Lounge made from velvet has a very smart and stylish appearance.[9]

It was cut on similar lines to the lounge jacket, with a roll collar and continuous lapel faced with silk or satin, and was worn with a white or black waistcoat and evening trousers. In time it became customary to wear

it with a black bow tie. On occasion the waistcoat could be discarded and a sash or cummerbund worn round the waist instead (but this did not become common until later in the twentieth century).

The dinner jacket was an innovation for informal evening occasions such as dinner and small evening parties, the theatre and concerts, but it was not worn for public dinners, assemblies or dancing. This convention was observed until the second half of the twentieth century. The white tie and tails of formal evening dress were a familiar sight on the stage and screen of the 1920's and 1930's; the singer and entertainer Jack Buchanan was thought to be one of the most elegant men of his time in his evening clothes, and Fred Astaire more or less immortalized them in his film *Top Hat* [**92**].

During the Second World War social life at night was restricted by the black-out, the frequent air raids and the fuel shortages. Most men were in uniform, and women found it more practical to wear short evening dresses, so the habit of changing into elaborate evening clothes was disrupted and it was never fully revived when the war was over. The dress suit gradually passed out of normal use altogether, while the dinner jacket took its place for most formal evening wear and a dark lounge suit, in its turn, became acceptable for restaurants and the theatre. Before the war it was the custom to change for dinner every night, but by the 1950's and 1960's few men changed into evening dress unless dining out or attending functions.

93 The London Skating Club at Regent's Park 1891 The morning coat, 'dressy without being formal', was considered suitable wear for skating in the 1890's. The group includes the Prince of Wales (later Edward VII).

149

Morning coats and frock coats also moved up the scale from the informal or ordinary daytime wear to become formal or ceremonial garments. The morning coat at the beginning of the nineteenth century was literally a coat for morning wear, or rather for riding, since that was a gentleman's chief morning occupation. Although it was a coat with tails it differed from the dress coat by its curved front edges which sloped back gently at the sides. The frock coat, unlike the dress and morning coats, had straight front edges which overlapped when fastened like an ordinary overcoat [63]. It began to be worn for informal day wear in the 1820's and by the middle of the century had become the most popular day coat. In the second half of the century it was regarded as formal and correct day wear whilst for informal occasions the lounge jacket could be worn. For a short period in the 1870's and 1880's the morning coat [93] was preferred, but during the last decade of the century the frock coat returned to favour and it was worn until the end of the Edwardian period. By the beginning of the present century both the frock and morning coats were counted as very formal wear while the lounge suit was becoming increasingly acceptable as a day suit. The frock coat continued to be worn by elderly and conservative men such as the Prime Minister or bank managers but after the First World War fell rapidly out of general use. The morning coat took its place, to some extent, and was worn for formal day occasions (especially at the races and for weddings, functions for which it was still correct in the 1960's) [64]. In the 1920's it was usual for men to wear a black morning coat, striped trousers, patent leather shoes, spats, a winged collar and a black tie for business and in the City, although a permissible variation was a black jacket and waistcoat. Ten years later fewer men kept to this rule and after the Second World War dark lounge suits were almost universally worn.

Undress Wear

It has already been noted that one recognizable way of dressing informally in the mediaeval period in Italy was to wear the shirt or chemise without further covering. In the warmer climate of southern Europe men worked out of doors and in the fields in their shirt sleeves and it was possible to relax at home in this form of undress.

The practice was less common in the colder northern regions and the shirt was rarely worn without an upper garment. Men were, however, accustomed to wearing déshabillé or undress and could replace the formal doublet, tunic or coat with a comfortable, informal gown. The loose, easy covering could be put on over the shirt in the early part of the day, before a man was formally dressed, and worn in the evening indoors when dress clothes were not required. This often provided necessary relief from stiff or heavy formal wear and was a practical measure preserving his most expensive garments. Sitting about in 'best' clothes is not only less comfortable but stretches, creases and wears the fabric. Suits of fine embroidered cloth or silk, were not intended for everyday use, and being costly and difficult to clean were worn only for short periods.

94 Sir David Wilkie by Andrew Geddes 1816 The nightgown or dressing-gown was a comfortable informal garment worn indoors. It was often made of silk or wool damask.

95 'A Rake's Progress –The Levée' (det) by William Hogarth *c* 1733
The banyan was an informal coat or house-gown more shaped and fitted than the dressing-gown. It could be worn with a soft, turban-like cap.

One of the most popular informal male garments was the nightgown or dressing-gown (also known as a morning gown, India gown or banyan) [**94**]. It figures in accounts and inventories in Britain from the beginning of the sixteenth century[10] and remained in fashion until about the middle of the nineteenth century, although the dressing-gown continued to be worn informally into the present century. The nightgown was a long, loose garment or house gown, originally kimono-shaped, which could be worn over the shirt and doublet or waistcoat in place of more formal covering. It was primarily worn for ease and comfort in the home but as undress wear it was also a permissible form of dress in which to receive visitors (a university don might see students in his study, dressed in a nightgown, for example). It is evident, however, that it was not considered strictly correct to appear out of doors or in public places so informally clothed. At Bath in the early eighteenth century it seems to have been possible for men to appear at the Pump Room in nightgowns but the habit was discouraged and the Master of Ceremonies, Richard Nash's rules for polite behaviour stated in 1742 'that Gentlemen of Fashion never appearing in a morning before the Ladies in Gowns and Caps shew Breeding and Respect'[11] ('gowns' and 'caps' here refer to a gentleman's nightgown and nightcap). In 1781 Parson Woodforde was embarrassed to be 'caught on the hop, busy in my garden, and dressed in my cotton morning gown, old wigg and Hat' by an unexpected visitor.[12]

In the seventeenth and eighteenth centuries men frequently sat for their portraits in nightgowns; Samuel Pepys hired a golden brown silk Indian gown when he sat to John Hales in 1666.[13] The drape of the garment appealed to artists, especially since the gown was usually loosely wrapped about the figure and only occasionally tied with a sash round the waist. As an informal, untailored style of dress it was also thought to be timeless and less 'dating', an important consideration in the second half of the seventeenth century when it became unfashionable to be painted in contemporary clothes.

An alternative form of house-gown, sometimes called a banyan, was an easy coat, either full or three-quarter length, which was more shaped and fitted than the nightgown [**95**]. It followed the general cut of the contemporary coat and was probably a degree more formal than the nightgown.[14]

These informal gowns were made in a variety of different materials. Silk was one of the most popular and a number of fine damask gowns still survive; wool and cotton were also worn. Some of the silks and cottons were imported from India and the generally oriental appearance of the nightgown accorded with the taste for other exotic imports such as porcelain, lacquer, chintz and tea. By the end of the eighteenth century cotton had become a fashionable dress material for both men and women and most of Parson Woodforde's morning gowns seem to have been of this material. On two occasions in 1781 he bought six yards of cotton (at two shillings and six pence and two and fourpence a yard) from a travelling salesman for the purpose.[15]

A soft cap was usually worn with the gown and was known as a night cap or morning cap. In the seventeenth century, informal caps were dome-shaped and often made of linen embroidered in coloured silks and metal thread [113]; in the eighteenth century a soft, turban-like cap was more fashionable [95]. The tradition of wearing a comfortable gown and cap was carried on in the nineteenth century but in a slightly different form. Dressing-gowns and a round night cap were worn until the 1850's but after this date the smoking jacket and smoking cap became popular (when cigarette smoking was commonly taken up during the Crimean War) [116]. The smoking jacket was a short, easy-fitting coat in the style of the lounge jacket. It was a distinctive garment since it was often quilted and decorated with silk cord or braid frogging. A description of 1898 states that as a rule it is 'trimmed with coloured silk facings and cuffs, the fronts, pockets, edges and sleeves being ornamented with various coloured cords. In many instances the rolls and cuffs are quilted, while in others flowers, birds, and so on are worked upon the silk by hand.'[16]

The smoking cap hardly survived the close of the century, but the smoking jacket continued to be worn, often in place of the dinner jacket as an informal coat for an evening at home (with day or evening trousers). Soft materials were used, such as velvet or wool in dark reds, greens, blues, brown or black, with quilted silk facings and cord trimmings. In 1956 Austin Reed's catalogue announced an updated version of the smoking jacket, renamed a 'Television Jacket', in 'wine wool velour with quilted collar and cuffs' [96]. This did not become a widespread fashion and few men felt the need to wear a special garment for watching television (or indeed for smoking by this date).

By the middle of the eighteenth century, the coat for ordinary day or outdoor use was made in two versions: the frock for informal occasions and the fashionable coat for dress wear. The frock was originally a working garment, a kind of smock or overall in the form of a loose coat with a collar. After the 1730's it became general as an informal or country coat [35] and although similar in shape to the coat it was plainer and easier fitting. Towards the end of the century, when the taste for extravagant decoration had subsided, a simpler, more natural and romantic look became fashionable and the frock was even more popular. By the 1780's the coat appeared only at the most formal occasions and at court. Men began to wear country clothes – riding coats and breeches – as ordinary day dress and town wear, and by the beginning of the nineteenth century this form of clothing was established as the basis of the fashionable male wardrobe [37, 38].

Another informal eighteenth-century coat was the shooting jacket, which was worn for sporting and country pursuits. John Willoughby was wearing one when Jane Austen's Marianne Dashwood first met him, and her immediate impressions were that 'his name was good, his residence was their favourite village and she soon found out that of all manly dresses a shooting jacket was the most becoming'.[17] It usually took the form of a short frock.

96 Television Jacket by Austin Reed 1956
An updated version of the dressing-gown or smoking jacket in wine velours with quilted collar and cuffs.

The lounge jacket was one of many informal coats and jackets which became popular in the middle of the century [63]. They were cut in easy-fitting styles and were often made from coarse tweeds or fancy coatings. The lounge suit was introduced in the 1860's as comfortable, informal wear for the country, and for watching or participating in sports and casual pursuits. It was shorter and looser than the frock coat or morning coat, and steadily increased in favour.

The reefer or yachting jacket – a short double-breasted coat with a low collar and small lapels – was fashionable in the last quarter of the nineteenth century. Even more in demand at this period was the Norfolk jacket with distinctive box pleat in the centre back and two pleats at the front, fastened by a belt which buttoned at the waist [97]. In the 1890's a yoke was added at the shoulders and the pleats started below it. Sometimes the sleeves buttoned at the wrist like a shirt and it always fastened high to the neck; there were patch pockets at each hip and a vertical breast-pocket concealed in the left-hand pleat. The pleats ensured a loose, comfortable fit across the chest without any loss in smartness, and the close buttoning made it warm so that the jacket was very suitable for country and sports wear. It was usually worn with knickerbockers and woollen stockings which were also practical for these purposes.

Knickerbockers were most popular for cycling, when trousers might have caught on pedals and spokes and were liable to get wet or dirty at the hem in bad weather; on the whole they were preferred to trousers for country wear of all kinds and continued to be worn during the first half of the twentieth century. (In 1944 George Bernard Shaw could still be seen in the country 'dressed in a pepper-and-salt knickerbocker suit'.[18]) In the 1920's knickerbockers took on a slightly different aspect and were cut longer and looser, to hang over the tops of the hose. They were called 'plus fours' (thought to have come from a golfing term) and were worn chiefly for golf. They were one of the most characteristic sports garments of the inter-war period.

The Norfolk jacket was worn for almost every kind of sporting or country occasion and remained popular during the first two decades of the present century, but it was an informal garment which was always retained for its original purpose and not taken up into fashionable or ordinary dress; unlike the lounge jacket it never left the country. The blazer, which came into use for seaside, boating and cricketing wear in the 1890's was another jacket designed to be worn with flannel trousers for casual town or country dress. It was a short flannel jacket with patch pockets, often brightly coloured or striped (in club colours). Later versions in dark blue flannel or serge could have a club badge on the outside breast-pocket and they tended to be double-breasted, fastening with brass buttons (army officers wore their own regimental buttons). After the First World War it was possible to wear the blazer as an alternative to the tweed sports jacket, both of which were less formal than the lounge suit. The blazer and flannels came to be thought of as typically British informal wear for men.

As the lounge suit established itself for ordinary day wear and then as a

formal suit, its original place was taken by the sports jacket and flannel trousers [98]. The sports jacket began to be worn in the early years of the present century, and by the 1920's had clearly ousted the Norfolk jacket. It was similar in shape to the lounge jacket but its cut was much easier and it was usually single-breasted. It could be worn with matching trousers or knickerbockers, but the most general version was a sports jacket of tweed (checked or plain) with flannel trousers. By the 1930's it might be worn with an open-necked shirt or pull-over for casual wear but was considered more respectable with a collar and tie. After the Second World War the sports jacket and odd trousers were increasingly worn in place of the more formal lounge suit.

Other styles of informal coats and jackets were popular during the 1950's and 1960's; most of these were borrowed from or directly inspired by service uniforms, or sports or working dress. Wind-proof anoraks and Canadian lumber jackets were adopted for casual wear in the 1950's, for instance, and the short leather or cloth jacket based on army battledress lines was one of the most fashionable styles during the later 1960's. When jeans came into widespread use these short jackets were made to match, in blue denim, and were worn over an open-necked shirt or T-shirt.

97 Norfolk Jacket 1905
This distinctive jacket had a box pleat in the centre back, and two at the front (a vertical breast-pocket was concealed in the left-hand pleat). The belt buttoned at the waist. It was usually worn with knickerbockers and woollen stockings.

98 *Gazette du Bon Ton* 1922
The lounge suit was replaced by the tweed sports jacket and flannel trousers for informal occasions in the early twentieth century. Short tapered trousers with sharp creases were fashionable.

Knitwear became a common feature of sports and leisure clothes for men during the twentieth century. Knitted woollen garments had been in use in the late nineteenth century for sports such as football and cycling but were not worn as a general fashion until after the First World War. In 1900, for example, the *Tailor and Cutter* thought the cycling sweater was 'neither smart nor sightly in appearance, and no man can wear it as it now stands without looking like a "bounder" or a "scorcher" or both'.[19] 'Home-Knit Jerseys ... suitable for Football and Boating' were advertised by the Army and Navy Stores in 1907 but they were 'to order only'; they were available in stripes or plain with full- or half-length sleeves. Jerseys for sports had at first been long-sleeved with a roll collar but were later made with a V-neck and were known as 'pull-overs' in the 1920's. At this time Shetland pull-overs in Fair Isle patterns became very popular, especially for golf, and the fashion was encouraged by the Prince of Wales who had at least two portraits of himself painted in one. 'I suppose the most showy of all my garments was the multicoloured Fair Isle sweater, with its jigsaw of patterns,' he later wrote; and he went on to say that he wore it for the first time when playing himself in as Captain of the Royal and Ancient Golf Club at St Andrews in 1922[20] [45].

Plain white or cream V-necked sweaters for sports often had a band in club colours at the neck and hem. Pull-overs with round or V-necks continued to be worn with sports jackets, blazers or tweed lounge suits during the 1930's, and sleeveless slip-overs were fashionable in place of a waistcoat (though only for informal wear) [46]. They were close-fitting and fairly short-waisted.

In the 1950's the sports shirt (that is, a tunic shirt with turned-down attached collar and, often, half-sleeves) was produced in knitted wool rather than flannel, linen or cotton. It could be worn as a shirt or a sweater and was either fastened to the neck with two or three buttons or left open. On its own or beneath a pull-over or cardigan jacket, it was one of the most popular garments for men during the 1950's and 1960's.

The post-war period saw the large-scale development of knitwear for leisure clothes and many new shapes and fabrics were introduced. Man-made fibres and knitting machinery made inexpensive garments easy to produce and a whole new industry came into being. Much of the impetus came from America but Italian designers (Brioni in particular) were credited with the inspiration and originality of the new knitwear styles.

In the later 1950's and early 1960's it was fashionable for knitted sweaters and cardigans to be large and bulky (an advertisement for a 'Chunky', pure Orlon sweater in 1962 stressed 'that firm hefty feel to it') – indeed, they were considerably longer and looser than ever before. Fancy stitching contributed to the effect. Plain polo-necked sweaters were also popular and were worn with a V-necked sweater or sports jacket, dispensing with the shirt, collar and tie. Otherwise, an open-necked shirt could be worn with a plain round or V-necked pull-over.

During the 1960's the T-shirt became a favourite casual garment for young men and women; it took the place of a vest, shirt or sweater in warm weather but also could be worn as an under-shirt in winter. The T-shirt appears to have originated from the working-man's vest or under-shirt – a short-sleeved, collarless shirt, fastening with two buttons at the neck, in knit or woven wool or cotton – but it may also have come into fashionable use through sports, for which round-necked, short-sleeved under-shirts were worn. The American fashion for wearing the T-shirt and jeans spread to Britain in the last years of the 1950's (since which time the two have almost invariably gone together). A decade later T-shirts were at the height of popular fashion; they were given additional and continued novelty by the printing of badges, names and slogans across the chest.

Perhaps the most significant new garment for informal wear after the Second World War was denim jeans. These trousers had never previously been worn for ordinary day wear, although they had been tough working clothing since the mid nineteenth century.[21] Levi Strauss, a Bavarian immigrant to America at the height of the gold rush, had the idea of making durable trousers from the stout canvas used for tents and wagon covers, but later adopted a stout cotton cloth or denim dyed indigo blue. Levis were the best quality American jeans available and the name became synonymous with them, although they have since been imitated by a number of other manufacturers.

Until the 1950's jeans were used by workingmen (miners, farmers and cowboys) as a kind of overall, but they were then adopted by young men in America for casual wear and in time became available throughout Europe. In the 1960's they were worn by young people everywhere and developed into a virtual uniform, especially amongst students. They were cheap, practical and in some ways a badge of rebellion against the Establishment. The idea of wearing 'anti-Establishment' trousers was not entirely new. In the 1890's men like William Morris and Walter Crane had attempted to express socialist principles and ideas by adopting or emulating the dress of working men, and thirty years later 'earnest young readers of the *New Statesman*' were wearing 'corduroy trousers and a rough jacket' with much the same aim in mind.[22] In fact, corduroy trousers remained an attribute of student or 'intellectual' dress until well into the 1950's when they were supplanted by the jeans. David Wincham, a bearded don at a redbrick university in Nancy Mitford's novel, *Don't Tell Alfred*, was typically clad 'in corduroy trousers, a duffle coat, a tartan shirt and sandals over thick, dirty, yellow woollen socks'.[23]

By the end of the 1960's jeans, although still a fashion mainly for the young, were worn by men and women of a much wider age-range and of all persuasions, so that they began to approach the status of a conventional rather than an unconventional casual garment.

CHAPTER NINE

Hair

The cut and arrangement of men and women's hair is one of the most important aspects of the fashionable image, and one acutely sensitive to change. Hair is an integral part of the image a man presents to the world. Facial features cannot themselves be altered except in most unusual circumstances, but hair can be dressed in countless different ways to change the whole appearance of the head. Hair styles have changed frequently, and sometimes very fast, and they have a direct bearing on the ways in which the ideals of beauty or elegance are expressed in each period.

A hair style can entirely change the emphasis of the face, to bring it closer to the ideal or mood of the period. It can also be a distinguishing mark denoting – or revealing – for instance, religious affiliation, nationality, occupation, degree of authority, aspirations in life and, of course, age. A full head of long, thick and curly hair, which has not lost its colour, is a sign of youth and has at most times been coveted – even imitated, when necessary, by artificial means.

Since a very early date hair has been dyed, curled or improved by the addition of false hair. Wigs appear to have been worn at various times, by ancient Egyptians, Assyrians and Persians, amongst others, but the hundred years or so from the late seventeenth to the late eighteenth century saw the most widespread use of false hair, when the wig was almost universally worn in Europe. The early form of the European wig, as worn in the last quarter of the seventeenth century was large and long with a mass of heavy curls; wigs were expensive and the most flamboyant were a mark of status (hence the expression 'big wig' used to refer to an important person). In the early decades of the next century this style of wig passed out of fashion, but it was retained for professional dress and, in particular, for legal costume (the judge's wig is still based upon the full-bottomed style) with the result that the large, long wig came to be regarded as a symbol of authority.

Long hair has had different significance at different periods. For example, during the Middle Ages it was usual for artists to depict orientals and biblical characters with long hair; at this time long blond hair was also associated with the German people, who had marked characteristics as a nation (in the south of Europe long hair was seen as a distinct feature of the northern 'barbarians'). In the nineteenth century, hair was often worn longer than usual by artists and intellectuals, and in the later decades this style was considered automatically to be somewhat effeminate and typical of the poet or aesthete. This attitude has prevailed to a great extent during the present century, although during the 1960's long hair for men assumed a more definite, even political significance, – like the jeans – becoming a badge of protest and defiance against the Establishment, and doubtless still holding, for many people, the connotation of barbarism.

There have also been fashions in the wearing of facial hair. Beards, side whiskers and moustaches have been regarded traditionally as symbols of virility and strength; evidence of the practice of shaving dates to earliest times, and attitudes towards hair on the face have always varied considerably. For a hundred years after the late seventeenth century beards and moustaches were virtually never seen; when the wig passed out of fashion in the late eighteenth century there was a gradual return to facial hair, and after the 1850's it became not only popular but highly respectable to wear a beard, by then taken to be the proper adjunct of every middle-class Victorian businessman [91].

By the beginning of the twentieth century beards were no longer favoured and they quickly disappeared, to be looked on largely with suspicion during the next sixty years ('beaver' was a rather derogatory term for a bearded man, in use from about 1910 onwards). Until well after the Second World War beards were worn by few men and usually signified artistic or intellectual ('bohemian') aspirations; by the 1960's a beard, worn with long hair, was taken either to express a rejection of established values, traditions and modes of dress or to underline quite blatantly a young man's masculinity – the reverse, in fact, of the attitude adopted a hundred years earlier.

The shape of the head and the appearance of the face play a part in the final effect of the fashionable silhouette, and this depends very largely on the relative length and fullness of the hair. An obvious example is the style worn in the early years of the sixteenth century when the squarely cut, shoulder-length hair (sometimes worn with a fringe over the forehead) ideally complemented the square, bulky shape of men's clothes and shoes [18].

There is often a direct relationship between the cut of men's hair and their clothes. In the sixteenth century, for example, men's hair was fashionably cut short and close to the head while collars were worn high, enclosing the neck [21]. Long, thick hair would almost certainly not have been pleasant to wear or to look at when combined with a tall, wide, starched and pleated ruff. In the next century, when the ruff was replaced by the falling band, or collar, men's hair was worn much longer; and by the last quarter of the century a cravat took the place of the collar which was almost totally obscured by the hair or wig which spread over the shoulders and chest [28]. During this time, hats, although essential to any costume, were often carried rather than worn because they were made awkward by a wig [34].

There are obvious basic differences between the hair arrangements of men and women. Men are far more likely to lose their hair and have rarely allowed it to be dressed in a style which would seriously hamper working or fighting (the long hair and cumbersome wigs of the seventeenth century would appear to contradict this but wigs could be, and often were, removed for strenuous activity or with comfortable, informal dress). There are, however, many instances where male and female hair arrangements have resembled each other and, as a rule, fashionable trends are reflected on the heads of both sexes. In the 1770's for example, the crown of the male wig was worn fuller and higher, rising in sympathy with the very tall styles in women's hair [35].

The Development of Hairdressing

It is evident that sophisticated techniques for cutting hair were in use from an early date. The ancient Romans paid considerable attention to the hair, which was usually cut short and could be artificially curled. Barbers practised a prosperous trade and their shops were favourite places for men to meet and exchange gossip. From the first century A.D. the hair was cut with iron shears and the shape could be quite elaborate; fashions tended to be influenced by the taste of the reigning emperor and changed frequently. Curls were fashionable and false hair was often used. Bronze and iron knives were in common use as razors, and during the first century A.D. Roman citizens were mostly clean-shaven; but beards were worn in the following century.[1]

The sixth-century mosaics of the court of the Emperor Justinian, in Ravenna, indicate that men's hair continued to be carefully cut and dressed; it was kept fairly short and neat, in a bowl-shaped crop which covered the tips of the ears. The tonsure (a shaved, circular patch on the crown of the head) was worn by ecclesiastics, and regulations concerning its exact form were laid down at the Synod of Whitby in A.D. 664.

Before the Norman invasion of 1066 Britons appear to have worn their hair long, to the nape of the neck or a little below it, parted at the centre and waved back. Most young men were clean-shaven but the older men wore beards and moustaches. The Bayeux Tapestry (c 1080) illustrates interesting differences between the hair arrangements of the Britons and the Norman French. The Normans were clean-shaven and cut their hair short, particularly at the back of the head which was shaved; when Harold's spies saw the Normans land in England, they thought they were an army of priests rather than soldiers.[2] After the Conquest, the British fashion for longer hair was adopted by the Normans and this became the accepted style on the Continent.

During the first half of the twelfth century men's hair was worn considerably longer than the style we see in the Bayeux Tapestry and could reach as far as the shoulders. However, the tympanum of Autun cathedral, which dates from the middle of the century, shows some variety in the treatment of hair, and by the thirteenth century the general length was to the nape of the neck (the hair had either a centre parting or a fringe and was usually waved) [99]. By the end of that century coifs were in common use to keep the hair neatly in place [51]: the head was covered by a close-fitting cap or bonnet of fine linen (or silk) which was tied under the chin; the hair

curled out from beneath the lower edge of the coif, and a small fringe could be exposed on the forehead. The coif appears to have been worn by men of all classes, including labourers, but men who were well-placed and fashionable had coifs of the finest quality linen which was almost transparent. This head-dress continued to be worn during the fourteenth century and it was clearly seen as an integral part of the hair arrangement (it could be worn beneath another covering such as a hood). In Boccaccio's *Decameron* (c 1350), a Florentine called Biondello is described as 'a dapper little fellow, elegant to a fault and neater than a fly, with a coif surmounting a head of long, fair hair exquisitely arranged so that not a single strand was out of place.'[3] Contemporary pictures indicate that the desired effect was a tight, smooth fit with no wrinkles or creases. By the 1330's Italian frescoes show most men wearing small, formal fringes; younger men might also have a lock of hair flicked across the cheekbone.

Beards had become less common in the previous century and by this time many men were clean-shaven. Towards the end of the century, pointed or forked beards, neatly trimmed and shaped, were fashionable, but they were not worn by all men. Chaucer's merchant in *The Canterbury Tales* had a forked beard, and the Westminster Abbey effigy of Edward III (who died in 1377) illustrates a beard carefully cut and divided in two.

In the later fourteenth century men's hair appears to have been arranged in a rounder, fuller, bowl-shaped cut, radiating from the centre of the crown, dipping backwards to the nape of the neck and curving up over the ears [**13**]. Early in the next century most men were wearing their hair fluffed out at the sides and it is evident from Chaucer's descriptions that curls were fashionable. A parish clerk in the Miller's Tale had hair which was:

> ... all in golden curls and shone;
> Just like a fan it strutted outwards, starting
> To left and right from an accomplished parting.

99 Effigy of Henry III in Westminster Abbey 1291
Men wore their hair long, to the nape of the neck, parted at the centre and waved back.

100 Effigy of Sir John Cressey 1444
Hair cut in the short, bowl-shaped crop resembled a smooth, round skull cap.

The handsome young squire, one of the pilgrims, had 'locks as curly as if they had been pressed'. By comparison, the Pardoner, illustrating the reverse of what was considered to be fashionable or attractive:

> ... had hair as yellow as wax,
> Hanging down smoothly like a hank of flax.
> In driblets fell his locks behind his head
> Down to his shoulders which they overspread;
> Thinly they fell, like rat-tails, one by one.[4]

Although it was fashionable, however, curled hair was not the only style. Hair was also cut straight in the short, bowl-shaped crop to resemble a smooth, round skull cap [100].

During the fifteenth century regional differences became noticeably apparent in the clothes and hairdressing of men and women throughout Europe. In the first decades of the century men in the Netherlands wore their hair cut short, well above the ears and shaved at the back of the head, with a fringe over the forehead. By the 1440's this cut looked almost like a tonsure [14, 100]. In Italy, the hair was worn fuller, often without a fringe, and was considerably bushier at the back of the head, but it too was cut short. A fashion in the 1420's, for dropping the neckline of the gown at the back, made the neck seem longer. The size of the head was greatly emphasized in both male and female fashions of the 1420's and 1430's when full hair cuts and large head dresses were worn.

In the second half of the century the fashionable length for men's hair increased both in the north and in the south of Europe, and by the 1470's it had reached the shoulders. In Italy the hair began to be worn longer in the 1450's, but it was also cut closer to the head. By the 1480's the fuller style was back in fashion, and hair was worn shoulder-length in a mass of fluffy and frizzed curls. False hair was used as an accessory by both sexes at the time, and this exaggerated fashion (at its most extreme in 1486) was often achieved by the use of wigs. A decade later the hair was still worn long but it had subsided to more normal dimensions. In the north of Europe during the 1480's men's hair was also both long and bushy. It was worn with flat caps pulled well down on to the forehead and sometimes almost tipping over the eyes, which gave young men a rather thuggish appearance [16, 17]. The 1490's were characterized throughout Europe by the flatness of men's crowns which underlined the squatter silhouette coming into fashion.

Men's hair was worn long, to the shoulders, until the 1520's, and on occasion it could be enclosed in a round cap or caul which prevented it from becoming cumbersome or impractical [112]. In Italy the soft, droopy appearance of the male haircut complemented the shape of the clothes, in particular the enormous, squashy sleeves and the softly-gathered, squared opening at the neck of the shirt. In northern Europe the fashionable line was squarer, harder and more Gothic in spirit, men's hair appeared to be rather blunter in cut and the image could be underlined by a straight fringe.

After about 1515 the hair gradually shortened; it was pushed back behind the ears and then cut quite short [19]. By the 1530's short, smooth hair was worn almost everywhere; male fashions generally during the middle years of the century were virtually international. The hair was cut close to the head and kept neatly trimmed until the 1580's.

In the 1550's the neckband of the shirt and doublet began to rise and attention was focused on the tall, wide ruff. With the advent of short hair, beards and moustaches returned to fashion and were as carefully cut as the head itself. The shape of the beard altered as different styles became fashionable: in the 1560's it was generally rounded, but a decade later it became more pointed. Forked or square, spade-shaped beards were also worn during the later sixteenth century and few young men were entirely clean-shaven.

During the 1580's men's hair grew a little longer again, loosening into close curls which added to the generally romantic aspect of their clothes [22, 23]. By 1600 even the older and more conservative men had also adopted the longer length and the hair curled out over the ears [55]. By 1615 the hair began to rise a little at the front and in the years to follow it steadily grew longer, reaching the shoulders by the 1630's [25, 26]. The new length of hair was combined with soft, loose curls; it was fashionable to grow one portion or lock of the hair rather longer on the left-hand side and this was commonly called a love-lock. Occasionally the lock was plaited; Christian IV of Denmark, for example, favoured this style for some time after it had passed out of fashion and wore a long, thin pigtail at one side until his death in 1648.

By the 1630's the longer hair was beginning to push the shirt collar – which spread across the shoulders – into folds towards the front of the chest [28, 57]; at the end of the decade men were beginning to tie the end of the collar together with ribbon and in due course the lace-edged collar was replaced by a long neckcloth or cravat [29]. With long hair it was more appropriate to wear the cravat around the neck, since the lace edges were displayed to better effect beneath the chin than across the shoulders where they now would be obscured [74].

During the 1650's fashionable hair became so long and curled [101] that it was necessary to add false pieces where the natural hair was deficient. By 1660 a whole head of false hair could be worn and the periwig was adopted; this proved to be a convenient and better-looking alternative to a mass of greasy natural hair (hair was not usually washed very often and powder was used to absorb the grease). When adopting a long wig, men could have their own hair cut short or completely shaved, which besides being more comfortable and hygienic made the wig easier to put on. The periwig came to England from the Continent with the restoration of the monarchy in 1660 but did not become a widespread fashion for several years. Samuel Pepys, for example, bought his first wigs (one at £3 and the other at forty shillings) in October 1663, and he felt self-conscious about wearing one for the first time to church the following month: 'I found that my coming in a periwigg did not prove so strange to the world as I was afeared it would, for I thought that all the church would presently have cast their eyes all upon me – but I found no such thing'.[5]

101 Man in Black by G. ter Borch 1656 (det of 57)
As men's hair increased in length it pushed the collar towards the centre front. (If the natural hair was deficient false pieces could be added and by 1660 a whole head of false hair, or periwig, was adopted).

102 'A Rake's Progress –The Levée' by Hogarth *c* 1733 (det)
The campaign wig was divided into two locks which hung over each shoulder and a third, shorter lock at the nape of the neck.

In the month of September two years later, Pepys wrote in his diary:

> Up and put on my colourd silk suit very fine and my new periwigg bought a good while since, but darst not wear, because the plague was in Westminster when I bought it. And it is a wonder what will be the fashion after the plague is done as to periwiggs, for nobody will dare to buy any haire, for fear of the infection – that it had been cut of the head of people dead of the plague.[5]

Despite these fears, wigs usually were made of human hair – horsehair and sheep's or goat's hair could be used but were not so common. Brown or black were the most general colours at this time, although blonde wigs became fashionable in the later 1660's. The hair was attached either to a base of parchment-like material or, more commonly, to a net structure; wig-making techniques developed to a high standard once the fashion became established [**104**]. The wig was not, at first, a fashion for the poor, since it often cost in the region of £5 and upwards, but by the middle of the eighteenth century it was worn in England by men of every social class.[6]

As men's hair grew longer during the seventeenth century the emphasis on facial hair decreased and by the time the wig was introduced the beard and moustache were out of fashion. Most men were clean-shaven for the greater part of the century but elderly or conservative men clung to the earlier style for some decades. Charles II has been portrayed with a pencil-line moustache, but this was not usual. In January 1664, Pepys 'began a practice which I find, by the ease I do it with, that I shall continue, it saving me money and time – that is to Trimme myself with a Razer – which pleases me mightily.' His wife was able to trim his hair from time to time but he still found the barber necessary to keep his wigs in good order, and in 1668 he came to an arrangement with him to do this on payment of twenty shillings a year.[7]

Fashions in men's hair styles altered whether it was natural or false and wigs changed their shape with considerable frequency. The style of wig known as the full-bottomed, was fashionable from the 1660's to about 1710 [**31**]. In the 1660's it was long and immensely curled (its appearance complemented by the florid 'gros point' lace of the collar); the crown remained flat until the mid 1680's. Hair in the 1670's was generally fuller, frizzed out at the sides to give a horizontal emphasis to the head, and it was worn long to the middle of the chest. During the 1680's the shape changed; the crown was built upwards, reflecting the increasing height of the women's tiered cap or fontange. By the end of the decade the wig formed a distinct point at the top of the head and the mass of loose curls was worn off the shoulder and down the back. The crown reached its highest point in the mid 1690's and in the last years of the century it was divided at the centre front, the hair rising in two peaks at either side of the parting [**31**]; it was also fashionable to wear the hair over one shoulder. A military and naval habit during the 1690's was to tie back the hair from the shoulders, in a tail or queue.

By 1710 the full-bottomed wig was decreasing in height and bulk but was also beginning to pass out of fashionable use; it was correct with formal dress and was retained by professional men such as doctors and lawyers. In following decades other styles of wigs, which were shorter and less full, were preferred for ordinary wear. The campaign or travelling wig, for example was in use until the 1750's [**102**]. It was a little shorter than the full-bottomed wig and the hair was divided into two locks which hung over each shoulder and a third, shorter lock or long curl, at the nape of the neck. Bob wigs, both short and long (the long wig covered the neck) were worn for undress wear [**32**]. There were also several wigs with queues, where the hair was drawn back in a tail. The hair could be simply tied back with a black silk ribbon bow (the tye wig), it could be plaited (as with the Ramillies wig) or it could be enclosed in a small, black silk bag with a draw-string and finished with a black bow at the nape of the neck (the bag wig) [**33, 103**]. This last was the usual style for dress wear, taking the place of the full-bottomed wig from about 1730 onwards.

For dress or formal occasions it was customary to powder the hair with finely ground starch or flour which was puffed on to the wig after it had been greased with pomatum [**103**]. This form of dressing could damage the clothes, so usually a powdering gown or jacket was worn over the coat when powder was applied; the bag enclosing the queue also afforded a measure of protection.

The wig was essentially a feature of formal dress during the eighteenth century. It could be removed for informal wear or at certain times indoors (the surgeon in Tobias Smollett's *Humphry Clinker* (1771), for example, removed his coat and wig before setting to work in a cap and apron[8]). A soft cap – called a night cap or morning cap – was worn in place of the wig, to cover a bald or closely cropped head and keep it warm, and it usually accompanied the informal coat or the nightgown [**115**].

At the beginning of the eighteenth century it was still possible for men to wear their own hair long and dressed, in a manner similar to the wig, with

103 Francis Beckford by Reynolds 1755–56 (det of 34) The mid-eighteenth century wig was dressed close to the head but curved up at the sides over the ears.

104 'Perruquier – Barbier' in the *Encyclopédie* by Denis Diderot 1771 Wig-making techniques developed to a high standard once the fashion for false hair was established.

powder and grease. By the end of the 1740's, however, almost all men in Britain, irrespective of their social station, were wearing wigs and this was usual until wigs passed out of fashion altogether in the last decades of the century. The few who did not wear wigs included young men, before the age of about eighteen, and those who belonged to non-conformist religious sects such as the Methodists. Social distinctions could be observed in the shape of the wig, its fit (badly fitting wigs were a mark of ill breeding) and its grooming (unkempt wigs tending to be worn by working men or the very poor). The professional classes were distinguished by the size of their wigs: the largest (in the full-bottomed style) were worn by judges as a completely formal head-dress, no longer intended to resemble natural or fashionable hair, and the next largest by doctors who wore it with the customary black suit and plain cravat.

The wig (or natural hair) was parted at the centre until the 1730's when it was brushed straight back from the forehead and temples in a *toupet* (that is, a roll of hair at the front) [33]. In the early eighteenth century the crown of the wig descended again, and by 1740 the wig was both shorter and flatter. The neater, closer shape of the male wig was in keeping with the small, tight shape of women's hair. In the 1750's the wig continued to be dressed close to the head [103] and the crown was flat, but the hair curved up at the sides, developing into horizontal clusters of sausage-shaped curls which covered the ears. The arrangement of women's hair during the 1760's became softer and fuller, with the crown gradually rising until the very tall heads of the 1770's. The crown of the male wig rose, and it was brushed up to its greatest height in 1776–77 (the young Macaroni exquisites took this fashion to its most extreme). Roll curls on each side of the head still covered the ear but were worn tighter and smaller; by 1781 the ear became visible with the hair built out in one curl from each side [36]. In the early 1780's women's enormously tall hair arrangements collapsed into a mass of soft, loose curls and men's wigs also became longer, softer and looser.

The last decade of the eighteenth century saw an end to the fashionable life of the wig and it began to be discarded by young men in favour of natural hair worn short and unpowdered. A tax on hair powder in 1795 is thought to have encouraged the trend, but it seems to have begun before this date and was more likely to have been the result of the changing mood in current fashions. The more natural and informal manner of hairdressing was an integral feature of the new enthusiasm for more 'democratic' styles of dress and country clothes and for the neo-classical taste (short curls in the antique style were worn 'à la Titus', 'Brutus' or 'Apollo') [105].

It is evident from Jane Austen's novels, written in the early years of the nineteenth century, that older and more conservative men clung to the habit of using powder, which was correct for formal occasions. In *The Watsons*, Mrs Robert Watson scolds her husband:

> "You have not put any fresh powder in your hair." "No," he replies, " – I do not intend it – I think there is powder enough in my hair for my wife and sisters." "Indeed, you ought to make some alteration in your dress before dinner when you are out visiting, though you do not at home." "Nonsense" [he returns, but a short while later he is overheard telling another guest] "You cannot be more in déshabille than myself. – We got here so late, that I had not time even to put a little fresh powder in my hair."[9]

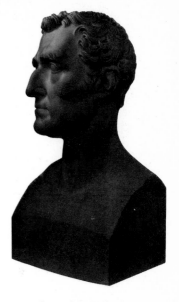

105 Bust of the Duke of Wellington by W. Pistrucci, early nineteenth century Short curls in the antique style were an expression of neo-classical taste. This apparently natural and casual manner of hairdressing was the result of skilful cutting. Once wigs were abandoned whiskers reappeared on the face.

A queue or pigtail continued to be worn by army officers until it was officially abolished in 1808. The order, however, did not reach the Royal Welch Fusiliers who were serving in Nova Scotia at the time, and a relic of the black silk wig bag still survives as part of their uniform. Known as the 'flash' (originally a slang word for the wig), it consists of five black silk ribbons which hang fanwise from the back of the collar.[10]

By the beginning of the nineteenth century most men were wearing their own hair closely cropped in a short, layered style. The effect was natural and casual, the intention to look carelessly windswept, as part of the overall romantic mood of both male and female dress [38]. This negligent appearance was, however, carefully contrived since to look effective the hair had to be cut and shaped most skilfully. Young men like Frank Churchill in Jane Austen's *Emma* could well need to give their hair frequent attention:

> Emma's very good opinion of Frank Churchill was a little shaken ... by hearing that he was gone off to London, merely to have his hair cut. A sudden freak seemed to have seized him at breakfast, and he had sent for a chaise and set off, intending to return to dinner, but with no more important view that appeared than having his hair cut. There was certainly no harm in his travelling sixteen miles twice over on such an errand; but there was an air of foppery and nonsense in it which she could not approve ... He came back, had had his hair cut, and laughed at himself with a very good grace, but without seeming at all ashamed of what he had done. He had no reason to wish his hair longer, to conceal any confusion of face.[11]

With the return to natural hair, whiskers appeared on the face, [105] although moustaches were not fashionable until the 1830's and full beards were uncommon before the middle of the century. The short male haircut coincided with the rising height of the shirt collar and cravat which enclosed the neck and part of the jaw.

From the later 1820's onwards men began to shed some of the romantic aspects of their appearance and adopted a more worldly image. The hair was worn a little longer and smoother, parted at the centre or the side and combed into loose curls or waves over the ears in the 1830's and 1840's [40, 62]. A side parting was common but there was a move towards the centre by the 1850's and the hair was loosely waved or smoothed down sleekly on each side with the aid of macassar oil; it was worn long enough to curl in to the neck. Facial hair became more prominent, full side whiskers were popular by the 1850's and moustaches and beards were grown during and after the Crimean War (1854–56). By the late 1860's beards were common and very few men were completely clean-shaven [42]. In the following decade there was increased variety in the styles of hair worn on the face; moustaches, whiskers and beards could be worn alone or combined in different shapes [106]. When the Rev. Francis Kilvert had his hair cut in 1870 he told the barber to trim his beard square. '"Now,"' replied the barber, '"this is very inconsistent. Your features are round and you want your beard cut square." "Still," I said, "I prefer it."'[12]

106 *The Tailor and Cutter* 1874 Moustache and mutton-chop whiskers.

Hair continued to be worn in a centre or side parting in a smooth or waved crop. During the 1850's it became fashionable for the centre parting to be drawn over the back of the head, and in the 1860's the hair was brushed out from it to either side. Towards the end of the century the side parting became more usual, but both side and centre partings were worn [107]. The hair was generally shorter by the 1890's and virtually every respectable middle-class man wore a beard which was regarded as the outward, visible sign of the philistine by aesthetes of the 1880's and 1890's, who were deliberately clean-shaven [87, 107] and very often wore their hair longer than was the respectable fashion. Beardless men were thought to look more sensitive and 'artistic' until the end of the century.

At the beginning of the twentieth century, beards began to disappear, hastened out to some extent by the invention and wider use of the safety razor [44]. The new ideal of a 'smooth-shaven, stern-faced, dogged-chin' man was effectively portrayed by Charles Dana Gibson, amongst other artists.[13] Some men of conservative tastes continued to wear beards until the 1930's, but they were thought to be very old-fashioned for doing so. Moustaches could be retained but they were usually small and toothbrush-like (similar to those worn by Charlie Chaplin and Clark Gable in the 1920's and 1930's) [133].

By 1900 the hair was worn short and neatly trimmed, and usually parted on one side [80], although a centre parting or no parting at all (with the hair combed straight back) were permissible styles in the following decades. The neat, smooth look was effected by the use of oil or brilliantine which gave the hair that patent-leather appearance often associated with Rudolph Valentino in the 1920's.

107 Aubrey Beardsley by
J. E. Blanche 1895
A deliberately clean-shaven
appearance was thought to
look more 'sensitive' at a time
when every respectable
middle-class man wore a
beard and this came to be
associated with artists and
poets.

Short hair remained fashionable during the 1930's [92] and there was little obvious change in the shape of men's heads, but the flattened hair of the 1920's tended to be replaced by waves for younger men aiming at a more casual elegance. During the Second World War the popularity of moustaches began to wane, possibly because of the association with Hitler, and by the late 1940's most men were clean-shaven. Beards were unusual and thought to be an eccentric affectation. In Anthony Powell's novel, *Books do Furnish a Room* (set in about 1947), the bearded young avant-garde novelist, X. Trapnel, was a striking figure: 'beards, rarer in those days than they became later, at that period hinted of submarine duty, rather than the arts, social protest or a subsequent fashion simply for much more hair . . . the beard, assessed with the clothes and the stick he carried, marked him out as an exhibitionist in a reasonably high category.'[14] The beard began to be adopted during the 1950's as a badge of association with 'the arts' or

'social protest', but did not become widespread until the 1960's. By the later 1960's much more hair had become fashionable as Anthony Powell says, and beards were accepted for ordinary wear without sinister implications.

Between 1939 and 1945 most men were serving in the armed forces and were obliged to wear their hair short. Beards which were strictly forbidden in the army, although moustaches were allowed. With general demobilization in the second half of the 1940's the standard haircut was 'short back and sides' which remained popular with conventional men during the next two decades. With its hint of service discipline this style became a mark of respectability and was virtually compulsory for all professional men and those who worked in offices [65].

During the 1950's there was more variety in the cut of young men's hair though it remained short and tidy. In America, styles ranged from the minimal crew cut to the longer, greased, combed-back arrangement worn, for example, by Elvis Presley. In England the crew cut had little if any appeal but Teddy Boys wore the so-called 'Duck's Tail' hair style (of which Elvis Presley's cut was a modified version). The hair was long, dragged back at each side and swept up in front, and kept in place with lavish greasing; this neo-Edwardian image even included long side-whiskers, or 'side boards'.

Short hair was general in the early 1960's and it was always worn off the brow, so the new cut popularized by the Beatles in 1963 [108] created a sensation with its long fringe covering the forehead and increased length at the back of the head. The contrast of styles was extreme, and the general effect at the time seemed quite barbaric; throughout the 1960's long hair produced startled and angry reactions from most sections of society. As a symbol of protest and badge of allegiance to new ideas, abundant hair (including beards, whiskers and moustaches) became one of the most significant features of the dress of young people (it was celebrated in the anti-Establishment Broadway musical *Hair*).[15]

Jimi Hendrix, the black rock-star, grew his hair until it resembled an enormous frizzy halo, setting the fashion for the curled, bushy 'Afro' cut. Hair was grown by some men to its natural limits, and might be worn to halfway down the back (sometimes needing to be tied in a pigtail), but once the fashion had been taken to its extreme it began to lose its hold and in 1969 moves were made towards short hair once again. Fashionable young men cropped their hair short, and it was now the 'Skinheads' who made an appearance. Like the Teddy Boys, Skinheads adopted a distinctive style of dress for working-class boys from the East End of London: old-fashioned collarless shirts, dungarees, heavy, laced boots and shaved heads or crew cuts.

The extremities of long hair bypassed conventional men but by the end of the 1960's hair in general was being worn an inch or so longer. Wigs were revived as a fashionable aid and there was a marked increase in the production of cosmetics and dressings for male hair.

108 The Beatles *c* 1964
A new haircut with a long fringe was popularized by the pop group.

CHAPTER TEN

Hats

Hats and other head coverings were originally worn for practical reasons. They protected the head and shoulders (including the neck, eyes and ears) from the weather and from knocks and blows (for example when riding or fighting). From an early date, however, a symbolic and decorative significance was attached to the placing of a covering or ornament on the head and the wearing of a hat has continued to be regarded as a mark of authority or respectability.

The term 'hat' is used in this chapter to refer to head coverings in general. There are different forms of head covering, such as hat, cap, bonnet, or hood, and these can be distinguished by certain features. A hat, for example, is generally considered to have a brim, while a cap has none and usually has a soft crown. A hood is also made of a soft or flexible material and covers both head and neck (often being attached to a cloak or coat). Hats or caps for men in the sixteenth century (or earlier) were called 'bonnets', a term which passed out of use in England in the seventeenth century (to be replaced by the word 'cap') but was retained in Scotland.[1] These terms are loosely defined and there are times when it is difficult to make a clear distinction between them, especially when some contemporary words (such as bonnet) are no longer in common use; but they will be used here in their general sense.

The main features of hats or head coverings of any sort are the crown, brim (when present) and fastening (if used). The crown and the brim can vary in shape, height, width and texture. Crowns, for instance, can be low, round and close-fitting or high to a point, conical or drum-shaped; brims may be narrow or wide, and may be worn curled at the sides, tilted, cocked or turned up close to the head. Hats can be hard or soft. Fastenings include methods of attaching a covering to the head or shoulders (usually by strings or straps) or securing the brim (for example, by buttoning it to the crown).

Hats, unless purely functional in nature (such as helmets or riding hats), are regarded as a piece of clothing to complement or complete the costume. The size and shape of a hat will therefore bear some relationship to the rest of the clothes worn and will in particular be affected by the current fashion of the hair.

The most usual material for hats has been felt, made either of wool or fur. Felting is an old process which was certainly known to the ancient Greeks. Unlike weaving it consists in the matting of wool or fur fibres by very firm compression to produce a fabric which does not fray or unravel and is reasonably impermeable. As a light, firm (but pliable), warm and weatherproof material, felt is particularly suitable for head coverings, and it can be stiffened to make a hard, protective crown. Until the eighteenth century fur felt was widely used; it was of a finer quality than wool felt, but it was also more expensive. The best felts were made of beaver fur (in the seventeenth century beaver was used almost entirely for the manufacture of hats[2]) but rabbit, or coney, was also used.

Straw is the other most important material for head coverings and it has a long history (straw, grass and rush hats have been worn since primitive times[3]). Whereas felt gave protection against the cold and wet, straw was the ideal shield against the sun. It is light and cool to wear and was a cheap, common material. Straw was worn out of doors, in hot climates or warm weather. In the Middle Ages straw hats were mainly worn by labourers and travellers and although they later became fashionable for ordinary wear they were always traditionally associated with the country.

Hats have also been made of a number of other materials such as leather and fur, knitted wool or woven cloth and silks of all kinds. Cottons, canvas, corduroy and certain man-made materials for informal caps and hats are among the more recent innovations. The usual stiffening agents for hats have been gum arabic or glue and shellac.

Hats can decorate and be decorated in a number of ways. Ornaments of various kinds have been fixed to the crown or brim; during the sixteenth century badges or brooches in finely-wrought metals set with precious stones were especially fashionable [139], and were worn in the hat as a piece of jewellery. Gold- or silver-tipped tags or 'aiglets', gold and silver lace and fringes could also be added and buttons on cocked hats were often very fine. Mary Delany noted at Queen Caroline's birthday in 1729 that: 'the King was in blue velvet with diamond buttons; the hat was buttoned up with prodigious fine diamonds.'[4] In the sixteenth and seventeenth centuries, hatbands too, although usually of silk, could be made of precious metals, and gold, silver or copper with a cable twist were placed round the crown. Silk ribbon or gold and silver braid was used to edge or bind brims. Some hoods and many caps were lined with fur during the Middle Ages and from this period onwards, feathers were a favourite trimming for hats and caps (ostrich plumes, in particular, were popular). Embroidery has also been used for the decoration of head coverings; Edward III, for example, had five hoods of white long cloth worked with blue dancing men made for him and his companions in 1347.[5] Night caps of linen were embroidered in coloured silks during the sixteenth and seventeenth centuries, and smoking caps of the nineteenth century could be worked in Berlin wools on canvas.

The ways in which a hat was worn might also be said to be decorative. The mediaeval hood, or chaperon, is one example. It could be draped and worn on top of the head (in the manner of a turban) in a variety of different ways [111]. Seventeenth- and eighteenth-century hats with broad brims were often cocked – that is, looped or buttoned up to the crown on one, both or three sides. Brims can also be curled or tilted and the hat worn at an angle, tipped forwards, backwards or sideways on the head. A slightly tilted hat is usually thought to add a touch of style or elegance to a costume, in the way, for instance, that Guards officers in civilian dress in London during the 1950's were noted for wearing a dark lounge suit, white shirt, Guards' tie and tightly rolled umbrella, with a black bowler hat tilted forward on to the forehead. At times, hats have been carried rather than worn, as an accessory to dress, the eighteenth-century *chapeau bras* was usually seen tucked under one arm.

A considerable amount of symbolic significance has been attached to hats or head dresses, which have been recognized as a mark of status, occupation or a distinctive type of dress. Laurel or olive wreaths were worn about the head in ancient Rome as a sign of victory or merit, while crowns or coronets have been one of the attributes of sovereignty and authority in Europe. The removing of hat or cap had been the traditional sign of respect or subservience, particularly in the presence of a monarch. At the Court of Elizabeth I in 1585, it was reported that men would put on their hats or bonnets to dance, but in the Queen's chamber no one could wear a hat, whether she was present or not.[6] Uncovering the head as a matter of courtesy to a person or a building (such as a church or a war-memorial) is a custom still observed, although it is often reduced to a momentary raising or touching of the hat (which is thought to be the origin of the military or naval salute). In some, but not all periods, it has been thought necessary to cover the head for the sake of decency or respectability; during the first half of the present century, for example, few men would be seen out of doors without a hat or cap.

During the Middle Ages hats were most usually worn by agricultural labourers or travellers, as protection against the weather, and were regarded as the distinctive apparel of these two occupations. Mediaeval manuscript illuminations sometimes depict Christ wearing a hat, but only in particular circumstances – such as at the supper at Emmaus, when He has met the travellers on the road, and is shown wearing a pilgrim's hat, or when He appears before Mary Magdalene after the Resurrection and is mistaken by her for a gardener [109]. Travellers wore hats of straw or felt and those of the pilgrims were usually decorated with badges or devices relating to the object of their pilgrimage. The cockle shell, the attribute of St James of Compostella, was the common distinctive badge of pilgrims, probably because his was the most popular mediaeval shrine to visit. The characteristic shape of the Roman Catholic cardinal's or bishop's hat has its origin in the mediaeval hat worn by travellers and was at first no different from it (since cardinals and bishops were obliged to travel in their work). Another hat which assumed particular significance was what is now called the Phrygian cap or cap of liberty: when a Roman slave was granted his freedom it was customary for his master to present him with a cap of this shape and subsequently it was adopted as a symbol of liberty by the First French Republic.

Certain articles of clothing become popularly associated with individual characters or are consciously adopted by them as a personal device. Several styles of hats during the past hundred years have featured in this way – for

109 Holkham Bible (det), early fourteenth century Mediaeval manuscript illuminations sometimes depict Christ wearing a hat. In this case He is dressed as a gardener.

110 Luttrell Psalter *c* 1340–45 (det of 9) By the fourteenth century the hood was one of the standard garments for men of all classes.

example, the homburg, usually associated with the Prince of Wales (later Edward VII); the deerstalker cap so often worn by Sherlock Holmes; the cloth cap adopted by the Labour M.P. Kier Hardie; Charlie Chaplin's bowler, Sir Anthony Eden's trilby and Maurice Chevalier's straw boater.

The Development of Hats and Head Coverings

There is evidence that the ancient Greeks and Romans wore close-fitting caps of wool or felt and head coverings of straw. During the early mediaeval period heads appear to have remained uncovered for the most part and it is not until the later mediaeval period that hoods and hats were fashionable.

In the Anglo-Saxon period the most usual form of head-covering, if one was worn at all, was a cap. It is likely that several different styles of cap were worn and there was some variation in materials and decoration. A cap very similar in shape to the Phrygian (that is, with a tall pointed crown tipped forward) was common until the eleventh century and may have been brought to Europe from the Middle East by Phoenician traders.[7] A cap excavated in Denmark, from Tollund bog near Silkeborg, dates from the first or second century A.D. and is probably representative of another type quite general at this time. The cap is conical, and made of several pieces of

111 Conquests of
Charlemagne by Tavernier
c 1460 (det of 15)
The hood or *chaperon* was
worn on top of the head (the
round opening for the face
was placed on the crown, the
edge was rolled back to form
a brim and the shoulder-cape
and long end were twisted or
draped on top).

leather thonged together. Leather and wool were the usual materials and there may have been distinctions in shape or ornament according to rank.

In the early mediaeval period hoods were mainly worn by travellers and working men as protective clothing. The hood was similar in shape to a monk's cowl and usually made of woollen cloth; a separate hood, covering the shoulders and head, could be open or closed at the neck in front. The hood became increasingly popular and by the fourteenth century was one of the standard garments for men of all classes [110].

Hats were making an appearance by the end of the eleventh century and there are illustrations of peasants wearing them in the twelfth-century Lambeth Bible. At this date the hat was worn for added protection and was regarded purely as a functional item of apparel.

During the thirteenth century the coif seems to have come into general use [51]. This was a close-fitting bonnet or cap which covered the head and ears and fastened under the chin with strings. It always appears to be white or light-coloured and was usually made of a fine, almost transparent linen (although silk may also have been used). The coif was worn by men and appears to have been an intrinsic part of the hair arrangement; it fitted tightly over the head and kept the hair firmly in place. Fourteenth-century illustrations reveal the transparency of the coif where it is pulled tightly over the ears. Caps and hoods could be worn over the coif, which remained in use until the early fifteenth century. After the coif passed out of fashionable use it became fossilized, as a feature of professional or official dress, especially of ecclesiastical or legal costume. There was, for example, an Order of the Coif to which all Serjeants-at-Law belonged until the end of the nineteenth century. The last vestige of the coif – the judge's black cap which was placed on the wig – was in fact worn until the abolition of the death sentence.

By the fourteenth century there was a considerable variety of fashionable head coverings. Hoods had changed in shape and were worn in more than one way. They were closer fitting around the face, neck and shoulders and the pointed end at the back of the head was gradually elongated, which suggests that they could be as fashionably tailored as other garments [110]. The end of the hood could be tipped forward or sideways, or the edge turned back from the face to reveal a contrasting lining. An imaginative development was to place the hood on top of the head. The round opening for the face was put over the crown and the edge rolled back to form a brim, while the shoulder-cape and long end were twisted or draped on top to complete the head dress [111].

Fur was used extensively for clothing in the Middle Ages and mediaeval hoods were often fur-lined (though the type of fur used would vary with different social groups or occupations). University graduates normally wore furred hoods and the custom has continued to the present day (the traditional form of the academic hood has, in fact, altered comparatively little from its original mediaeval shape). Hoods could also be lined with silk or cloth – materials which were used for the outer part and which afforded scope for embroidery or other decoration. By the last decades of the fourteenth century, hoods fitted tightly over the head, neck and shoulders, the end was very long and narrow and the edge of the shoulder-cape could be scalloped or dagged.

Hats of straw or felt were worn for various outdoor pursuits during the fourteenth century [109]. The characteristic shape for straw hats was similar to the cardinal's hat (into which it developed). A long cord hung from the brim, beneath the chin, allowing the hat to be pushed back and suspended from the shoulders (for later ecclesiastical wear the cords of cardinals', bishops' and abbots' hats were lengthened and knotted with terminating tassels arranged in particular formations to indicate rank[8]). The straw-plaiting industry seems to have originated in Tuscany and was probably established by the fourteenth century. The technique of plaiting straws into long narrow strips which were sewn in spiral rows to make a hat was a comparatively late development.[9]

Another distinctive hat, worn over the hood for riding, had a long pointed brim or peak at the front. This was worn by both men and women. Also fashionable by the middle of the century were tall conical hats with close, turned-up brims. Beaver for felt hats was certainly in use by this time and Chaucer's merchant had a 'Flemish beaver hat'.

Wreaths or chaplets were worn by men on certain occasions during the early fourteenth century. It was traditional for both bridegrooms and brides to wear a wreath of fresh flowers for a betrothal. Circlets of gold set with stones in the form of flowers were worn as a piece of jewellery, although probably only by the nobility.

The International Gothic period (c 1390 – 1420) was, as we have seen, a time of extravagance and exaggeration in male and female dress. The grandeur and bulk of fashionable clothes was balanced and emphasized by the size of men's hats which reached very large proportions by the 1430's. Straw hats which had formerly only been worn in the country were adopted for high fashion. In the 1420's and 1430's they became larger, with tall crowns and wide brims (van Eyck's Arnolfini portrait of 1434 shows a deep-crowned, finely plaited black straw hat) [83]. Enormous hats made of cloth or felt were fashionable in Italy in the early 1430's, and fur hats could be worn in the Netherlands.

Rolled hoods or chaperons, which equalled the size of hats, were also worn. The hood worn on top of the head was elaborately draped to form a turban-like head dress which became more and more formalized. By the middle of the fifteenth century the chaperon was worn in the Netherlands as a conventional hat which, when removed as a mark of respect, could be hung over one shoulder by the long end which dangled from the crown [53]. (There is some evidence in fifteenth-century Flemish and French manuscript illuminations to suggest that there were regional differences in the wearing and arrangement of the chaperon.) By the 1470's, however, the chaperon was passing out of fashionable use; by the 1480's it was considered outmoded, but it was retained as a feature of official dress. In time, a conventionalized form of the chaperon, considerably diminished in size, was merely fixed to the shoulder of the gown or mantle. This may still

112 Danish tombstone, sixteenth century
Long hair could be enclosed in a round, turban-like cap for practical purposes.

be seen in Britain today on the official mantle of the Order of the Garter.[10]

After the 1430's men's hats grew smaller and by the middle of the century the fashionable silhouette presented a longer, slimmer line. Gowns were less bulky and becoming shorter, shoes were longer and thinner with pointed toes, and in the 1460's tall, pointed caps had appeared in the Netherlands [16]. Mid fifteenth century hats and caps could be lavishly decorated with jewellery and embroidery (in 1454, for example, Philip the Good had so many jewels in his hat for the celebrations of the Feast of the Pheasant that no more could be added). By the late 1460's the eccentric, spiky character of dress in the Netherlands passed its peak and the tall cap began to collapse about the crown. During the 1470's flatter, low-crowned caps and hats were worn, sometimes well on to the forehead, and this contributed to the new squatter look. In the 1480's men's hair was worn considerably longer and fuller and the bushy shoulder-length style was topped with a round, low, flat cap [17].

It is evident from contemporary pictures that men's head covering in the fifteenth century varied from region to region and country to country throughout Europe. There was a variety of different shapes and styles of hats and caps. Fringed straw hats were fashionable in France in the middle of the century, for example, and another distinctive head dress, in Germany, was a forehead band of metal with a feather attached to the front.

At the beginning of the next century, men's hair was worn long and a practical fashion was to enclose it in a round, turban-like cap or netted caul (in Italy the cap was called a 'balzo'). A Danish tombstone from the time shows a man wearing a similar head dress with armour and no doubt it made fighting or active pursuits more practicable [112].

Low-crowned hats or caps were fashionable at this period and the flat-topped look emphasized the generally square outline of the clothes and silhouette. A new form of cap was the biretta or four-cornered, soft-crowned cap, which could be turned up at the lower edge over the ears and back of the neck [18]. This was fashionable during the first two decades of the century but was then relegated to official and professional use, associated in particular with ecclesiastics, scholars and teachers [19]. A formalized version of the cap, with the crown flattened and hardened, became the mortar board of academic dress.

During the sixteenth and seventeenth centuries (until about 1680) hats and caps were worn by men indoors as well as out, at meal times and in church. Low-crowned caps or hats with slashed and turned-up brims, which supplanted the biretta after the 1520's, were lavishly decorated with jewels, ornaments and plumes for formal wear [19]. The hats themselves could be made of rich materials such as velvets, damasks, brocaded silks or satin; the slashed brims were often fastened with ornamental buttons or tied with aiglets, and it was fashionable to fix a medallion, badge or jewel at one side [20].

By the middle of the sixteenth century hats had generally decreased in size, possibly because men's hair by this date was universally worn short and neat. Small, flat caps could be worn tilted to one side of the head. In the

1560's crowns were made a little fuller and higher and had a softer, squashy appearance. Hats with narrow flat brims and gathered crowns were worn until the 1590's but in the last quarter of the century stiffer, taller felt hats with conical ('sugar loaf') crowns were increasingly the fashion. Beaver was popular despite its expense and was available in black, white, grey and brown (but black was the most usual colour). In the 1580's hats with deep, round crowns, similar to a bowler, were worn and in the 1590's tall, square-topped crowns were fashionable [23]. Both these hats had moderately wide brims which could be slightly curled.

Hatbands were made of ribbon, silk cord or circlets of gold or silver, finished with a plume or jewels. Fastidious Brisk, in Ben Jonson's *Everyman out of his Humour* (1600), had his new hat and fancy hatband all but demolished by an opponent in a duel: 'He again lights me here - I had on a gold cable hatband, then new come up, which I wore about a murrey French hat I had – he cuts my hatband, and yet it was massy goldsmith's work – cuts my brim, which by good fortune, being thick embroidered with gold twist and spangles, disappointed the force of the blow.'[11]

Flat caps of the mid sixteenth century could be made of wool, and some were knitted (it is thought that knitted caps were originally imported).[12] To stimulate the wool and cappers' trades an act of Parliament in 1571 ordained that on Sundays and holidays all males over six years of age, except the nobility and persons of degree, were to wear caps of wool manufactured in England. The act was repealed in 1597, but flat woollen caps were already recognized as the distinguishing mark of a citizen, tradesman or apprentice. Fine cloth and silks were generally used for the gentry and nobility. The caps which form part of the present Beefeater's uniform originate from the Tudor period.

Night caps began to be worn during this century, not simply for bed, but for informal day or evening wear. Usually made of linen (which was often embroidered), they were close-fitting, conical caps with a close, turned-back brim. Night caps continued to be fashionable in the following century [113].

Hats of the early seventeenth century were mostly tall-crowned, with fairly wide brims and decorative hatbands [24, 139]. Jewelled buckles were a popular form of decoration (in 1615, for example, Christian IV of Denmark sent his chamberlain three packets each containing diamond-and-ruby hatbands and two buckles – one mounted like an oakleaf, the other in the form of a leopard – for the three princes, with instructions to order the hatter to make a band of silk to fix them on[13]). The steeple-crowned hat was worn during the first half of the century [27, 57, 84]; it is often popularly associated with the Puritans, but they wore no form of special dress and it was only in the avoidance of extravagance that their clothes differed from contemporary fashionable styles.

There were several different types of hats to be seen during the period but generally speaking the crowns descended gradually and the brims widened, until the high, conical hat passed out of fashion altogether in the second half of the century. Very wide, soft brims were often cocked or

113 Phineas Pett by an unknown artist 1612 Night caps were usual for informal day or evening wear. They were often made of linen embroidered with coloured silks and metal thread.

turned up and fastened to the crown at the front or side [25, 114]; this allowed some variety in the manner of wearing the hat although it was primarily a practical measure. A cocked brim prevented the hat from being lifted by the wind when riding, and from getting in the way of the use of a sword. Plumes remained a favourite trimming and this style of hat is traditionally associated with the dress of the Royalists or Cavaliers in the English Civil War. By the 1690's wide brims were cocked on three sides of the hat and arranged to form an equilateral triangle (with a point to the front of the head). The plume was reduced to a fringe of feathers along the top edge of the brim (which was often bound with braid).

The finest quality hats were still made of beaver which had become synonymous with hats of this kind, but rabbit was also used (black rabbit skins were exported from England to France and Italy during the sixteenth

century to supply the industry manufacturing felt hats[14]). 'Castor' was a term which referred to hats either made of beaver or intended to be taken as such, but castors and demi-castors were probably inferior to beavers and made only of rabbit.

During the second half of the seventeenth century men's hair was worn longer and by the 1660's it was being replaced by the long periwig. In 1664, Pepys was convinced he had got a strange cold in his head by flinging off his hat at dinner and sitting with the wind in his neck,[15] which indicates that the practice of wearing a hat at meals was beginning to die out. By the last decades of the century the increasing emphasis on hair was undermining the status of the hat, which was less easy to wear with the tall-crowned, full-bottomed wig. In the century to follow, variety and attention was focussed more on men's hairdressing than on their head coverings.

114 Prince Rupert of the Rhine by Gerard van Honthorst *c* 1635
Very wide, soft brims were cocked (turned up) at the front or side.

The three-cornered hat, fashionable until the 1780's, had a low, round, hard crown with a wide brim evenly cocked [34]. The firm, neat and completely symmetrical nature of the hat was in keeping with the spirit of earlier eighteenth-century dress with its orderly, formal and essentially classical lines. It was often not worn, but simply carried under the arm, as a mark of good breeding. Beaver continued to be used for the best quality hats and was usually black or dark brown. Cream-coloured beaver could be worn but was uncommon. Richard Nash, the Master of Ceremonies in Bath during the first half of the eighteenth century, affected a white beaver to distinguish himself from the crowd – an eccentricity which was apparently applauded but not copied. For dress wear the button and loop fastening on the cocked brim [34] were decorative and the button was often a jewel. Brims could be edged with gold or silver braid or lace. There were slight variations in the width of the brim and the way in which it was cocked, and these styles were given names such as Nivernois, Kevenhuller or Dettingen. Hatbands were entirely obscured by the cocked brim and as a result disappeared from this form of hat.

An alternative form at the time was the round hat, with a round crown and wide, uncocked brim, which could be worn in the country and was generally adopted by professional men. This was probably the kind of hat worn by Parson Woodforde (he frequently mentions in his diary the black crepe or satin hatbands he was obliged to wear for funerals). During the 1770's the round hat became more fashionable and began to replace the three-cornered hat for riding [36]. In the last decades of the century the crown changed again, becoming taller and straighter with a narrower brim; by the 1790's the popularity of country clothes brought the conical hat into greater prominence, and it was adopted for fashionable town wear and was to develop into the top hat so characteristic of the nineteenth century [1].

For formal and Court wear in the later eighteenth century, the *chapeau bras*, a flattened three-cornered hat designed to be carried under the arm, was the correct accessory. In the daytime, the three-cornered hat gave way to the bicorne, that is a two-cornered hat simply turned up and flattened at the back and front.

Night caps became an important item of informal clothing during the eighteenth century. Wigs had been fashionable since the 1660's and it was usual for men to crop their own hair short or completely shave the head. A soft cap was worn in place of the wig before a man was formally dressed, or if he was relaxing at home in a nightgown (or morning gown) [115]. Night caps were often made to match the nightgown in materials such as wool or silk damask and velvet; unlike the conical cap of the seventeenth century they were generally fuller and more turban-like. When wigs were abandoned towards the end of the eighteenth century the night cap began to lose its purpose, and it passed out of fashion in the next century. It was eventually replaced, to some extent, by the smoking cap, after smoking became more common: it was usual for men to put on an informal jacket and cap in a room set aside for smoking or when the ladies retired after

dinner. It has been supposed that a smoking cap was worn to prevent the hair from smelling strongly of smoke but it may just have been a natural continuation of the old idea of wearing a cap with an informal gown. The cap was generally round and shaped like a pork pie, with a tassel on the crown (rather similar to a fez [**116**]). It provided considerable new scope for canvas work and embroidered decoration and many fashion journals of the period included patterns for smoking caps to be worked at home.

By the beginning of the nineteenth century the top hat was usually worn by day [**117**]. The two most fashionable forms were either a fairly tall, flat-topped crown with a moderately wide brim turned down at the back and the front, or a lower-crowned hat with a slightly broader brim gently

115 Captain Lord George Graham in his cabin (det) by William Hogarth *c* 1745 The wig was a feature of formal dress. It could be removed and replaced by a nightcap when relaxing indoors.

116 Smoking Saloon, Great Northern Railway 1879
The smoking cap was usually round and shaped like a pork pie with a tassel on the crown.

117 'Fashionable Full Dress and Fashionable Morning Riding Dress' in *Le Beau Monde* 1806
A crescent-shaped opera hat was correct for full dress wear. The top hat was worn by day.

curved up at each side. For full dress wear a semi-circular or crescent-shaped opera hat was worn. This hat folded flat and could be carried under the arm as a *chapeau bras* [**117**].

During the century there were slight variations in the shape and size of the crown and brim of top hats. Crowns could have tapering, waisted or vertical sides and varied in height according to the fashion, while brims narrowed and widened and were curled gently or sharply at the sides. The fashionable shape of the 1820's was cylindrical with a slight widening at the top and a narrow, curved brim. In the 1830's the crown was tall, generally between seven and eight inches high; in the mid 1860's it was lowered to an average of about six inches, but went up again in the 1880's and down again in the 1890's. The top hat was correct day wear with the frock coat and morning coat and by the 1840's was worn at night with the dress coat. Variations in colour were permitted and black, grey, brown and beige were worn. Top hats could also be made of straw for the summer.

During the 1850's a change was made from beaver to silk, or what was called 'hatter's plush'; that is, a very fine silk shag was applied to the felt to give it a nap. Top hats made of hatter's plush continued to be called 'silk hats' in the twentieth century, and although the collapsible top hat for evening wear was covered with black corded silk it was referred to as an 'opera hat'. Both types were fragile and had to be handled carefully.

The crescent-shaped opera hat or *chapeau bras* began to be replaced by the crush opera hat in the later 1830's. The invention of a Frenchman, Gibus, in 1835, allowed the top hat to be folded flat by means of a spring in the crown; this form was used for dress wear and was especially useful at the opera or theatre where it was no longer in danger of being damaged in the crush, or under seats. The cocked hat remained in use only for ceremonial Court wear.

The growing uniformity and sombre colouring of men's dress during the nineteenth century can only have been accentuated by the widespread use of the black top hat. James Laver once compared the general shape and impression of a collection of top hats to a row of factory chimneys and when viewed in those terms they certainly seem to add to the mood of a new industrial age [**79**]. The stiff, uncompromising and almost unchanging shape of the silk hat imparts an air of formality – and a certain elegance – to men's clothes. Hats, like collars and shirt fronts in the later Victorian period, had to be stiff to be formal and respectable.

Lower-crowned, wider-brimmed and softer hats were worn for informal occasions or in the country, and these were normally made of felt or straw [**127**]. A low-crowned, broad-brimmed hat called a 'wideawake' was a popular style (so-called, asserted *Punch* in 1849, 'from the fact of its having no nap'[16]). Straw hats with straight brims, similar in shape to sailor's hats , were worn during the 1850's and later developed into the 'boater', a very stiff straw hat for informal wear with a round flat crown and moderately wide, straight brim. The boater was at first worn for sports and recreations such as tennis and boating but it became accepted for informal town wear with a lounge suit in the 1880's and was at the height of its popularity in the 1890's.

The bowler was introduced for informal wear in the 1860's and was a new form of hat, made of hard felt with a bowl-shaped crown and narrow, curled brim. In unison with the top hat, the crown of the bowler also rose in the 1880's (and came down likewise in the following decade). The bowler (which was known as a 'Derby' in the United States) was usually black but could be light brown for summer wear [**44**].

In the 1870's a hat with a dented crown and curved brim presented another fashionable style for less formal wear [**63**]. This could be made in hard or soft felt, or in straw. By the 1890's two variants of this general shape were known by the names of 'Homburg' and 'Trilby'. The homburg was made of stiff felt with a silk-bound brim; it was particularly favoured by the Prince of Wales. The trilby was similar but it was made in a softer felt and could have an unbound brim. The name Trilby originated from the title of George du Maurier's novel published in 1894; the book was immensely popular and 'trilby' was adopted as a name for several different articles (but has only survived in the form of the hat). In the 1880's, artists (such as Van Gogh) had worn a soft, wide-brimmed hat and it was from this that the fashionable trilby appears to have developed.

For strictly country or sporting wear, tweed or cloth caps could be worn and were sometimes made to match the lounge or Norfolk suit. One style of tweed cap had peaks at the front and back; another, the deerstalker, had ear-flaps which could be fastened under the chin or tied together over the crown. Nautical, peaked caps were taken up as an accessory to the reefer or yachting jacket. Peaked caps had appeared at the end of the eighteenth century, and became popular during the next (especially amongst

Scandinavian students); they were also adopted for standard wear by railway porters (illustrated, for example, in W.P. Frith's 'Railway Station' of 1862). The peak provided a useful eye-shade.[17] Men continued to wear hats for all outdoor occasions during the first half of the twentieth century although the more informal versions were increasingly preferred [118].

During the Edwardian period the top or silk hat remained the correct accessory to the frock or morning coat but was less usual for ordinary day wear as the lounge suit increased in popularity. The opera hat was worn with a dress suit or dinner jacket. The bowler was still usually black, but grey or fawn were also possible colours; the homburg and the trilby continued to be fashionable; and straw boaters and panama hats were worn during the summer. Cloth caps in various styles were confined to sports and country wear or for motoring (George Bernard Shaw, 'always old-fashioned in dress', wore 'a motoring cap of a style suited to the horseless carriages of the nineties' when he visited Russia in 1931[18]).

In the 1920's the black bowler began to replace the top hat for correct day or business wear; it could be worn with the black jacket and striped trousers or with a dark lounge suit [64]. Tweed suits for the country were usually accompanied by a soft felt hat, and tweed caps were usual for golf with a knickerbocker suit. In the mid 1920's when very wide trousers and a square, loosely-cut jacket were worn, a felt hat with a squarish crown was fashionable. Panama hats in fine straw, similar in shape to the soft felt hat, were worn with flannel trousers in summer as the boater passed out of fashion. By the 1950's the panama tended only to be worn by elderly or conservative men. In Barbara Pym's novel, *Excellent Women*, Mildred noticed that her vicar, Julian, had 'a rather new-looking panama hat', hanging in the hall. 'I had never seen him wearing it and it occurred to me that perhaps he bought it to keep until its ribbon became rusty with age and the straw itself a greyish yellow. My father had worn just such a hat and it always seemed to me to epitomise the wisdom of an old country clergyman.'[19]

By the 1930's the trilby had become the favourite shape of hat for ordinary day wear while the homburg and the bowler were regarded as rather more formal [118]. A black homburg could be worn with a dinner suit in the evening (although to be correct, a dress coat required an opera hat) and with a business suit by day. (This hat became popularly associated with Sir Anthony Eden.) Black hats were always worn with black footwear. A soft grey or brown felt hat could be worn with brown shoes and a lounge suit. Trilbys were available in various shades to harmonize with tweed suitings. The 'pork-pie', with a low, round dented crown, was another popular shape during the decade; the 'snap brim' was turned down at the front and up at the back. Crowns were a little higher and brims slightly broader than during the 1920's to balance the squarer shoulders of men's jackets and wider trouser legs.

The importance of the hat diminished considerably after the Second World War for both men and women, but there were still some occasions when men might want to wear one. With the narrower suit and tapered

Town hats are lighter

Homburg hats
21/- 25/- 30/-

Light weight
Sports hat (under 2oz)
Showerproof 17/6
Other qualities slightly
heavier 21/- 27/6

Tweed Fishing hat
14/6

Sports hats are weather-proof

Tweed caps
7/6 10/6 12/6

Silk hats
35/- 42/- 50/- 55/-

Rough finished
pork pie
12/6 21/- 25/-

Bowler hats
21/- 25/- 30/-

Soft hats
21/- 25/- 30/-

trousers of the 1950's a trimmer looking hat was fashionable, in the pork-pie, snap-brim style [65]. Homburgs were less popular and the bowler was mostly confined to business or formal town wear. Top hats were worn with morning coats for formal or ceremonial occasions, weddings and the races. Informal hats and caps, especially for holiday and beach wear, were still being produced but many men preferred to go bareheaded whenever possible and it was no longer considered necessary to wear a hat to look respectable.

These general trends continued during the 1960's when hats were even more uncommon. There were attempts in the middle of the decade to revive the hat as a fashionable accessory – a high-crowned, broad-brimmed felt hat made a brief appearance and was to some extent made popular by the jazz musician George Melly – but essentially the hat was in decline and by 1970 it could no longer claim a significant place in any man's wardrobe.

118 Hats by Simpson (Piccadilly) Ltd 1938
Men wore hats for all outdoor occasions during the first half of this century.

CHAPTER ELEVEN

Shoes

Some sections of the human race have never found it necessary to adopt any kind of footwear, but men in the West have covered all or part of their feet since earliest times. The purpose of shoes is to protect the sole and the upper part of the foot from extremes of heat and cold, from wet and dirt, from rough ground and from dangers such as animal and insect bites.[1] The simplest means of doing this was either to fix an additional layer or sole under the foot (in the form of a sandal) or to enclose the foot in a bag of material (as a kind of moccasin). For climatic reasons, primitive sandals were generally developed in hot countries and the moccasin in colder, northern regions. At some point these two forms of footwear were combined and modified to produce what can be properly called a shoe: that is, a closed covering for the upper part of the foot attached to a separate sole.

The word 'shoe' can be used as a general term for footwear (and will be throughout this chapter) but a distinction can be made between the shoe and the boot. A boot covers a part of the leg as well as the foot, while the shoe covers only the foot.[2] At some periods overshoes (in the form of pattens or galoshes) have also been worn to protect both the feet and shoes from damp and dirt.

Apart from its protective function the shoe has served to complete or enhance male and female costume (sometimes contributing a very decorative effect) and has been used to indicate rank or office. As with other items of Western clothing shoes have altered with fashion; in the course of its history, the shoe has varied quite considerably in shape and appearance. The formation of the foot and the essentially functional nature of the shoe imposes some limitations on footwear design but the main features of sole, toe, heel and fastening can be adjusted to produce different effects.

The shape of the sole is probably the most striking feature of the shoe and the toe can range from a sharp point to a blunt square [**121, 124**]. The sole can also be elongated, beyond the natural length of the foot. The back part of the sole itself has altered very little, but at the very end of the sixteenth century it began to be raised and the heel came into general use. Since then, the shape and height of the shoe has varied considerably with the use of different forms of heels.

It is possible to make shoes and boots in such an easy-fitting style that they can be put on or pulled off without any means of loosening or tightening them (Wellington boots and women's court shoes, for example); but most footwear is more comfortable and adaptable with some type of fastening. Boots and shoes can be opened and closed by buttons, ties, laces, buckles or elasticated gussets. The appearance of the 'upper' will differ according to the method used and the fastenings themselves can be made to look decorative. Eighteenth-century shoe buckles, in particular, became ornaments in their own right and were designed to be worn more or less as pieces of jewellery. Shoes can, of course, be decorated in other ways: they can be made in different colours and the uppers patterned with punched or cut-out designs, embroidery or ribbons.

A number of materials – including grass, wood, rubber, cloth and silk – have been used to make shoes but the most usual has always been leather. Leather is undoubtedly the most suitable material and as long as animals are killed for their meat there will be a steady supply of hides. Skins were almost certainly the first material available to primitive man for clothing, once he had learned to convert the rawhide into leather by tanning. At first the hides were softened with oils and fats from the same animal but in time it was found that by steeping them in an infusion of oak-bark they could be prevented from putrefying. A refined version of the process of vegetable tanning is still in use today.

Leather has several qualities which recommend it as an almost ideal material for footwear. It is strong and durable, in varying degrees of weight and texture; it is flexible, making it comfortable to wear and walk in; and it is both elastic and plastic, that is, it can be moulded into any shape but is elastic enough to keep its general form. It is also permeable, allowing air and water or water-vapour to pass through its surface – a necessity for warm, perspiring feet – and it is a slow conductor of heat; in winter it retains the warmth inside the shoe and in summer repels it from the outside. From a decorative point of view, it has a range of natural textures and surfaces but it can also be dyed any colour and highly polished. It can be sewn and worked without difficulty and can be punched or cut out into fanciful patterns[3] [129].

The art of tanning leather and making shoes was developed to a high standard by an early date. Examples of excavated Roman footwear give evidence of skilled workmanship and suggest that there was more variety then in footwear styles for men than there has been during the twentieth century; and a Cordwainers' Guild was certainly in existence in England before the end of the thirteenth century.

The two most basic forms of shoe construction were the sandal and the moccasin. The sandal was essentially a sole held to the foot by thongs or straps, which passed over the toes or the instep or between the first and second toes (all similar to the types of sandals still worn today). The sandal protected the sole of the foot rather than the upper while the moccasin could do both. A piece of leather or other material was placed under the foot and drawn up and around it. It was either closed by a draw-string method or the upper material was cut away and a seam sewn at the centre front of the foot. The moccasin effectively covered the foot but having no separate sole it could not give further reinforcement to the base of the shoe.

The sole of a sandal could be made several layers deep and even studded with nails (as were the sandals worn by the Roman armies).

It seems likely that in the Romano-British period the two forms were combined to produce a kind of shoe which was both warm and sturdy, covering the upper part of the foot and providing a firm sole by sandwiching the moccasin between a sole and insole.[4] A second step was to alter the process: instead of the upper passing under the foot and being closed on top, the underpart was removed and the upper was joined along its lower edge to a sole. The upper was thonged or sewn to the sole over a wooden, foot-shaped mould called a last. At first it was attached inside out and the shoe then turned so that the seam faced inwards; this was the turnshoe method, which was used until the end of the fifteenth century when it was replaced by the welted construction. It was realized that the upper could be attached to the sole the right way out by introducing a welt, or narrow strip of leather, between the two layers; the welt was sewn to the lower edge of the upper and then the sole was stitched to the welt. A later variant of the welted method was the Veldtschoen (which is still in use for golf shoes and desert boots): the upper is stretched over the welt and stitched down flat on to it.

The usual method of attaching the sole to the upper has been stitching, with a firm waxed thread. Primitive shoes were originally thonged, with a leather thong threaded through holes in each section; but with the use of a needle the more satisfactory stitched seam could be made. The Romans used nails to rivet the layers of sole and upper together and much later, in the early nineteenth century, metal rivets were again used to construct heavy army boots. Since the end of the Second World War certain man-made materials have been developed and some modern shoes are attached by an adhesive of synthetic cement.

It is sometimes thought that shoes shaped to the right and left feet are a comparatively recent development and that 'straights' were always worn in the past. Straights were certainly worn in the early mediaeval period and were again universal in the seventeenth and eighteenth centuries but in the later Middle Ages shoe bottoms were made left and right and in the nineteenth century both types were worn. Straights are made symmetrical, to be worn on either foot, but regular use often moulds them to the shape of right and left foot.

The general appearance of the shoe is to a large extent governed by the purpose for which it is intended. Dress shoes are usually light and decorative while heavyweight high shoes or boots are used for outdoor wear and certain kinds of work. Until the nineteenth century, boots were more often worn by men than women, especially for riding and fighting. Shoes for indoor wear and particularly for dancing need to be light and flexible, not only for the comfort of the wearer but to safeguard carpets and floors. Francis Kilvert was understandably distressed in 1870 when 'after dinner the carpet was taken up in the drawing-room and there was a dance on the slippery dark oak floor which was sadly scratched and scored by the nailed boots of the gentlemen and some of the ladies'.[5] Hard, sturdy leathers are used for practical boots and shoes and the softer, finer grades for indoor or dress wear; uppers of silk, velvet and cloth (with light leather soles) may also be worn and are used for slippers. At some periods rank or status was indicated by the type or decoration of the footwear worn. Senators in Republican Rome, for instance, wore black shoes while magistrates wore red.[6] Shoes of the nobility in the early and later Middle Ages appear also to have been distinguished by shape and elaborate decoration. In the eighteenth century it was thought that a man's social position could be judged by the quality of his shoe buckles.[7]

Fashionable shoes bear a close relationship to the clothes with which they are worn and almost always contribute to the successful effect of the costume. The shape and appearance of the shoe is an important element in the fashionable silhouette and will usually reflect or complete the desired outline. Two obvious examples are the long pointed toes of the mid fifteenth century and the squat, square shoes of the Tudor period, with their respective emphasis on vertical and horizontal lines [15, 19]. The mediaeval pointed toe underlines the spiky appearance of male and female dress and seems to echo the Gothic taste in contemporary architecture for tall pinnacles and pointed arches. The solid, square and heavy look of men's dress in the early sixteenth century with its enormous padded shoulders, is nicely balanced and complemented by the flat, wide-toed shoes with geometrical slashed decoration. Rather more subtly, in the twentieth century, shoe shapes have altered in relation to the cut of the trouser leg: narrow, pointed shoes being worn with a narrow, cuffless trouser and blunter, broader toes with the wider, turned-up legs.

The Development of Footwear

During the Romano-British period there appear to have been many different styles of shoe giving the foot varying degrees of cover.[8] A light sandal – with a thong passed between the first and second toes and looped around the ankle – was worn indoors and for warm weather. This was usually made in soft leathers and bright colours. Of the more substantial shoes the three main types were the *caliga*, *calceus* and *gallica*.

The caliga was the military sandal worn by the Roman army on its arrival in Britain: it had a sole heavily reinforced with nails, it was attached to the foot by straps over the instep and it was laced up the front of the leg, to the calf, with leather thongs; the toes were exposed and the upper had a lattice-work appearance. It is probable that the caligae were standardized like modern army boots.[9] The calceus was a high shoe with a closed toe and it covered the foot with an upper of cloth or leather. It was the correct wear with the toga for Roman citizens and there were different forms of the shoe according to rank. The gallica was an alternative to the calceus, and gradually replaced it as formal rules governing dress was relaxed. It was a shoe of Gallic rather than Roman origin and was better suited to the climate of Northern Europe: it had a closed toe and a sole of several layers reinforced with nails.

119 Roman sandal,
Museum of London

Nails were a characteristic feature of Roman footwear and fulfilled a dual purpose. They were a means of firmly attaching the layers of sole to the upper and provided additional protection to the sole. Nailed soles were hard-wearing on marches and gave a grip similar to spiked climbing boots. As a rule the nails were set in decorative patterns on the sole. Bronze or iron nails were hammered in over an iron last which acted as a kind of anvil; when the point of the nail struck the last it curved over and the surface of the insole remained smooth, ensuring that no sharp points would dig into the foot.[10]

Most Roman shoes were rounded or foot-shaped but pointed toes were not unknown. There were no heels, but that part of the sole could be repaired or reinforced with additional layers of leather. The lattice-work uppers were cut by hand or stamped out but such elaborate shoes would have been expensive and were probably restricted to the rich. A wide range of colours, including gold, appears to have been worn and some shoes had iron or bronze buckles.

According to the ancient Greek historian Herodotus, in the fifth century B.C., styles in footwear varied with the climate and geography of different regions in Europe. The Romans imposed a degree of uniformity throughout the Empire but adapted their dress, when necessary, to local conditions. After the break-up of the Roman Empire regional styles developed; in Britain the closed shoe was re-adopted for standard wear and the use of nails discontinued.

During the early mediaeval period shoes followed the natural shape of the foot; they remained flat and were made as straights [4]. The usual form of shoe was closed, reaching to the ankle where it was fastened with a thong or lace, but lower-cut, slip-on shoes and boots were also worn [50]. The uppers were often stamped with decorative geometrical patterns and there was a high standard of craftsmanship. Shoes were constructed by the turnshoe method but by the end of the eleventh century the upper was being stitched to the sole by thread, rather than thonged with leather. Spanish or cordovan leather was being used increasingly by this time; it was a soft leather, usually black, red or tawny, and is the source for the term 'cordwain'. Ecclesiastical and ceremonial footwear, however, tended to be made of embroidered cloth and silks.

During the later Middle Ages shoes were made to fit the right and left feet and the pointed toe was fashionable for most of the period. A sharp point began to be worn in the 1090's and was described as a 'scorpion's tail'. (It has been suggested that the fashion was introduced from the East by Crusaders). The ankle shoe remained the general form for ordinary wear but there were calf-length boots (which were turned over at the top to reveal a lining of another colour) and low-cut shoes were worn with formal dress by the upper classes. Shoes could be lined with fur for warmth. Ankle shoes were usually slit at the sides or centre front and were fastened by thongs passing round the ankle or tied over the instep; but some had a strap and buckle.

In the twelfth century, shoes which were low at the front were cut high at the back, well up the heel, to give a securer fit. This distinctive shape was worn again in the mid fifteenth century. Sometimes hose were fitted with a leather sole and were worn without other footwear [8], a practice which continued until the middle of the fifteenth century. In the late fourteenth century the Italian merchant, Francesco Datini, listed amongst the accomplishments necessary for his daughter to acquire: to 'embroider in silk and cut out linen and woollen cloth and put soles to hose.'[11] Many different colours were worn, including green, blue and yellow, black, brown and red; purple and gilded leathers were used for ceremonial wear.

The point of the toe was elongated during the fourteenth century, exaggerating the lozenge-shaped appearance of the foot; because mediaeval shoes were flat and soft they tend, to the modern eye, to look more like stockinged feet and seem rather broad across the base of the toes [9]. The toe began to lengthen in the 1320's and remained long enough to be banned by sumptuary legislation in the 1360's. These toes were referred to as 'pikes' or 'crackowes' (supposedly because of the Polish origin of the fashion) and the toes were stuffed with wool or hay to preserve their shape. In the last decades of the fourteenth century toes were worn enormously long, with elaborate hose and the very short male tunic. Shoes during this century were also cut out in elaborately patterned uppers which Chaucer, amongst others, compared with finely-traced church windows. In the 'Miller's Tale' a parish clerk had:

...shoes cut out in tracery, as in use

In old St Paul's. The hose upon his feet

Showed scarlet through ...[12]

The cut-out work was now more common than the stamped patterns or applied embroidery. The Merchant, another of Chaucer's characters, had boots which were 'clasped' or buckled; a few button fastenings were also used on fourteenth-century footwear. Wooden pattens or galoshes came into use during the period to wear over the light-weight shoes, both indoors and out; these were made with wooden soles attached to the foot by a leather toe-band (examples may be seen in the Luttrell Psalter of c 1340–45).

120   Pattens 1434 (det of 83)

With the start of the fifteenth century piked toes passed out of fashion for a short time and an oval shape was preferred for several decades. During the 1430's and 1440's both rounded and pointed toes were worn; but by the middle of the century long toes had returned to full favour and they reached their most eccentric form in the 1460's when they were again subject to sumptuary legislation. Laws of 1463 and 1464 restricted the pikes, or 'poulaines' as they were now called, to a length of two inches. It has always been maintained that shoe-toes grew so long that it became the custom to fasten them up to the leg by a cord or chain just below the knee; but there is little or no positive evidence to support the idea and historians are inclined to doubt it.[13] Wooden pattens – fastened with a leather strap and buckle over the toes – continued to be worn and were made with long toes to support the fashionable length of shoe. A well-known illustration appears again, in van Eyck's portrait of Giovanni Arnolfini (1434) [120].

121   Late fifteenth-century pointed shoe, Museum of London

By the early 1470's pointed toes could hardly grow any longer [121]; once they had reached their limit, the fashion was dropped. By the end of the decade the new shape was a rounded toe, adopted in the Netherlands and most of Europe (although German fashions retained the points through the 1470's and 1480's). By the 1490's men's feet had a distinctly blunt appearance [17].

In the second half of the fifteenth century boots became generally more fashionable and could be worn to the thighs as well as (more usually) the calf. In the 1450's and 1460's the toes were long and pointed. The fashion in the last quarter of the century was for soft, close-fitting boots with rounded toes; the tops were turned down and were usually lined with another colour or had a scalloped edge [17]. These boots, worn with the skin-tight doublet and hose and a mantle loosely draped over one shoulder were subtly reminiscent of classical antiquity and contributed to the general effect of this fashionable image.

The shape of the early sixteenth-century toe can be seen as part of a complete reaction against the spiky silhouette of the mediaeval period [19]. The square-toed shoe complemented the new softness and immense bulk of fashionable male dress which induced a sturdy, almost swaggering stance. In place of length, shoes now pursued extreme width (and in time fell under the stricture of sumptuary legislation for this excess too). The rounded toe of the 1490's gradually flattened and broadened, becoming increasingly splayed until the 1540's when the fashion ended. At its widest the toe could measure up to six and a half inches across. As usual, the fashion was taken to a further extreme in the north than in the south of Europe (toes were less exaggeratedly square in Italy, for instance, during the 1530's). With the new geometrical shape many shoes could be made straights. The slip-on type of shoe continued to be cut high to the ankle but there were also lower-cut versions which required a strap over the instep with a buckle fastening or ribbon ties. The welted construction was adopted in favour of the turnshoe method by about 1500. The most popular form of ornament was to slash the upper in patterns of vertical, horizontal and diagonal cuts which added to the angular appearance of the shoe.

The 1540's saw a return to a more natural, rounded or almond-shaped foot until the end of the century [20]. Slashing remained in fashion and was very popular in the 1590's. In common with the fashion in clothes, favourite colours for shoes in the Tudor period were black, red and white. Black shoes were given further depth of colour and shine by the application of blacking, a thick, oily composition which contained lamp-black. White was often worn at Court (the Elizabethan song 'Greensleeves' mentions 'pumps as white as was the milk'). For formal wear, shoes were made with silk or velvet uppers which were slashed or embroidered. It appears that the reverse side of the leather (known as suede) began to be used at this period. Boots were not fashionably worn except for riding and travelling.

During the last quarter of the century the latchet fastening began to replace the slip-on type of shoe [23, 24]. The heel leathers developed straps which were brought across the front of the shoe and tied over the vamp or tongue. In the last decades of the century the sole of the shoe was thickened and a wedge-shaped formation lifted the heel at the back. At the very end of the 1590's a separate heel began to form as the sole curved up under the arch of the foot. Cork was used a great deal to thicken soles but some were raised by multiple layers of leather.

122   Shoe 1613 (det of 24)

The raised heel had made a general appearance by about 1600; at first it was low and rounded but it was to grow to a height of two or three inches, with a square base, made of leather or wood. Wedge heels of cork continued to be worn until the 1620's. Early seventeenth-century shoes opened up at the side seams and were made rather narrow under the arch; all shoes were made straights. The ribbon ties fastening the latchets over the tongue grew large enough to become decorative features in themselves and large bows or rosettes adorned the front of the shoe [122]. Shoe-roses could be edged with gold lace or spangles to give additional colour and sparkle to the shoe. By 1610 there was considerable emphasis on knees and feet, and both were given a ruffle or rosette ornament. Red heels came into fashion for court or dress wear and were worn until the middle of the eighteenth century.

During the middle of the century the boot predominated and from the 1620's to the 1660's was fashionable for both indoor and outdoor wear. At this period of warfare throughout Europe men's footwear was undoubtedly influenced by military dress, although boots could be made to look extremely decorative and elegant. Unless they were strictly practical, boots were worn in fine supple leathers to give an easy fit around the leg and fall into soft creases [25]; they were made long but were turned over below the knee, either in a double fold (down and then up) or in a cup or

123 Boots *c* 1639 (det of 26)

bucket shape over the calf. In the 1640's bucket tops became very wide and when turned down fell almost to the ankle. Heel spurs were attached to the foot by large, butterfly-shaped leathers which covered the instep [**123**]. Boots were also lined, with inner boot-hose of linen to protect the stockings from the rough or greasy surface of the leather. The tops of the boot-hose appeared above or were turned down over the boots and were usually trimmed with a border of lace or embroidery, which continued to focus attention on the knee. Boot-hose had been fashionable in the late sixteenth century and Stubbes, in his *Anatomy of Abuses* (1583), had written a satirically sour description of them:

> of the finest clothe that may be got, yea, fine enought to make any band, ruffe or shirte, needlefull to be worn; yet this is bad enough to weare next their greasie boots. And . . . they must be wrought all over from the gartering place upward, with needle worke, clogged with silke of all colours, with byrdes, foules beastes and antiques portraited all over sumptuous sorte.[14]

In the 1630's toes were squared rather than round and after the 1640's they tapered to a square toe; heels were worn high. Some shoes and boots were worn with an additional mule or patten in the form of a flat sole with a covered toe [**123**]. More functional heavy jack-boots for fighting were made in hard black leather.

With the end of the Civil War in England shoes returned to fashion for ordinary wear and boots were chiefly worn on horseback [**27**]. Toes were long, shallow and square-ended, the open sides closed up and the front vamp was cut high to the ankle. The large round shoe-roses were replaced by ribbon ties or stiff bows but by the 1660's these in turn were succeeded by buckles (Samuel Pepys first 'began to put on buckles to my shoes' on 22 January 1660). Small square or rectangular buckles of metal (usually silver) with spiked bars were used to secure the straps or latchets and became the distinctive feature of men's and women's shoes until the end of the eighteenth century [**30**]. In the second half of the seventeenth century most men's shoes were black leather but the tongue could be lined with a contrasting colour; in the 1690's the tongue was cut very high and could be

124 Late seventeenth-century shoe, Museum of London

turned over at the top to show the lining and a scalloped edge [137].

For most of the next century the shape and construction of men's shoes altered comparatively little and variety and effect depended on the buckle. These were produced with care and imagination and a standard of craftsmanship usually reserved for jewellery (many silversmiths and jewellers announced on their trade cards that they were specialists in buckle-making[15]). Unlike modern buckles they were completely removable and interchangeable with any pair of shoes and could be lent, borrowed or given as presents to other people. In Richardson's novel, *Pamela* (1740–41), for example, the heroine's father arrives without suitable clothes for her wedding but the bridegroom, Mr B., lends him all he needs and 'he was then pleased to give him the silver buckles out of his own shoes'.[16]

With the changing fashions in men's dress it was the size and appearance of the buckle that altered more rapidly than the shoe itself. Until the 1720's the buckle was small, rectangular and fairly plain; after the first quarter of the century buckle-frames gradually became larger [125] until in the 1770's they reached a maximum size; they were then made square, oblong and oval [36]. Frames grew smaller again from the 1770's until the 1790's when they passed out of fashion altogether. Most buckles were made of silver, but Sheffield plate, steel and pinchbeck were amongst other materials also used and all these could be finely wrought and worked. After the 1740's, when buckles were growing larger, they could be set with stones, paste or marcasite; by the 1750's this was being done in an increasingly flamboyant manner. For mourning dress buckles were japanned black or set with faceted jet.

The shape of the shoe was gradually modified during the century. After the 1720's the square, blocked toe fashionable since the end of the previous century was abandoned in favour of a natural rounded shape. The long tongues which had risen high over the ankle were cut much lower and the corners were rounded off. Heels were also reduced to a height of about one inch in the second half of the century and became virtually flat in the 1790's. After the 1750's the uppers were not cut so high over the instep and the quarters lengthened to shift the buckle nearer the toe (so that by the end of the century the shoe began to resemble a low-cut slipper). The mid-eighteenth-century shoe was much lighter and more graceful in appearance than the heavy baroque shape of the early decades and fashionable young men (such as the Viscount in Hogarth's series of paintings, 'Marriage à la Mode' – *c* 1743) wore quite pointed toes [33]. Shoes continued to be made almost exclusively of black Spanish leather and red heels were worn with formal dress.

Until the last two decades of the century boots were not fashionably worn indoors or for town, although the rules of polite society were not always observed in the country. In Bath, for instance, Richard Nash, the Master of Ceremonies, had to work hard to prevent local squires attending balls and evening assemblies in riding boots. After the 1780's, however, boots of several types became acceptable and popular with fashionable

125 Buckled shoes *c* 1733 (det of 95)

dress and by the 1790's riding and military boots were worn everywhere. The top boot, for riding, with its buff-coloured, turned-over top, was adopted for day wear with the riding coat and breeches, in the new vogue for country clothes. Military styles were also introduced for civilians: the Hessian, for example, was a short riding boot worn with pantaloons; it curved up to the knee at the front and was finished at the top with a tassel [61]. Unlike the soft, creased seventeenth-century boots, hessians and top boots were worn closely fitting with skin-tight breeches and pantaloons to give a smooth effect.

At the same moment, shoe buckles fell into disuse and, once trousers were adopted in the early nineteenth century, they never returned to general wear. Shoe buckles and laced wrist-ruffles were two features of eighteenth-century male attire which had been particularly indicative of social status; but the idea of such distinctions lost favour in the last decade of the century with the rising tide of republican sentiment, and attempts were made to introduce greater simplicity and equality (or democracy) into clothing. This encouraged the adoption of country or working styles of dress; at the same time the military influence was felt with almost the whole of Europe at war.

In the first two decades of the nineteenth century top boots, hessians, hussar boots or buskins, Wellington boots and half-boots (or Bluchers) were all worn. Both hessians and hussar boots were cut lower at the back of the knee than in front, to allow the leg to bend freely, and both were worn with pantaloons. Hussar boots were similar to short hessians but had no decorative tassel. In 1817 the Wellington boot was introduced [126]; like the top boot it was knee-high with a straight top but it was not turned over or finished with a tassel. This basic shape has continued into modern footwear although the rubber version was not in common use until the beginning of the present century. Half-boots, or Bluchers (named after another military commander), fastened at the front with a tie over the tongue. Boot toes were rounded and heels were low and square. All these styles remained in general use, especially for walking, until the 1830's when half-boots were more usually preferred; long boots were gradually relegated to the hunting field and after the middle of the century were rarely worn other than for sport.

Shoes were eclipsed by the popularity of boots in the late eighteenth century and once buckles were left off they assumed a much plainer appearance. Shoes were still fastened by latchets over a tongue but were tied instead of buckled [39]; however, low-cut buckled shoes or pumps were worn for Court or dress wear, with knee-breeches. Dress shoes were low-heeled and had round toes. Boots were more commonly worn than shoes throughout the nineteenth century and for day wear were considered to be the more formal of the two.

Several different styles of half-boot were fashionable during the Victorian period. In 1837 the elastic-sided boot appeared, mainly as a result of the experiments made with India rubber cloth (see Chapter 7). Gussets of elasticated material were inserted at each side of the boot which required no

other fastening. These boots were popular but laced and buttoned styles were also fashionable: apart from Bluchers there were Alberts (cloth topped boots with side lacing), button boots (from the 1830's onwards) and Balmorals (which laced at the front [128]). Men's half-boots were similar to those worn by women. Metal eyelets, which made lacing considerably more practicable, were patented in 1823 [127].

Apart from the different methods of fastening, there was variety in the materials used for uppers. Leather was combined with cloth tops and in the later part of the century plain, suede and patent leathers were worn. Black continued to be the usual colour until the last decades of the century, when brown began to be worn as an alternative for day wear, but it was

126 Wellington Boot 1817 A knee-high boot with a straight top. The rubber version was not in common use until the beginning of this century.

127 'Measuring for the Wedding Ring' (det) by W. H. Simmond 1855 Metal eyelets were patented in 1823 and made lacing for boots and shoes more practicable.

considered to be extremely informal and only really permissible with a lounge suit, in the country.

The shape of boots and shoes was changing gradually. By the 1830's the rounded or slightly pointed toe was made square but the shoe remained long and narrow. Until the 1860's, when there was a return to a wider, rounder shoe, men's feet were obviously intended to appear as neat and small as possible (fashion plates depict them as dainty and mice-like as women's were thought to be [62]). In the 1880's a blunt point was fashionable for both men and women and the rather long, narrow shoe was worn until the end of the century.

Shoes were worn during the century for informal and sports wear and, perhaps, on occasion had the advantage over boots. Beatrix Potter, for example, was sharply observant of untidiness in dress and wrote an unfavourable report of John Ruskin in her diary for 1884: 'one of the most ridiculous figures I have seen ... He had on high boots, and one of his trousers was tucked up on the top of one. He became aware of this halfway round the room, and stood on one leg to put it right, but in so doing hitched up the other trouser worse than the first one had been.'[17]

Low-heeled pumps were still worn for full dress and for dancing. The undress shoe was tied with latchets until the late 1840's when lacing up the front appeared, and button fastenings were introduced in the 1860's. In the last quarter of the century the two most usual styles of front-laced shoe were the Derby and the Oxonian, or Oxford. The distinction lay in the construction of the two: whereas the Derby had the quarters and facings (which carried the eyelet holes) stitched to the vamp, the Oxford, in reverse, had the vamp stitched over the quarters and facings.

In the country, extra protection from dirt or rain was provided by cloth or leather gaiters which buttoned up the leg. Short gaiters, or spats, which covered the ankles were fashionable for town wear from the 1870's; they were sometimes made of the same cloth as the trousers but more usually were of light grey or fawn box-cloth or canvas, buttoned at the side and fastening under the instep with a buckle and strap [43]. Overshoes or galoshes of rubber were available for bad weather and outdoor wear and after the 1830's soles of India rubber began to be used for boots (in 1874 Francis Kilvert bought a pair of 'ten shilling gutta-percha-soled elastic boots' from Decks of Salisbury[18]).

From the middle of the century onwards, with the invention of the sewing machine, footwear could be mass-produced. By the end of the 1850's a machine to close the seams had come into general use; the firm of C. & J. Clark, for instance, bought three treadle machines in 1856 and in 1858 also imported from America machines for cutting soles.[19] Leading shoemaking towns over the country were quick to introduce equipment of this kind although it met with considerable opposition in its early years. Greater numbers of cheaper lines in footwear became available but most men who could afford it still preferred to have their boots and shoes made by hand.

In the first decade and a half of the present century styles in men's footwear remained similar to those fashionable in the late 1890's. Until the outbreak of the First World War, black boots in light kid or patent leather were correct for dress wear [128]; slightly heavier boots were made of calf and there were some cloth tops in buff or grey. Brown or tan was increasingly worn with lounge suits and at the end of the Edwardian period shoes were becoming more popular. Both laced and buttoned boots and shoes were in use but the less convenient button fastening was losing favour. The prevailing fashionable line was long, with a spade-shaped toe: here follows perhaps one of the most delightful recorded descriptions of a man's feet, and it exemplifies the ideal of this period. The Duke of Dorset, in Max Beerbohm's *Zuleika Dobson* (1911), was every inch an aristocrat and a dandy: 'the ducal feet were beautiful on the white bearskin hearth rug. So slim and long were they, of instep so nobly arched, that only with a pair of glazed ox-tongues on a breakfast-table were they comparable.'[20]

Shoes worn for sport or the country were blunter-toed and after about 1910 the toe-cap bulged upwards. A popular form of decoration,

128 Advertisement for boots 1901
Cloth-topped boot with front lacing. Men's boots were similar to those worn by women.

brogueing, involved punching the upper with a pattern of small holes and double-stitching the seams. Brogues with fringed tongues became a favourite shoe for golf in the 1920's.

The 1914–18 war encouraged the adoption of more comfortable, practical footwear and the round toe replaced the narrow point. Only the more elderly and conservative men continued to wear boots in post-war years, while lace-up shoes came into increasing use as the lounge suit replaced the frock and morning coats. Plain black calf or brogues in the Oxford style were worn in town [133] and brown in the country for informal dress; spats were still considered correct with a morning coat but were worn far less in the 1920's and became virtually obsolete by the 1930's. For summer and sports – especially tennis and cricket – shoes were made of white buckskin (and were usually worn with white flannel trousers). During the 1920's two-toned shoes (later called 'co-respondents') – either white and tan or white and black (the toe-cap, saddle-strap or vamp made in the contrasting colour) – were also fashionable for sports wear and they became even more popular in the 1930's (although they were not universally considered to be in the best of taste [129]). Suede, or 'reversed calf', was another type of shoe thought to be somewhat extrovert, in fact, 'a totally reliable sign of a cad'.[21] The Prince of Wales, who was fond of both, caused a sensation in 1924 by wearing suede shoes to America and was told that it was thought to be a mark of great effeminacy.[22] Suede became gradually more acceptable and was widely advertised in catalogues of the 1930's but it was usually confined to less formal dress. In 1956 Harrods could advertise evening shoes (to be worn with a dinner jacket) in black suede, but this was not a common fashion.

Patent leather retained its popularity for evening and formal dress wear [69, 90]. Low-cut dancing pumps trimmed with a flat silk bow and worn with the dress coat were generally less common after the end of the First World War, but plain laced shoes in black patent leather were correct with the morning coat, dress and dinner suits. By the late 1930's the fully-laced shoe (that is, with six pairs of eyelet holes) was the accepted version for formal dress, but a shoe with two ties could be more informally worn with a dinner jacket. In the 1960's patent leather was still correct for formal evening wear (Harrods advertised the two-tie shoe in 1961, elastic-sided shoes in 1964 and even the elastic-sided Chelsea boot in 1963, all in black patent) but plain leather was increasingly worn as an acceptable alternative. In 1969 'wet-look' patent leather or man-made material became fashionable for casual, day shoes, with a gilt trim on the instep. The narrator in John Braine's novel, *Queen of the Distant Country* (1972) describes a typical informal outfit chosen by a smart young man at this time: 'a light blue Crimplene jacket in check, a pair of navy blue slacks, a pair of yellow socks, a yellow nylon polo-neck sweater and a pair of black Bally wet-look casuals.'[23]

The Oxford shoe, with or without brogueing, was the style most commonly worn by men in the 1930's but the 'monk' shoe, with a plain vamp and buckle and strap fastening over the instep, provided some

129 Shoes by Simpson (Piccadilly) Ltd 1938 Brogued and two-toned shoes were popular between the wars.

How many pairs should you have?

As with your suits, so with your shoes—the more you have the lower the cost in the long run. Remember, too, that nothing is so expensive as cheap shoes. Here, then, are sensible suggestions for the average man. Monks and reversed calf are, of course, not essential—but are increasing in popularity.

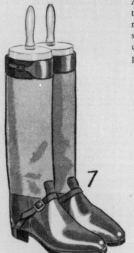

1 Oxford shoe. Black or brown calf and brown reverse calf. 30/-, 35/-, 42/- Hand-made 75/-
2 Semi-Brogue in black, brown, or brown reverse calf. 35/-, 42/- Hand-made 75/-
3 Also in full brogue.
4 Brown and white Semi-Brogue. Brown willow calf combined with white buckskin. 35/-, 42/-, 50/- Hand-made 75/-
5 Monk shoes. Willow calf, leather lined through to toe. Black, brown and reverse calf. 35/- and 50/- Bench-made 70/-
6 Waterproof Calf Veldtschoen Golf Shoe. Sole, ⅜" thick, waterproof and suitably spiked for a true stance. 25/-
7 Newmarket boot. Willow calf golosh, with fawn waterproof canvas leg. 84/-
8 Tibet Monastery Sandal. Natural coloured cowhide. 21/-
9 Heavyweight Willow calf for walking. Thick crêpe sole and heel. Repairable. Also for golf. 30/-

variety [**129**]. In the mid 1930's Americans adopted the Norwegian-model shoe for informal wear – a slip-on, moccasin type of shoe with an apron vamp, a version of the peasant shoe made by fishermen – and it was adapted for use in England as a golf shoe with a moulded rubber sole. Fabric shoes and leather sandals (some with crepe soles) were also introduced for summer wear. In the late 1930's the chukka or desert boot – an ankle shoe with a two-tie fastening – began to be worn; it was to become a popular casual shoe in following decades.

Men's shoes in the 1930's and 1940's were heavier in shape and character to balance the wider trouser leg. When trousers became narrower in the early 1950's fashionable shoes altered correspondingly: the very tight, rather short 'drainpipe' trousers were accompanied by narrow, sharply pointed 'winklepicker' shoes. A few years before these 'Italian' shoes were introduced, the Teddy Boys were wearing large, boat-shaped shoes or 'creepers' with thick crepe soles. A more conservative new shoe in the 1950's was the casual slip-on. The laced shoe was still worn but a more informal version (in plain or reversed calf) had only three ties.

The elastic-sided shoe became very popular in the 1960's [**65**] but a more novel idea was the re-introduction of the ankle boot with elastic gussets. The 'Chelsea' boot was being advertised by Harrods as early as 1961: it was 'styled for the tapered trouser' the firm announced, and went on to say that, 'this elegant boot has sprung sides and uppers of finest box calf.' In the following year the Beatles made their first hit record and immediately became fashionable figures. Their clothes were not original but they were extremely influential and caused, above all, the widespread popularity of the collarless jacket and the Chelsea boot with a high cuban heel. By the mid 1960's blunt or squared toes were the preferred shape and heels were raised to provide a suitable shoe to wear with the new flared trousers.

During the Second World War composition soles had been introduced in an attempt to conserve leather and during the 1950's attention was turned to using man-made materials for footwear as well as for other clothing. 'Corfam' for example appeared in 1963 and proved to be a successful substitute for leather.

CHAPTER TWELVE

Other Accessories

An accessory to dress is an extra item which may be either worn or carried, the function of which is to complete or adorn a man's or woman's costume. As an addition to the basic garments it can be both useful and decorative. Many accessories were purely functional originally, and only later put to fashionable use. The walking stick, for example, was a practical aid for the mediaeval traveller, but in the fifteenth century it began to be carried with ordinary dress, and by the eighteenth century it had become a feature of a gentleman's wardrobe. Sticks and swords, although fashionably worn, were essentially protective weapons; some accessories such as gloves and umbrellas, were used as a guard against the weather; belts and sashes or bags and purses were intended to support or transport objects; and many items of jewellery which would appear to have been ornamental fulfilled a purpose such as fastening or securing the clothes.

Once adopted for general wear, dress accessories can play an important part in the overall effect of a costume, contributing to the shape of the fashionable silhouette and the decorative nature of the clothes. Belts can affect the fit of a garment and emphasize the waist or hips. Accessories have been used to add novelty to a costume (without altering the garments themselves) and to distinguish formal from informal dress. Hats and gloves, in particular, became significant items, considered necessary to complete a formal suit of clothes. Jewellery was a conspicuous means of displaying wealth and could make a garment appear rich and splendid.

Apart from adorning a costume, an accessory might be an instrument in the fashionable gestures or deportment of a certain period. Swords, sticks and snuff boxes of the eighteenth century were especially important in this way. A man of fashion or breeding knew how to handle these objects with grace and style and they could draw attention to his hands, the whiteness of his skin, his sparkling jewels and the lace of his ruffles [134]. These accessories to dress were generally associated with the gentleman. In the nineteenth century they were replaced by the walking stick or cane and the monocle. Joseph Chamberlain, for instance, 'was immensely dapper. His clothes were perfect, he always wore an orchid in his button-hole and a gold-rimmed monocle in his eye. Disraeli once likened him to "the cad of the omnibus", but had to admit that "he wore his monocle like a gentleman"'.[1] The Frenchman, Charles Haas, in Tissot's painting of the Jockey Club in Paris (1868), was described as 'tall and svelte, wise, sad and arrogant; he cocks his walking-cane on his right shoulder; he lolls astride in the French window of the balcony, ineffably elegant in grey top-hat and striped trousers'.[2]

Rules of social etiquette have also involved the use of dress accessories; not only has it been considered more formal and polite to don extra garments, such as coverings for the head and hands, but it is a mark of courtesy or respect to remove them in the presence of particular people or buildings. At some periods, hats and gloves have been merely carried in the hand and were not intended to fulfill a useful purpose.

A number of accessories came to be recognized as a distinguishing mark or badge. In early periods gloves were worn only by men of rank or royal blood; in the seventeenth century the sash or scarf draped diagonally across the chest was a distinctive feature of military dress [28]; in the nineteenth century the umbrella habitually carried by Louis Philippe of France was considered to be degradingly bourgeois.

Several important male accessories such as neckties, hats and shoes have been discussed already; in this chapter, additional items, including belts and sashes, bags and purses, swords, walking sticks, umbrellas, snuff boxes, smoking accessories and jewellery will be mentioned.

Belts, Sashes and Scarves

The belt is probably one of the oldest accessories; it is known to have been worn since the Bronze Age[3] and seems to have had considerable mystical significance in the mediaeval period when it was associated with potency and strength (in *Sir Gawain and the Green Knight* a girdle was believed to possess magical properties and was worn by Sir Gawain to safeguard his life); it has sometimes had other connotations. By the fourteenth century, elaborately wrought belts worn low around the hips had become the badge of the knight [130]; these were usually made of square plates of precious metal linked over a base of leather and they could be finely ornamented with chased work, stones or enamel. It seems likely that these belts were attached in some way to the garment since it would have been difficult otherwise to keep them in place. The knightly belt was similar to but not identical with the sword belt which was worn either about the waist or passed over one shoulder. Both types of belt were a feature of military dress.

Belts were also worn by civilians during the Middle Ages and were an important element in fashionable dress. When clothes became closer fitting the belt served to emphasize the waist; in the fifteenth century, with the fashion for longer, looser and heavier garments, the belt relieved the shoulders of some of the weight which, with a lining entirely of fur, could be considerable [14]. By this period the belt was recognized as a mark of rank or respectability; for a man to be deprived of his belt was considered degrading.[4] The belt was used to enhance the general appearance of a man's costume and was often decorative and expensive; it served also to carry a purse, pouch or money-bag in varying sizes, from at least the eleventh century onwards [10, 52]. There are frequent references to belts and purses in Italy in Boccaccio's *Decameron*: in one story a lady 'fastened a dainty and

beautiful little silver girdle round his waist, with a fine purse to go with it' and in another, a character was not pleased to be sent a belt and purse 'as though I didn't have enough belts and purses already'.[5] A dagger might be suspended from the girdle and it appears that gloves, when not in use, could be tucked into the waist. Belts were made of leather, silk or precious metals (sometimes set with jewels when intended to be ornamental).

It is often the case that one item of clothing is separated from another by a belt; when the doublet and hose became the principal male garments, a break was clearly indicated at the level of the waist. The fashionable silhouette of the later sixteenth century, for example, had a small, well-defined waist with swelling hips and 'peascod belly', all of which were enhanced by a belt [23]; but the line for the next two centuries was longer, narrower and smoother and had no need of a belt for this purpose [27, 30]. During this period, belts or girdles mostly only tied loose gowns or carried a sword.

As a fastening device the belt was not yet used for suspending or closing the trunk-hose or breeches; even in the nineteenth century belted trousers were generally worn only for sports. Trousers were originally supported by braces and waist belts were not a common fashion until the later 1920's when high-waisted, full-cut trousers began to be worn. Belts became a popular alternative to braces when the two-piece suit gained favour, for without the waistcoat the braces were exposed. During the 1960's belts were a fashionable accessory to male dress; they were worn just below the waist and were made wide, with large buckles.

The baldrick was a broad shoulder belt worn diagonally across the chest

130 Effigy of Sir Humphry Littlebury 1360 Elaborately-wrought belts were worn low on the hips in the later fourteenth century.

either as a decorative accessory, as in the mediaeval period, or more commonly, as a functional item of military dress [130] used (especially in the fifteenth and sixteenth centuries) to carry a horn, weapon, powder-flask or tinder and lead. Long, broad scarves or sashes of silk, either worn over one shoulder or around the waist became a feature of military costume during the second half of the sixteenth century and in the seventeenth century [28]. The military sash was a means of identification before uniform clothing was introduced for armed forces; colours could indicate allegiance or rank and orders or decorations were sometimes attached to it. It is thought that the modern cummerbund, originally worn with evening dress by British officers serving in India, may have been a continuation of the military waist sash.

During the nineteenth century large neckties or cravats were often referred to as scarves but the long scarf of knitted wool or silk with fringed ends was not a usual accessory until the present century. White silk scarves were worn with outdoor evening clothes – cloak or coat, top hat and cane – until the dress suit ceased to be fashionable after the Second World War. Coloured or striped woollen scarves were adopted for sports or country wear and in particular for motoring.

Gloves and Muffs

Gloves are an important accessory to dress, to protect the hands and complete a costume, but they have also, from an early date, had great symbolic significance. It is evident that at first they were worn only by men of high rank in the church or state; they were probably not in common use in England until the end of the twelfth century.

There is mention of gloves in the Anglo-Saxon period (for example in *Beowulf* [6]) but they appear not to have been articles of everyday wear; they were worn by royalty – kings were crowned and buried in elaborate gloves – and by bishops, from at least the sixth century. These gloves were expensive items made of fine leather or silk, embroidered or embellished with precious stones, and were possibly imported from the Continent. Until the thirteenth century there seems to have been little desire to use gloves for practical purposes and men and women protected their hands, when necessary, with long sleeves which reached over the fingers. A glove, therefore, was regarded as a significant object; it could be given to another man as a pledge of security or confidence, exchanged by lovers as a token of fidelity or flung down as a challenge or gesture of defiance. Often gloves were given as presents and it became the practice to give and wear them at funerals.

By the fourteenth century, gloves with gauntlet cuffs were worn by both sexes and all social classes, although the more elaborate, embroidered pairs were reserved for the nobility and were still considered a luxury; sturdy leather gloves were worn for sports such as hawking and archery. During the fifteenth century gloves became indispensable to the dress of the gentry [17] but it was in the following two centuries that they reached a high point

of design and decoration. Gloves usually were made of soft leathers such as sheep, doe or goat skins and the cuffs or gauntlets were lined with silk. By the second half of the sixteenth century fashionable gloves were worn with long, soft gauntlets trimmed with embroidery, lace or fringes of silk or gold and silver thread. The most ornamental gloves were carried rather than worn [24] and little distinction was made between the lengths of the fingers; the little finger was almost as long as the rest and the tips were stuffed to keep their shape.[7] Perfumed gloves, which had been known since the Middle Ages, became very popular (especially for present-giving) during the sixteenth and seventeenth centuries and were imported to England. Knitted gloves were made with the introduction of knitted hose; but leather continued to be the form for elegant wear.

During the seventeenth century gloves were available in a fairly wide range of leathers but doeskin was the most popular [25]; silk and worsteds were also used and linings were made of silk (sometimes velvet). Embroidery in coloured silks and metal threads, lace, fringes and ribbon trimmings remained in fashion and the gloves of the earlier decades were as rich as those of the Elizabethan period [131]. The gauntlet style prevailed, although less elaborate gloves with a small turned-back cuff could be worn. The gauntlet or long cuff was divided into stiffened tabs or sections which were individually embroidered and fringed. The cuff widened towards its base and was left open at the back. Plain gloves (for example in wash leather or dogskin) were made for ordinary or practical wear [26, 27].

Fashionable dress from the late seventeenth to the late eighteenth century had a direct effect on glove design. The laced sleeve-ruffles of the

131 English seventeenth-century gloves. Victoria and Albert Museum
Leather gloves with gauntlet cuffs of satin embroidered with coloured silks, metal thread and spangles.

132 Conquests of
Charlemagne by Tavernier
c 1460 (det of 15)
Although the purpose of a
bag or purse was mainly
functional, it was also
regarded as a decorative
accessory and was a feature of
the belt.

shirt and deep wide cuffs of the coat discouraged the use of heavily embroidered gauntlets [**30**]; there was no longer a need to wear elaborate gloves and the fanciful trimming was gradually toned down. Gloves became plain and were shorter in the cuff [**36**].

Plain cotton, silk, worsted or leather gloves were common wear throughout the nineteenth century. White or light-coloured silk or kid gloves were correct with evening dress and buff, yellow or pastel shades in a slightly heavier weight were usual by day (kid, dogskin and doeskin leathers and worsteds were fashionable).

During the first three decades of the present century gloves remained an essential item of both male and female dress [**64**]. They were worn with evening or town clothes, in the country and for motoring. The shape and material of the gloves varied according to their purpose. Coarse leathers (hogskin or pigskin) and knitted wool or string gloves (with leather palms) were usual for country and informal wear or very cold weather. Smoother leathers – mainly kid and chamois – were correct for formal day wear and in town; light colours were worn in the summer or on festive occasions, for weddings and the races, while darker shades were preferred for the autumn and winter. Evening dress required white gloves. By the time war broke out in 1939 gloves had become less popular and once peace was restored they were gradually abandoned for ordinary wear. During the 1950's and 1960's men wore gloves for practical reasons (for motoring and outdoor pursuits, and for keeping warm generally), or for very formal occasions, but as an accessory to dress they were no longer obligatory to complete an outfit.

Hands could also be kept warm by fur muffs which were used by men as an accessory to dress during the seventeenth and eighteenth centuries [**30**]. They were worn as early as 1600 but were more common after the Restoration. During November 1662, Pepys wrote in his diary: 'this Day I first did wear a muffe, being my wife's last year's muffe, and now I have bought her a new one this serves me very well.' They reached a large size in the 1680's and 1690's and could be suspended from the waist. They could still be seen during the eighteenth century but on the whole were regarded as an affectation, to be worn by beaux. By the early nineteenth century muffs were confined to female dress and passed entirely out of the male wardrobe.

Bags, Purses and Cases

Bags and purses are not usually associated with male costume. After the seventeenth century, certainly they were not common: in general men preferred to carry small items in their pockets and liked to have their hands free. During the Middle Ages, however, wallets or pouches of silk, cloth or leather were often attached to the belt or girdle. From at least the ninth and tenth centuries men carried money, writing materials or small, valuable objects in a bag at the shoulder or waist. The bags varied in size but were generally a little larger in the thirteenth century. At the end of the fourteenth, Chaucer's Franklin, for example, wore a dagger and a little purse of silk on his belt. Although the purpose of a bag or purse was mainly functional, it was also regarded as a decorative accessory and was a feature of the belt or girdle [**132**].

The practice continued during the sixteenth century and some purses could be elaborately embroidered and tasselled. By the next century small bags might be carried in a sleeve or in the breeches' pocket. The more fanciful purses were probably intended as decorative containers for presents of jewellery or sweetmeats; they were small, and either square, oblong or pointed.

In the later seventeenth century pockets became a more important feature of male dress and were included in the coat and waistcoat as well as the breeches. Small pockets in the waistband of the breeches carried a watch with a fob or seals and the larger pockets in the coat and waistcoat transported other objects such as coins, handkerchiefs, snuff boxes, spectacles or books. Most of the small items a man needed to carry about could be hung or attached to his clothes or put in a pocket and there was no need to use a separate bag for the purpose. In the nineteenth and early twentieth centuries men found their pockets quite adequate although containers of various kinds were used for coins, snuff, tobacco or visiting cards. The etiquette of leaving cards when making a social call was established in England by the seventeenth century and specially designed cases for carrying cards were a fashionable accessory. The cases were made of precious metals (which could be jewelled and monogrammed), ivory, mother-of-pearl, tortoiseshell and papier maché.[8]

There was a general male aversion to the carrying of bags except for travelling (with light hand-luggage such as the Gladstone bag of the later nineteenth century) or for professional reasons (a doctor, for instance, needed a case of his equipment). Papers and documents often had to be carried separately and by the 1920's it was acceptable for a businessman to transport these in a brief or attaché case [**133**].

From the later 1920's until the 1950's men's clothes were loosely cut and pockets were fairly capacious; when a slimmer line and closer fit returned to fashion, a problem arose. Even the smallest objects cause unsightly bulges in the pockets of tight clothes and, in the course of the 1960's, fashions made it necessary to introduce a handbag for men. Shoulder-bags or purses with wrist straps were designed, and although they were viewed with a certain amount of suspicion and hostility they began to have a small following; in holiday resorts, for example, they were found to be of use in carrying sun-glasses, cameras, papers and other essential items.

Snuff Boxes and Smoking Accessories

The habit of taking tobacco accounted for a number of different accessories from the seventeenth century onwards. The tobacco leaf was used in two ways: it was either ground to a fine powder and taken in the form of snuff, or it was smoked in a pipe (and later in cigars or cigarettes).

133 Grafton Fashions for Gentlemen 1926
Three-piece business suit with black bowler hat, rolled umbrella and attaché case.

Snuff (imported from South America) was used as early as the sixteenth century in Europe though originally only for medicinal purposes, to clear the head. In the following century it passed into fashionable use but in England the habit did not become common until the early years of the eighteenth century. The snuff was carefully prepared, blended and perfumed and it was thought necessary for a gentleman to develop a discerning taste (like a palate for wine); he was also expected to take the powder gracefully [134]. Snuff was carried in a small box and some men went so far as to use their own rasp or grater; a handkerchief, for dusting the clothes, face and hands was indispensable for most snuff takers.[9]

134 'The Marriage Contract' by Hogarth *c* 1743 (det of 33) A man of fashion handled his snuff box with grace and style.

The box was the most important feature of snuff taking and during the eighteenth century quantities of elaborately-wrought examples were produced [30, 134]. The finest were made of gold, silver and other metals, enamel, lacquer or tortoiseshell but plainer materials such as wood, bone, horn or ivory were also used. The boxes were a favourite present and could be collected in great numbers; Beau Nash, for example, was said to have had 365, a different one for each day of the year. 'In the year 1738', wrote Oliver Goldsmith, 'the Prince of Wales came to Bath, who presented Mr. Nash with a large gold enamelled snuff-box ... upon this some of the nobility thought it would be proper to give snuff-boxes too; they were quickly imitated by the middling gentry, and it soon became the fashion to give Mr. Nash snuff-boxes'.[10]

Snuff handkerchiefs were often dyed a light brown or printed in bright colours to disguise the stains. They were made of lawn, cambric or cotton and were intended to be plain and serviceable, but handkerchiefs decorated with popular scenes, events or slogans were produced in great quantities by the calico printers in the nineteenth century. After smoking became more usual in the 1860's these handkerchiefs were manufactured as souvenirs or commemorative items.[11]

Pipe smoking was introduced into England in the sixteenth century but it was overshadowed by snuff taking until the early nineteenth century when the habit began to wane. It now became more popular to smoke tobacco in a pipe or cigar [40] and by the 1850's cigarettes were fashionable. New accessories were produced in the second half of the nineteenth century and included cigar and cigarette cases (in morocco, calf, lizard or crocodile leather, gold and silver), cigar cutters, 'smokers' companions' and match boxes. Cigarette cases, petrol-filled lighters and cigarette holders made in expensive materials, mounted in precious metals and chased or monogrammed, were still made and given as presents in the twentieth century but after the Second World War they began to pass out of fashion. Cigarette cases and holders were used far less during the 1960's although pocket lighters fuelled by gas were popular with smokers.

Handkerchiefs

Apart from their use with snuff, handkerchiefs were carried by men and women from the mediaeval period onwards. Fashionable examples were made of fine white linen such as cambric, lawn or holland and could be embroidered and trimmed with lace; they were kept in a sleeve or pocket or in the hand [135]. More serviceable handkerchiefs, for actual use rather than display were made in coarser linens or cotton. Men of all classes could carry handkerchiefs; in 1783 for example, the philanthropist, Jonas Hanway, recommended that 'cheque handkerchiefs for the pocket, however small' should be distributed to all naval ratings because they were considered 'necessary for cleanliness'.[12]

In the nineteenth century handkerchiefs for the evening might be embroidered or edged with lace and scented; for less formal wear they were produced in coloured or patterned linens and cottons. When an outside breast-pocket was included on a lounge jacket it was possible to put a handkerchief in it and this became fashionable practice in the early decades of the present century. In time the handkerchief was carefully folded and arranged so that the corners were placed neatly and symmetrically at the top of the pocket. The touch of contrasting colour lightened the generally sober effect of the suit (until the 1960's when the fashion was discarded by younger men). The handkerchief carried in the breast-pocket was, however, purely decorative, and it was correct to keep the one for blowing the nose in the left sleeve (between the Wars the etiquette was never to put it in a pocket which might not be entirely clean).

135 Lord Darnley by Eworth 1563 (det of 21) Handkerchiefs were carried by men in a sleeve, a pocket or in the hand.

Swords

The sword is an exclusively masculine accessory. For centuries it was the distinguishing mark of a knight or a gentleman and it was worn with civilian dress until the later eighteenth century.

In the mediaeval period the sword was a feature of military clothing and was carried as a badge of knighthood [130]. It was suspended from a sword-belt fastened round the waist or across the chest. Civilians did not wear swords with ordinary dress but small daggers might be attached to the waist belt [10, 11].

Both swords and daggers were used increasingly in the sixteenth century and either could be carried with fashionable clothes. It became usual for gentlemen to master the art of these weapons as a social accomplishment. By the next century the dagger had passed out of ordinary use and a light, small sword (a 'Town', 'Court' or 'walking' sword) was adopted for everyday wear [30]. It was probably first employed in France and taken up in England after the Restoration. Pepys, for example, wrote in February 1661, 'this day I first begun to go forth in my coate and sword, as the manner now among gentlemen is.' Pepys' sword was apparently a fine one; in 1669 he went to the cutler's and 'there did give Tom, who was with me all day, a sword, cost me 12s. and a belt of my owne – and sent my own silver-hilt sword agilding against tomorrow.' His sword-belts also were carefully chosen and in 1668 he wore 'a shoulder-belt according to the new fashion' with his new stuff suit, and so, very handsome to church.'[13]

The sword was a necessary accoutrement for every gentleman in the eighteenth century and those designed for fashionable civilian use could be expensive and decorative [136]. However, when Tom Jones (in Henry Fielding's novel of that name, 1749) entered the army he had no sword and asked the serjeant to procure one for him: 'I will give you any reasonable price; nor do I insist upon its being silver-hilted, only a good blade, and such as may become a soldier's thigh.' The serjeant agrees that a silver-hilted sword does not become a soldier and finds him one which, 'tho' the blade might be composed of well-tempered steel, the handle was composed only of brass, and that none of the brightest.' Wearing this with a suit of coarse fustian, Jones was not taken to be much of a gentleman.[14]

Attempts were made during that century to suppress duelling by discouraging the wearing of swords. After the 1750's the fashion declined; the sword had in any case lost some of its importance with the introduction of the pistol as an alternative weapon of defence. In the nineteenth century it was worn only with ceremonial or service dress. A nephew of Jane Austen's was to write that 'old gentlemen who had survived the fashion of wearing swords were known to regret the disuse of that custom, because it put an end to one way of distinguishing those who had, from those who had not, been used to good society. To wear the sword easily was an art which, like swimming and skating, required to be learned in youth. Children could practise it easily with their toy swords.'[15]

Canes, Sticks and Umbrellas

The sword, as a decorative accessory to dress, was replaced by canes and sticks in the nineteenth century and their place in turn was taken by the umbrella in the twentieth.

A plain wooden staff with a handgrip was used by foot travellers in the Middle Ages and it was not until after the mid fifteenth century that the walking stick became a fashionable accessory [132]. Sticks of polished wood, or lightweight cane imported from the West Indies, were known in the sixteenth century but were not common before the first quarter of the next [25]. Walking sticks were made to look ornamental rather than functional: the finer quality woods were used and they were mounted in silver or silver gilt; sometimes precious stones were added, and it was usual for the late seventeenth-century examples to be trimmed with ribbons at the handle. Sticks made of ebony or white wood were known as 'walking sticks' while those of malacca or other types of cane were generally called 'canes'.[16] Very long and beribboned canes were, on the whole, only carried by fops or dandies.

During the first quarter of the eighteenth century a stick could be carried at the same time as a sword [137] and gradually replaced it as a badge of gentility. Slender canes were mounted in precious metals with heads or knobs of stone (marble, onyx, agate or jasper, for example), porcelain, ivory or amber. 'Clouded' or opaque amber handles were probably the most fashionable of all. Alexander Pope gives a telling description in *The Rape of the Lock* (1712–14) of:

Sir Plume, of Amber Snuff-box justly vain,
And the nice Conduct of a clouded Cane.[17]

136 Francis Beckford by Reynolds 1755-56 (det of 34) Swords were worn with civilian dress by gentlemen until the second half of the eighteenth century.

137 Louis XIV and his Heirs (det) by Largillière 1710 A walking stick or cane could be carried at the same time as a sword.

Canes continued to be trimmed with ribbons or tassels and were attached to the wrist with a loop of silk cord. A small box or pomander, to provide a sweet smell, could be fixed to the head of a stick. Holding the cane to the nose became a familiar gesture characteristic of the time, especially amongst men whose professions might not always be altogether savoury. Undertakers and doctors, for instance, are portrayed with this mannerism by Hogarth, and Christopher Anstey wrote of the physicians in Bath in 1766: 'thus they brush'd off, each his cane at his nose.'[18]

Canes and sticks remained fashionable throughout the nineteenth century and were always carried by gentlemen with formal day and evening dress [78, 87]. Ebony, polished blackthorn, bamboo and cane with decorative mounts, handles and tassels were the most usual. A famous portrait of the French Count Robert de Montesquiou by Boldini in 1897 showed the Count wearing blue porcelain cuff-links to match the handle of his walking cane. In the last two decades of the century, a tightly rolled umbrella might be substituted for a stick; but canes were popular until the outbreak of the First World War. The Army and Navy Stores, for example, advertised a large variety of sticks and canes in 1907. There were canes of rattan, partridge cane, malacca and bamboo; sticks of cherrywood, ebony, ash and oak, with silver or gilt mounts. Sticks designed specifically for walking were rather sturdier and had crook, staghorn, crutch or plain topped handles. After the war, with the increasing use of motor cars, sticks began to be abandoned but they lingered as an elegant accessory to evening dress (that is, top hat and tails) until the end of the 1930's [**64**].

The place of the stick was generally filled by the tightly furled umbrella. Umbrellas for men had been known since the late sixteenth century but they were not common until some 200 years later. (Thomas Coryate saw an umbrella for the first time in Italy in about 1607 and recorded the marvel in his *Crudities*[19]). It is evident that umbrellas were in use in England throughout the eighteenth century (Jonathan Swift mentions one carried by a sempstress in his *City Shower* of 1710[20]), but Jonas Hanway is usually credited with the introduction of the umbrella for men when he adopted his own in 1756. At that date the accessory was regarded as effeminate and ridiculous, but by the beginning of the nineteenth century it had become perfectly respectable. In Jane Austen's *Persuasion* (1818), Captain Wentworth tells Anne Elliot, '"though I came only yesterday, I have equipped myself properly for Bath already, you see," (pointing to a new umbrella)'.[21] In a town like Bath, which was small enough to go almost everywhere on foot, an umbrella was, of course, a convenient alternative to using a carriage or sedan chair for protection when it rained.

As nineteenth-century umbrellas were produced in cheaper materials and larger numbers their use became widespread. The early shape of the umbrella was not particularly elegant; it was bulky and clumsy with its whalebone frame and canopy of oiled cloth, and it was not until the introduction of fine steel spokes in 1852 that it was possible to fold the material into a long, slender line.[22] *Punch* cartoons of the later 1850's show both new and old styles being carried. Men were better disposed towards the umbrella once the narrow shape was achieved; when tightly rolled up, it could be made to resemble the more fashionable cane. By the 1880's an umbrella was often carried instead of a stick with day dress. The best quality umbrellas were made with silk canopies and fine wood handles but cheaper versions were available in cotton. The Reverend Francis Kilvert had his umbrella taken by mistake (to his advantage) in 1876: 'no sooner had Lady Hertford and her party gone than I found she had taken my umbrella and left me a much better one, a fine silk umbrella in place of my zenilla.'[23]

While the stick declined in the early decades of the present century, the umbrella gained favour and it became very popular after the Second World War, especially when carried with a formal lounge suit and bowler hat for town or business wear [**133**]. Although invaluable for bad weather in town, the umbrella was not correct, as a rule, for country walks; in *Noblesse Oblige* (1956) Christopher Sykes pointed out that 'to this day it is thought a fitting thing ... to wield an umbrella in the streets of London, but unspeakably un–U for the same man to wield it in country fields, unless he be a clergyman.'[24]

Jewellery

Men have adorned their clothes and bodies with precious stones and metals since the very earliest times. Until the second half of the sixteenth century, jewellery was worn in greater profusion by men than women [25] and it is only in the present century that the habit has almost disappeared.

Early forms of jewellery were both functional and decorative. Pins and brooches (*fibulae*) of precious metal were worn in pre-Christian times to fasten clothing and the brooch remained the common means of closing a mantle [4, 5]. Buckles and clasps were also used during the Middle Ages and girdles could be very ornamental [10, 11]. Bracelets and finger rings, which were purely decorative, were worn by men from a very early date. The use of jewellery and ornaments was, nevertheless, restricted to men of high rank, in the Middle Ages.

In the early mediaeval period it appears that jewellery was not worn in great quantities. The luxury of dress lay more in the quality of the textiles and furs – which could be very expensive – and clothes were decorated with embroidery. Precious stones and metals tended to be incorporated in the clothing (as part of the embroidery or sewn on to the garments in the form of bezants) rather than worn as separate articles of jewellery. By the later Middle Ages stones were available in larger numbers and the techniques of cutting and mounting had improved so that the emphasis began to shift. In the fourteenth century increasingly elaborate belts were worn (by the knighthood and the nobility) and badges, devices and pendants were fashionable. In particular, it was the practice of pilgrims to attach badges to their hats. The badges, usually representing the attribute of a saint, were produced in quantities at the places of pilgrimage and were bought and worn as a kind of souvenir (probably also assiduously collected). Amongst Chaucer's pilgrims, for example, the Yeoman wore a medal of St Christopher, in shining silver, on his breast, and the Pardoner had sewed a holy relic on his cap.

Badges or devices were also displayed on chains or collars. These were adopted as the insignia of knightly or charitable orders; the links of the chain or collar could be made in the shape of a device (most commonly the initials SS) and a pendant or badge was fixed to it. Elaborate collars were worn by royalty and the nobility for ceremonial occasions [17, 19, 139].

It was the custom for royalty or ambassadors of the Crown to distribute presents of jewellery amongst officials or servants. When Eleanor, the sister of Edward III, married the Count of Guelders in 1332, gifts were presented to her entourage and included brooches, buckles and belts (of silk of 'subtle work', 'powdered with pearls and mounted with silver gilt enamelled').[26] Until the seventeenth century gold chains were handed out as a standard reward for rendering the monarch a service.

During the fifteenth and sixteenth centuries pendants were important items of jewellery for both men and women. Many were designed with a devotional theme (such as the religious letters IHS) or personal initials or devices. Jewels in the shape of hearts or ships made from large stones or pearls were particularly popular. Some were worn around the neck on chains, silk cord or ribbon but others, in the form of badges or medallions, were fixed to hats and caps [139]. Hats also were decorated with aiglets, that

138 The Ambassadors by Holbein 1533 (det of 19) Badges of knightly orders were worn on chains or collars. In this example, the ambassador wears the French Order of St Michael.

is, tags or ties with tips of silver or gold. Lavish hat ornaments began to pass out of fashion in the second half of the sixteenth century.

In the later sixteenth century men began to wear fewer elaborate jewels and a profusion of ornament became more characteristic of women's dress.[27] Seventeenth-century male fashion was much more restrained in this respect although watches and rings continued to be worn and mourning jewellery was popular. Mourning or memorial rings, for example, were distributed amongst friends and relations at a funeral.

Pendant or fob seals and seals set in rings were worn increasingly during the seventeenth century. Seals bearing a coat of arms or other device had been in use since at least the fourteenth century (and were essential for business purposes) but they were not always small or portable enough to be carried on the person. If they were set into a finger ring or attached by a long chain to a watch and put in a pocket they might be kept safe and permanently available. After the Restoration a pair of seals were suspended from a chain or ribbon looped to the watch carried in a 'fob' pocket at the waistband of the breeches.[28] [37, 39, 61, 140]

During the eighteenth century the decorative emphasis of male fashion was placed more on the clothes than on jewellery. Garments were lavishly embroidered, woven or trimmed with metal threads which caught the light and provided much of the sparkle thought necessary for formal dress [60]. Gem stones were applied mainly to buttons and buckles: buttons (sometimes of diamonds) were worn in the hat or on the suit, and buckles fastened shoes, knee-breeches and stocks. Pins and brooches could be worn in the shirt front. In the last decades of the century fashionable dress was plainer and less formal, and country and casual clothes were preferred to stiff and elaborate dress suits; all things 'aristocratic' were carefully avoided (partly as a result of the revolution in France). The new taste in jewellery reflected these ideas: precious stones and metals gave way to cut steel and pinchbeck (imitation gold from a copper and zinc alloy).

At the opening of the nineteenth century men were wearing significantly less jewellery. Buckles, which had been so important during the previous century, were no longer used to fasten shoes, and as the stock was replaced by the cravat and knee-breeches by trousers, their original purpose disappeared. Men's dress was much more sombre and the taste for lavish decoration passed out of fashion. Jewellery still could be added to evening dress but was less conspicuous for daytime wear. Rings, cravat pins and watches were the most usual items; in the evening, pins and brooches, studs and cuff-links were added to the dress shirt.

Cravats or neckties were held in place by brooches or vertical pins of gold or silver with ornamental heads [40, 42, 141]. The pins might be headed with a pearl or precious stone, glass, enamel, cameo or miniature (and sporting motifs such as fox-masks were popular in the mid nineteenth century[29]). When Queen Victoria died in 1901 the Kaiser wore a tie-pin with his deceased grandmother's initials on it.[30]

The dark matt cloth used for men's evening clothes was lightened in the second half of the nineteenth century by a sparkle of gem stones in the studs

139 James I, attributed to J. de Critz c 1605 Jewelled pendants and medallions were fixed on hats or hung from gold chains.

140 'Morning Walking
Dress' in *Le Beau Monde* 1807
A pair of seals were
suspended from a chain
looped to the watch (which
was carried in a fob pocket at
the waistband of the
breeches).

and cuff-links of the dress shirt. They might also be made of gold and silver, pearls, mother-of-pearl and jet. After the dinner jacket was introduced separate sets of studs and links could be worn; the more elaborate with the white tie and tailcoat and less formal or more subdued versions with a black tie and dinner jacket.

Mourning jewellery, containing locks of hair or suitably inscribed with symbols, mottoes or initials, was worn by both men and women in the nineteenth century. Mr Wemmick in Charles Dickens' *Great Expectations* (1860–61) was partial to it and 'he appeared to have sustained a good many bereavements ; for, he wore at least four mourning rings, besides a brooch representing a lady and a weeping willow at a tomb with an urn on it. I noticed too that several rings and seals hung at his watch chain, as if he were quite laden with remembrances of departed friends.'[31]

A single, gold-rimmed eyeglass, or monocle, was another accessory to fashionable dress (until the outbreak of the First World War) [63]. A rimmed or rimless monocle was attached to a long black silk cord or ribbon round the neck. In the later nineteenth century in France, for example, the Prince de Sagan – 'generally considered the most consummate grand seigneur and arbiter of elegance of his time' – might be seen in the foyer of the Comédie Française 'in his velvet-collared greatcoat with white rose buttonhole, twirling his monocle on a sensationally broad black ribbon'.[32] Monocles became popularly associated with diplomats, army-officers and members of the upper-classes and often featured in caricatures of these types.

By the early twentieth century jewellery for men was restricted to a signet ring, cuff-links, studs and tie-pins [141] but as dress tended towards more informality even these became less frequently worn. Tie-pins or clips and collar bars (a gold bar pin which held the points of the collar down beneath the tie) were popular during the 1920's and 1930's but declined after the Second World War. In the 1950's and 1960's the dress suit was worn far less often, and ornamental studs and cuff-links were no longer compulsory for formal evening dress. Cuff-links could be worn with day

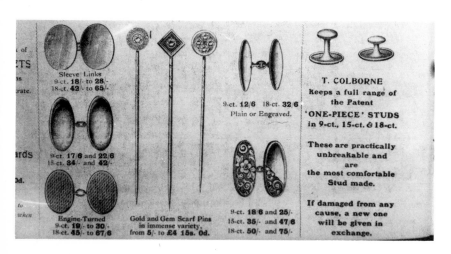

141   Jewellery by T. Colborne *c* 1910
Pins with ornamental heads kept the cravat, or scarf, in place. Cuff-links and studs were usual fastenings for shirts and collars.

clothes but the buttoned cuff became acceptable for ordinary use and was found to be much more practical.

During the 1950's and early 1960's men's jewellery was reduced to a minimum but it underwent a revival in the later 1960's when clothes were generally more colourful. Men began to wear chunky identity bracelets (similar to those worn during the war), fancy watch straps, gold and silver neck chains and medallions; wedding rings for men also became more usual. Many of these items were adopted by younger rather than older men and at the first they were seen only with informal dress. Chains and pendants, for instance, could not be worn with a tie and appeared with open-necked shirts and polo-necked sweaters.

Watches

Watches were made first in Germany at the end of the fifteenth century and came gradually into use; the early versions were spherical and were worn on a chain round the neck. They were amongst the most expensive and luxurious pieces of jewellery. They continued to be extremely popular and during the eighteenth century they were carried in a pocket at the waistband of the breeches.

During the nineteenth century the watch was carried in a waistcoat pocket and had a long curb chain with seals, fobs or trinkets attached (though more for the sake of ornament than utility). Pelham, the fictional dandy of the late 1820's, despised the watch: '*do* you think *I* could ever wear a watch? I know nothing so plebeian; what can any one, but a man of business, who had nine hours for his counting-house and one for his dinner, ever possibly want to know the time for? an assignation, you will say, true; but (here I played with my best ringlet) if a man is worth having he is surely worth waiting for!'[33] The man of business, however, was the backbone of Victorian society. A gold watch and chain was perhaps one of the best known symbols of his profession and status; they were acquired and worn with considerable pride (especially if presented as a reward for service or on retirement). The short watch-chain or 'Albert' was introduced in 1849; it passed through a buttonhole and was fixed by a hook or bar [63].

Wrist watches for men began to appear during the early years of the present century [142]. The idea of fixing a watch on a leather strap to the arm seems to have been encouraged by the popularity of cycling and motoring and by the rigours of the Boer and First World Wars.[34] Pocket watches were inconvenient when a man needed both hands free and could not delve beneath his overgarments for his waistcoat pockets. By 1907 the Army and Navy Stores were advertising wrist watches for sporting wear, but they were not generally accepted for ordinary use until the 1920's. The pocket watch was gradually abandoned although it was correct wear with a dress suit and formal dress until the second half of the century.

142 Advertisement for wrist watch 1910
Wrist watches were introduced for sporting and military wear at the beginning of this century.

Conclusion

Any work on the general history of fashion must be selective and it is inevitable that some interesting aspects must be left out. It has not been possible, within the scope of this book, to discuss details of regional or occupational dress and it has had to be confined to the development of fashionable styles. The subject of underclothing has been only briefly mentioned and so too has the dress for special occasions (such as weddings, funerals and for Court) but these are features which must be left to studies of a more detailed nature. There are references in each chapter to some of the most useful sources of further information and a general bibliography has been included at the end.

The items and aspects which have been discussed in this survey are those that seemed to be the most important. Many of the garments are difficult to sort out (there are endless variations in the male suit of clothes) but they have been put into categories for the sake of clarity and convenience. It is hoped that a discussion of different types of dress can provide a broader view of the whole sweep of men's fashions and enables the reader to relate earlier garments to modern clothes.

Fashion, of course, does not organize itself into such neat compartments; all these garments in reality belong together and ought to be considered as a whole. By turning back to the *Pictorial Survey* with which the book began fashion may perhaps be seen in its correct perspective. The fashionable image consists of both the man and his clothes – the way the garments are combined and how he chooses to display them.

Notes to the Text

INTRODUCTION

1 N. Waugh, *The Cut of Men's Clothes 1600–1900*, Faber, 1964, p. 35.

2 D. de Marly, 'King Charles II's own fashion: the theatrical origins of the English vest', in *Journal of the Warburg and Courtauld Institutes*, vol. XXXVII, 1974, pp. 378–382.

3 *The Tailor and Cutter*, London, 18 November 1897.

4 S. M. Newton, *Health, Art and Reason. Dress Reformers of the 19th Century*, John Murray, 1974, ch. 8.

5 *Observer Magazine*, 5 June 1977.

6 *The Ambassador* (British Export Magazine), London, no. 5, 1957.

7 D. de Marly 'Couture and Environment', in *The Times Literary Supplement*, 12 December 1975.

8 C. Baudelaire, *Le Peintre de la Vie Moderne* (Paris, 1860), trs. and ed. Jonathan Mayne, Phaidon, 1964, p. 2.

THE SUIT I

1 H. C. Broholm and M. Hald, *Costumes of the Bronze Age in Denmark*, Oxford University Press, 1940, ch. 5.

2 L. Wilson, *The Clothing of the Ancient Romans*, Johns Hopkins Press, Baltimore, 1938, ch. 1.

3 Broholm and Hald, op. cit., ch. 3.

4 See D. K. Burnham, *Cut My Cote*, Royal Ontario Museum, Toronto, 1973.

5 Broholm and Hald, loc. cit.

6 Burnham, op. cit.

7 Wilson, op. cit., ch. 5.

8 J. Liversidge, *Britain in the Roman Empire*, Routledge and Kegan Paul, 1968, ch. 6.

9 J. Evans, *Dress in Mediaeval France*, Oxford University Press, 1952, ch. 1.

10 ibid. See also C. Hawkins, 'A Fifteenth Century Pattern for "Chausses"', in *Costume*, no. 6, London, 1972, pp. 84–85.

11 Evans, loc. cit.

12 J. R. Planché, *History of British Costume*, Charles Knight, 1847, ch. 8.

13 J. L. Nevinson, 'Buttons and Buttonholes in the 14th century', in *Costume*, no. 11, London, 1977, pp. 38–44.

14 Evans, op. cit., ch. 2.

15 Paulin, ed., *Grandes Chroniques de France*, Paris, 1837, vol. V, pp. 462–63, and *The Brut Chronicle*, Early English Text Society, 1908, p. 296.

16 *Sir Gawain and the Green Knight*, trs. Brian Stone, 2nd edition, Penguin Classics, 1974, Fit I, 7 and 8.

17 M. Leloir, 'A Mediaeval Doublet', in *Apollo*, London, March 1936, pp. 157–160.

18 Evans, op. cit., ch. 3.

19 G. Chaucer, *The Canterbury Tales*, trs. Nevill Coghill, Penguin Classics, 1951, Prologue.

20 *Sir Gawain*, op. cit., Fit II, 36.

21 I. Origo, *The Merchant of Prato*, Cape, 1957, ch. 6.

22 E. Birbari, *Dress in Italian Painting 1460–1500*, John Murray, 1975, ch. 3.

23 C. W. and P. Cunnington, *Handbook of English Mediaeval Costume*, Faber, revised edition, 1973, p. 108.

24 R. Hakluyt, *Voyages and Discoveries*, 2nd edition, 1598–1600, Penguin Books, 1972, Glossary.

25 Birbari, op. cit., ch. 7.

26 ibid., ch. 3.

27 See J. Arnold, 'Decorative Features: Pinking, Snipping and Slashing', in *Costume*, no. 9, London, 1975, pp. 22–26.

28 See A. W. Murray, 'From Breeches to Sherryvallies', in *Waffen-und-Kostümkunde*, vol. XVI, 1974, pp. 87–106.

29 N. Waugh, op. cit., p. 14.

30 See J. L. Nevinson, 'A Gap Filled', in *Apollo*, London, August 1947, pp. 42–44.

31 *Life and Times of Anthony Wood, antiquary of Oxford, Described by Himself*, Oxford Historical Society, 5 vols, 1891–1900, vol. I, p. 509.

THE SUIT II

1 F. Moryson, *An Itinerary* (1617), Glasgow, 1907, vol. IV, pp. 217–238.

2 D. Cecil, *Max. A Biography*, Constable, 1964, p. 254.

3 G. D. Painter, *Marcel Proust*, Chatto and Windus, 1959, vol. I, p. 170.

4 See D. de Marly, 'King Charles II's Own Fashion: the theatrical origins of the English Vest', in *Journal of the Warburg and Courtauld Institutes*.

5 S. Pepys, *Diary*, ed. R. Latham and W. Matthews, Bell, 1970, entry for 4 November 1666.

6 R. Holme, *The Academy of Armory or, a Storhouse of Armory and Blazon*, Chester, 1688.

7 M. Davenport, *The Book of Costume*, Crown, New York, 1948, p. 653.

8 E. Green, 'John Wilkes and his visits to Bath', in *Proceedings of Bath Antiquarian Field Club*, Bath, 1905, vol. X, pp. 375–411.

9 J. Austen, *Sense and Sensibility*, 1811, vol. I, ch. 8.

10   See S. M. Newton, 'Costume in the Late Georgian Era', in *Britain in the 18th Century*, Treasures of the World Series, Macdonald and Jane's, 1970.

11   See A. W. Murray, 'From Breeches to Sherryvallies', in *Waffen-und-Kostümkunde*, vol. XVI, pp. 87–106.

12   E. Moers, *The Dandy*, Secker and Warburg, 1960, p. 221.

13   ibid., p. 99.

14   W. Collins, *The Woman in White*, London, 1859–60, 2nd Epoch, II and VI.

15   N. Waugh, op. cit., p. 114.

16   *The Tailor and Cutter*, London, 13 May 1897.

17   ibid., 20 May 1897.

18   ibid., 13 October 1898.

19   B. Potter, *Journal*, transcribed by Leslie Linder, Warne, 1966, entry for 4 February 1890.

20   F. Donaldson, *Edward VIII*, Weidenfeld and Nicolson, 1974, ch. 12.

21   F. Cowles, *Edward VII and his Circle*, Hamish Hamilton, 1956, ch. 7.

22   A. Bennett, *The Old Wives' Tale*, 1908, Book 4, ch. 1.

23   Cowles, op. cit., ch. 11.

24   Donaldson, op. cit., ch. 3.

25   Cecil, op. cit., p. 435.

26   J. Laver, *Concise History of Costume*, Thames and Hudson, 1969, ch. 9.

27   H. Acton, *Memoirs of an Aesthete*, Methuen, 1948, p. 118.

28   A. Powell, *The Military Philosophers* (*A Dance to the Music of Time*, vol. IX), Heinemann, 1968, ch. 3.

29   *Vogue*, April 1950, p. 108.

30   ibid., February 1961, p. 81.

31   N. Mitford, *Don't Tell Alfred*, Hamish Hamilton, 1960, chs. 9 and 17.

32   See N. Cohn, *Today There are No Gentlemen*, Weidenfeld and Nicolson, 1971, ch. 6.

33   See J. Dorner, *Fashion in the Forties and Fifties*, Ian Allan, 1975, p. 105.

34   *Men in Vogue*, November 1965, p. 58.

35   *The Ambassador* (British Export Magazine), 1961, no. 10, p. 42.

36   *Vogue*, 1 April 1969, p. 20.

THE SHIRT

1   See E. Birbari, op. cit., ch. 5.

2   S. M. Newton, *Renaissance Theatre Costume*, André Deutsch, 1975, ch. 4.

3   H. Fielding, *Tom Jones*, 1749, Book 1, ch. 3.

4   R. Herrick, 'Delight in Disorder', from *Hesperides* (1648), in the *Oxford Book of English Verse*, Oxford, 1900.

5   Cecil, op. cit., p. 425.

6   Q. Bell, *On Human Finery*, Hogarth Press, 1976, ch. 2.

7   Rev. J. Woodforde, *Diary of a Country Parson, 1758–1781*, ed. J. Beresford, Oxford University Press, 1924, entry for 9 October 1762.

8 Quoted in J. Laver, *Dandies*, Weidenfeld & Nicolson, 1968, p. 21.

9 Cecil, op. cit., p. 11.

10 C. W. and P. Cunnington, *The History of Underclothes*, Michael Joseph, 1951, ch. 8.

11 *The Workwoman's Guide, by a Lady*, London, 1838, 2nd edition revised and enlarged, 1840, ch. 6.

12 Cunnington, *The History of Underclothes*, ch. 3.

13 Burnham, op. cit., p. 9.

14 L. E. Tanner and J. L. Nevinson, 'On Some Later Funeral Effigies', in *Archaeologia*, vol. LXXXV, 1935, pp. 169–202.

15 A. Buck, *Victorian Costume and Costume Accessories*, Herbert Jenkins, 1961, ch. 19.

16 W. Blunt, *Cockerell*, Hamish Hamilton, 1964, p. 54.

17 Donaldson, op. cit., p. 44.

18 D. L. Sayers, *Gaudy Night*, Gollancz, 1935, chs. 13 and 17.

19 *Men in Vogue*, 15 March 1966, p. 95. *Vogue*, 15 March 1969, p. 133.

20 *Vogue*, July 1969, p. 17; June 1969, p. 26; January 1969, p. 7.

THE NECKTIE

1 Painter, op. cit., vol. I, ch. 9.

2 Blunt, op. cit., p. 34.

3 *The Tailor and Cutter,* London, 22 September 1898.

4 G. Etherege, *The Man of Mode*, 1676, Act I, scene i.

5 G. and W. Grossmith, *The Diary of a Nobody*, London, 1892, ch. 3.

6 J. Austen, *Emma*, 1816, vol. II, ch. 11.

7 *The Tailor and Cutter*, London, 22 September 1898.

8 ibid., 23 September 1897.

9 Donaldson, op. cit., ch. 3.

10 Mrs F. Nevill Jackson, 'Cravats', in *The Connoisseur*, London, August 1904, pp. 226–232.

11 Tanner and Nevinson, op. cit., pp. 169–202.

12 Holme, op. cit., 1688.

13 C. Anstey, *The New Bath Guide*, 1766, Letter X.

14 Woodforde, op. cit., entry for 9 October 1972.

15 R. W. Chapman, ed., *Jane Austen's Letters to her Sister Cassandra and Others*, Oxford University Press, 1932, 17 January 1809.

16 J. Austen, *Northanger Abbey,* 1818, vol. II, ch. 15.

17 C. Dickens, *Bleak House*, 1853, ch. 14.

18 H. Le Blanc, *The Art of Tying the Cravat*, 1828, Introduction.

19 D. L. Moore, 'Byronic Dress', in *Costume*, no. 5, London 1971, pp. 1–13.

20 Acton, op. cit., ch. 5.

21 *The Tailor and Cutter*, London, 23 September 1897.

22 ibid., 8 March and 24 May 1900.

23 J. Braine, *Queen of the Distant Country*, Eyre Methuen, 1972, p. 49.

24 See Cohn, op. cit., ch. 2.

25 *The Ambassador* (British Export Magazine), 1961, no. 3, pp. 57 and 64.

MANTLES AND OVERCOATS

1 J. Boswell, *The Journal of a Tour to the Hebrides with Samuel Johnson*, 1773, Introduction.

2 *Kilvert's Diary 1870–1879*, ed. W. Plomer, Cape, 1944, entry for 26 February 1870.

3 G. Boccaccio, *The Decameron*, trans. G. H. McWilliam, Penguin Classics, 1972, 6th Day, 5th Story.

4 ibid., 7th Day, 3rd Story.

5 Chaucer, op. cit., Prologue.

6 Pepys, op. cit., entries for 7 October 1660, 1 July 1660, 29 November 1663, 6 April 1668 and 22 and 31 October 1663.

7 ibid., 21 August 1668.

8 F. A. de Garsault, *Description des Arts et Métiers, L'Art du Tailleur*, Paris, 1769.

9 C. Brontë, *Jane Eyre*, 1847, ch. 12.

10 See Acton, op. cit., and M. Holroyd, *Lytton Strachey, a Biography*, 2 vols, Heinemann, 1967.

11 See C. H. Spiers, 'Deer Skin Leathers and their use for costume', in *Costume*, no. 7, London 1973, pp. 14–23.

12 J. Evelyn, *Tyrannus; or The Mode*, London, 1664.

13 Austen, *Northanger Abbey*, vol. II, ch. 5.

14 ibid., vol. I, ch. 11.

15 *The Whole Art of Dress by a Cavalry Officer*, 1830.

16 C. Brontë, *Villette*, 1853, ch. 29.

17 *The Tailor and Cutter*, London, 9 December 1897.

18 ibid., 10 November 1898.

19 ibid., 18 August 1898.

20 K. Grahame, *The Wind in the Willows*, Methuen, 1908, ch. 6.

21 M. Beerbohm, *Zuleika Dobson*, 1911, ch. 5.

22 *The Tailor and Cutter*, 4 January 1900.

DRESS AND UNDRESS

1 A. Bennett, *The Journals*, Penguin Books, 1971, entry for 7 March 1904.

2 H. Mayhew, quoted by J. Morley, in *Death, Heaven and the Victorians*, Studio Vista, 1971, p. 63.

3 S. Richardson, *Pamela*, 1740, vol. I, ch. 27.

4 Duke of Windsor, *A Family Album*, Cassell, 1960, p. 13.

5 Pepys, op. cit., entries for 2 February, 1 July and 25 August 1660 and 22 April 1661.

6   *The Autobiography and Correspondence of Mary Granville, Mrs Delany,* ed. Lady Llanover, 6 vols, Richard Bentley, 1861, entries for 16 March 1734 and 22 January 1940.

7   Richardson, op. cit., vol. I, ch. 32.

8   Cowles, op. cit., chs 1 and 11.

9   *The Tailor and Cutter*, London, 23 August 1900.

10   See M. H. Swain, 'Nightgown into Dressing Gown', in *Costume*, no. 6, London, 1972, pp. 10–21.

11   O. Goldsmith, *Life of Richard Nash of Bath Esq.*, London, 1762, p. 32.

12   Woodforde, op. cit., entry for 5 October 1781.

13   Pepys, op. cit., entry for 30 March 1666.

14   See N. Tarrant, 'Lord Sheffield's Banyan', in *Costume*, no. 11, London, 1977, pp. 92–97.

15   Woodforde, op. cit., entries for 21 November and 12 December 1781.

16   *The Tailor and Cutter*, 25 August 1898.

17   Austen, *Sense and Sensibility*, vol. I, ch. 9.

18   J. Lees-Milne, *Prophesying Peace*, Chatto and Windus, 1977, entry for 9 February 1944.

19   *The Tailor and Cutter*, 24 May 1900.

20   Duke of Windsor, op. cit., p. 130.

21   See E. Ratner, 'Levis', in *Dress*, no. 1, vol. 1, New York, 1975, pp. 1–5.

22   Newton, *Health, Art and Reason*, ch. 8.

23   Mitford, *Don't Tell Alfred*, ch. 11.

HAIR

1   See Liversidge, op. cit., ch. 6.

2   Planché, *History of British Costume*, ch. 5.

3   Boccaccio, op. cit., 9th Day, 8th Story.

4   Chaucer, op. cit., Prologue and Miller's Tale.

5   Pepys, op. cit., entries for 31 October 1663, 8 November 1663 and 3 September 1665.

6   See J. Arnold, *Perukes and Periwigs*, H.M.S.O., 1970.

7   Pepys, op. cit., entries for 6 January 1664 and 30 May 1668.

8   T. Smollett, *The Expedition of Humphry Clinker* (1771), Everyman's Library, Dent, 1968, p. 158.

9   J. Austen, *The Watsons*, in *Minor Works*, Oxford University Press, 1954, pp. 353 and 357.

10   E. L. Kirby, *The Royal Welch Fusiliers*, Pitkin Pictorials, 1974, p. 20.

11   J. Austen, *Emma*, 1816, vol. II, chs. 7 and 8.

12   *Kilvert's Diary, 1870–1879*, entry for 3 December 1870.

13   O. E. Schoeffler, and W. Gale, *Esquire's Encyclopedia of 20th Century Men's Fashions*, McGraw-Hill, 1973, p. 478.

14 A. Powell, *Books do Furnish a Room* (*A Dance to the Music of Time*, vol. X), Heinemann, 1971, ch. 3.

15 See Cohn, op. cit., ch. 11.

HATS

1 See J. H. Murray, ed., *New English Dictionary*, Oxford, 1888–1933.

2 E. M. Veale, *The English Fur Trade in the Later Middle Ages*, Oxford University Press, 1966, ch. 8.

3 C. H. Freeman, *Luton and the Hat Industry*, Luton Museum, 1964, p. 7.

4 *The Autobiography and Correspondence of Mary Granville, Mrs Delany*, entry for 4 March 1729.

5 Great Wardrobe Accounts, PRO E101/391/15, in *Archaeologia* vol. XXXI, p. 41.

6 H. K. Morse, *Elizabethan Pageantry*, Studio, 1934, p. 13.

7 H. Amphlett, *Hats*, R. Sadler, 1974, ch. 2.

8 J. R. Planché, *Cyclopaedia of Costume*, Chatto and Windus, 1876–79, vol. I, Dictionary.

9 Freeman, op. cit., p.8.

10 See S. M. Newton, 'The Order of the Garter', in *A Closer Look into History Series*, Visual Publications, London, 1970.

11 Quoted in Morse op. cit., p. 10.

12 C. W. and P. Cunnington, *Handbook of English Costume in the 16th Century*, Faber, 1964, p. 47.

13 H. Marryat, *A Residence in Jutland, the Danish Isles and Copenhagen*, London, 1860, vol. I, p. 360.

14 Veale, op. cit.

15 Pepys, op. cit., entry for 22 September 1664.

16 Quoted in C. W. and P. Cunnington, *Handbook of English Costume in the 19th Century*, Faber, 1959, p. 189.

17 Newton, *Renaissance Theatre Costume*, p. 97.

18 C. Sykes, *Nancy. The Life of Lady Astor*, Collins, 1972, p. 338.

19 B. Pym, *Excellent Women*, Cape, 1952, ch. 2.

SHOES

1 See J. Thornton, ed., *Textbook of Footwear Manufacture*, National Trade Press, Manchester, 1964, ch. 1.

2 Murray, ed., op. cit.

3 See Thornton, op. cit., ch. 2.

4 ibid., ch. 3.

5 *Kilvert's Diary*, 1870–1879, entry for 21 June 1870.

6 See J. Swann, *A History of Shoe Fashions*, Northampton Museum, 1975.

7 B. and T. Hughes, *Georgian Shoe Buckles*, London, G.L.C., 1972.

8 See Liversidge, *Britain in the Roman Empire*, ch. 6.

9   Swann, op. cit.; and 'Shoe Fashions to 1600', in *Transactions of the Museum Assistants Group*, no. 12, 1973, Belfast, 1975, pp. 14–24.

10 J. Thornton, 'The Examination of early shoes to 1600', in *Transactions*, op. cit., pp. 2–13.

11 Origo, op. cit., ch. 2.

12 Chaucer, op. cit.

13 Thornton ed., *Textbook of Footwear Manufacture*, ch. 4.

14 P. Stubbes, *Anatomy of Abuses in England* (1583), ed. F. J. Furnivall for the New Shakespeare Society, 1882.

15 Hughes, op. cit.

16 Richardson, *Pamela*, vol. I, ch. 32.

17 *Journal of Beatrix Potter*, entry for 5 March 1884.

18 *Kilvert's Diary*, 1870–1879, entry for 11 July 1874.

19 B. Lehane, *C & J Clark 1825–1975*, C. & J. Clark Ltd., Street, Somerset, 1975, p. 11.

20 Beerbohm, op. cit., ch. 3.

21 Donaldson, op. cit., ch. 9.

22 Duke of Windsor, op. cit., p. 35.

23 Braine, op. cit., ch. 17.

OTHER ACCESSORIES

1   Cowles, op. cit., ch. 12.

2   G. D. Painter, op. cit., vol. I, p. 93.

3   See Broholm and M. Hald, op. cit.

4   Cunnington, *Handbook of English Mediaeval Costume*, p. 105.

5   Boccaccio, op. cit., 8th Day, 10th Story and 3rd Day, 3rd Story.

6   S. W. Beck, *Gloves: their Annals and Associations*, Adams, 1883, ch. 2.

7   Cunnington, *Handbook of English Costume in the 16th Century*, 1954, p. 143.

8   See B. Howe, 'The Days of the Card Case', in *Country Life*, 1 October 1959, pp. 424–25.

9   See S. Groves, 'The Evolution of Snuff Taking', in *Country Life*, 4 April 1952, pp. 992–93. J. R. Yorke-Radleigh, 'On Taking Snuff', in *Country Life*, 14 June 1956, pp. 1308–11.

10 Goldsmith, op. cit., p. 121 and p. 126.

11 See G. B. Hughes, 'Old English Snuff Handkerchiefs', in *Country Life*, 17 November 1955, pp. 1154–58.

12 P. Cunnington and C. Lucas, *Charity Costumes*, A. & C. Black, 1978, p. 204.

13 Pepys, op. cit., entries for 3 February 1661, 4 November 1666, 17 May 1668 and 30 April 1669.

14 Fielding, op. cit., 1749, Book VII, ch. 14 and Book XIII, ch. 2.

15 J. E. Austen-Leigh, *Memoir of Jane Austen*, Richard Bentley, 1871, ch. 2.

16 See G. B. Hughes, 'Old English Walking-Sticks', in *Country Life*, 18 October 1956, pp. 879–83.

17 A. Pope, *The Rape of the Lock,* 1712-14, IV, 123.

18 Anstey, op. cit., Letter IV.

19 T. Coryate, *Coryat's Crudities* (1611), James MacLehose, 1905, vol. 1, p. 257.

20 G. M. Trevelyan, *English Social History*, Longmans Green, 1942, ch. 11.

21 J. Austen, *Persuasion*, vol. IV, ch. 7.

22 M. von Boehn and O. Fischel, *Modes and Manners: Ornaments*, Dent, 1929, ch. 5.

23 *Kilvert's Diary, 1870–1879*, entry for 28 April 1876.

24 N. Mitford, ed., *Noblesse Oblige*, Hamish Hamilton, 1956, p. 100.

25 J. Evans, *History of Jewellery 1100–1870,* Faber, 1953, ch. 5.

26 E. W. Safford, 'An account of expenses of Eleanor, sister of Edward III, on the occasion of her marriage to Reynald, Count of Guelders', in *Archaeologia*, London vol. LXXVII, 1927.

27 Evans, op. cit.

28 See G. B. Hughes, 'Seals for Business and Adornment', in *Country Life,* 22 May 1958, pp. 1116–17.

29 See G. B. Hughes, 'Sporting Scarf Pins', in *Country Life*, 15 February 1952, pp. 418–19.

30 Cowles, op. cit., ch. 12.

31 C. Dickens, *Great Expectations*, 1860–61, ch. 21.

32 Painter, op. cit., vol. I, pp. 154–5.

33 E. Lytton Bulwer, *Pelham* (1828), quoted in E. Moers, *The Dandy*, Secker & Warburg, 1960, Ch. 3.

34 P. Cunnington and A. Mansfield, *English Costume for Sports and Outdoor Recreations*, A. & C. Black, 1969, p. 254.

Select Bibliography

GENERAL

BELL, Q., *On Human Finery*, Hogarth Press, 1976.

BINDER, P., *The Peacock's Tail*, Harrap, 1958.

BOEHN, M. VON, *Modes and Manners* (from the Middle Ages to the end of the eighteenth century), 4 vols, trs. J. Joshua, Harrap, 1932–35.

COLLE, D., *Collars, Stocks, Cravats. A History and Costume Dating Guide to Civilian Men's Neckpieces 1655–1900,* White Lion, New York, 1974.

CUNNINGTON, C. W. and P., *The History of Underclothes*, Michael Joseph, 1951.

DAVENPORT, M., *The Book of Costume*, Crown, New York, 1948.

HALLS, Z., *Men's Costume 1580–1750*, London Museum, H.M.S.O., 1970. *Men's Costume 1750–1800*, London Museum, H.M.S.O., 1973.

MOERS, E., *The Dandy,* Secker & Warburg, 1960.

PLANCHÉ, J. R., *Cyclopaedia of Costume*, 2 vols, Chatto & Windus, 1876–79.

SEELEY, SERVICE & CO. LTD, *The Book of Ties*, 1968.

SWANN, J. M., *A History of Shoe Fashions*, Northampton Museum, 1975.

WAUGH, N., *The Cut of Men's Clothes*, Faber, 1964.

ANCIENT WORLD

BROHOLM, H. C. and HALD, M., *Costumes of the Bronze Age in Denmark*, Oxford University Press, 1940.

HOPE, T., *Costume of the Ancients,* 1809, reprinted as *Costumes of the Greeks and Romans*, Dover, New York, 1964.

WILSON, L. M., *The Roman Toga*, Johns Hopkins Press, Baltimore, 1924. *The Clothing of the Ancient Romans*, John Hopkins Press, Baltimore, 1938.

MEDIAEVAL

BIRBARI, E., *Dress in Italian Painting 1460–1500*, John Murray, 1975.

CUNNINGTON, C. W. and P., *Handbook of English Mediaeval Costume*, revised edition, Faber, 1973.

EVANS, J., *Dress in Mediaeval France*, Oxford University Press 1952.

SIXTEENTH AND SEVENTEENTH CENTURIES

CUNNINGTON, C. W. and P., *Handbook of English Costume in the 16th Century*, revised edition, Faber, 1970. *Handbook of English Costume in the 17th Century,* 3rd edition, Faber, 1972.

LAVER, J., ed., *Costume of the Western World*, 6 monographs, Harrap, 1951: Blum, A. 'The Last Valois 1515–1590'. Blum, A., 'Early Bourbon 1590–1643'. Laver, J., 'Early Tudor 1485–1558'. Reade, B., 'The Dominance of Spain 1550–1660'. Reynolds, G. 'Elizabethan and Jacobean 1558–1625'. Thienen, F. van, 'The Great Age of Holland 1600–1650'.

MORSE, H. K., *Elizabethan Pageantry: a pictoral survey of costume and its commentators from 1560–1620*, Studio, 1934.

EIGHTEENTH CENTURY

CUNNINGTON, C. W. and P., *Handbook of English Costume in the 18th Century*, Faber, 1957.

NINETEENTH CENTURY

BOEHN, M. VON and FISCHEL, O., *Modes and Manners of the 19th Century*, 4 vols, trs. M. Edwardes, Dent, 1927.

BUCK, A., *Victorian Costume and Costume Accessories*, Herbert Jenkins, 1961.

CUNNINGTON, C. W. and P., *Handbook of English Costume in the 19th Century*, revised edition, Faber, 1970.

NEWTON, S. M., *Health, Art and Reason. Dress Reformers of the 19th Century*, John Murray, 1974.

TWENTIETH CENTURY

COHN, N., *Today There Are No Gentlemen*, Weidenfeld & Nicolson, 1971.

MANSFIELD, A. and CUNNINGTON, P. *Handbook of English Costume in the 20th Century 1900–1950*, Faber, 1973.

SCHOEFFLER, O. E. and GALE, W. *Esquire's Encyclopaedia of 20th Century Men's Fashions*, McGraw-Hill, New York 1973.

Index